M O N E Y

MONEY

Understanding and Creating Alternatives to Legal Tender

THOMAS H. GRECO, JR.

Foreword by Vicki Robin

CHELSEA GREEN PUBLISHING COMPANY

White River Junction, Vermont

Designed by Dede Cummings Design.

Printed in Canada

First printing, October 2001.

04 03 02 01   1 2 3 4 5

Library of Congress Cataloging-in-Publication Data

Greco, Thomas H., 1936-
Money : understanding and creating alternatives to legal tender /
Thomas H. Greco.
p. cm.
Includes bibliographical references and index.
ISBN 1-890132-37-3 (alk. paper)
1. Money. 2. Legal tender. I. Title.
HG221 .G77 2001
332.4'2042–dc21
2001042155

Chelsea Green Publishing Company
P.O. Box 428
White River Junction, VT 05001
800-639-4099
www.chelseagreen.com

Dedicated to champions of
justice,
equity,
and freedom,
everywhere

CONTENTS

⟋

List of Illustrations   *xiii*

Foreword   *xv*

Preface   *xviii*

Introduction   *xx*

Part I. Monetary Realities and Official Illusions

1. What's the Matter with Money?   3

    Symptoms of Disease   4

    Three Ways in Which Conventional Money Malfunctions   4

    How Money Is Created   4

    Sidebar: An Example of Money Creation   8

    Why There Is Never Enough Money   8

    How Money Is Misallocated   9

    How Money Pumps Wealth from the Poor to the Rich   11

    Sidebar: For Whom the Debt Tolls   12

2. Community Currency and the New World Order   13

    Why Community Currencies?   13

    The New World Order   14

    Gaia Consciousness and Human Unity   15

    Correcting Past Errors   16

3. The Power and Place of Money   18

The Power Inherent in Money   18
The Place of Money in Human Interaction   19
The Body Economic   20

4. What Is Money?   22
    Definitions   23
    The Essential Nature of Money   23
    The Exchange Process and the Purpose of Money   24
    Historical Forms of Money   25
    The Money Circuit   26
    Bank Credit Money and the Interest Burden   29

5. The Disintegration of Local Economies   34
    Levers of Power, Then and Now   34
    The Evolution of Money   35
    Social Control through Control of Money and Finance   37
    Social Disintegration   37
    The End of Empires   39

6. Money, Power, and the U.S. Constitution   41
    Measuring Value and Defining the Dollar   43
    The Consolidation of Money Power   43

7. Restoring Local Economies   46
    Healthy Communities, Healthy World   47
    Two Fundamental Strategies   48
    Small (and Local) Is Beautiful   49
    How to Bring Money under Local Control   50
    Community Banking and the Liberation of Money   50
    The Role of Community Currencies   51

Part II. Complementary Currencies, Past and Present

8. A Brief History of Community Currencies
        and Private Exchange Systems   57
    Scrip of the Great Depression   58

WIR: The Swiss Wirtschaftsring   67
Legal Considerations   68
Lessons Learned   68
The Deflation Dilemma   70
Railway Notes   70
Sidebar: The "Constant" Currency of Ralph Borsodi   73
An Early Proposal for a Credit Clearing System   74

9. Global Finance, Inflation, and Local Currencies   76
   Why Central Governments and Central Banks
       Don't Like Local Currencies   76
   The Argentine Experience   82

10. New Wave Pioneers   86
    Barter, Reciprocal Trade, and Mutual Credit   86
    Commercial "Barter" or Trade Exchanges   87
    LETS: Local Employment and Trading System   89
    The Berkshire Experiments   94
    Ithaca HOURS   95
    Service Credits and Time Dollars   98
    Update on the Pioneers   99

11. Recent Models and Developments   101
    Tucson Traders   101
    The döMAK "Barter" Circle   106
    Toronto Dollars, "Money That Builds Community"   107
    Friendly Favors   112
    Equal Dollars (=$s)   114
    The Developing World Takes the Lead   115

Part III. Monetary Transformation and
          Community Empowerment

12. Currency Fundamentals   127
    Basis of Issue   128

Regulation of the Amount of Exchange Media Supplied   128
Power to Issue   129
What Gives a Currency Credibility?   130
Forms and Devices   134

13. Mutual Credit: The Foundation for
        Community Currencies   136
    What Is Mutual Credit?   136
    How a Mutual Credit System Works   138
    Basic Steps in Organizing a Mutual Credit System   140
    Continuing Issues in Mutual Credit Systems   142
    Strategies for Enhancing Mutual Credit Systems
        and Gaining Acceptance   144

14. Basic Currency Types: A Classification Scheme   145
    Different Breeds of Cat: Community Currencies
        Are Not All Created Equal   145
    Good Paper vs. Bad Paper   146
    Types of Currencies   146
    Sidebar: Harvey Bucks   158

15. A Note on Interest   164
    Interest or Usury?   165
    Toward Better Forms of Exchange   167
    What about Charges on Credit Balances?   167
    Sidebar: A Story of Robinson Crusoe   168

16. Medium of Exchange or Savings Medium?   172
    Conflicting Roles of Money   172
    Saving and Investment   173
    How Do We Save?   173
    Preventing Stagnation in Mutual Credit Systems   174
    Current Account vs. Capital Account   175
    Sidebar: Mutual Credit Loans: An Example   176
    Interest Revisited   176
    Basis of Issue Revisited   177

Part IV. Currency Design, Improvement, and Innovation

17. Improving Local Currencies, or How to
    Make a Good Thing Better   181
    Gift Exchange vs. Reciprocal Exchange   182
    Money Is an IOU   182
    Basis of Issue   183
    Mutual Credit and Paper Notes   183
    Essential Differences between LETS and HOURS   183
    How HOURS Work   184
    Fish or Fowl?   185
    How Are Ithaca HOURS Issued?   189
    Adding a Capital Cushion   191
    Using Excess Business Capacity to Support Local Currency   191
    Combined Bases of Issue   195

18. How to Design and Implement a Community
    Exchange System   197
    Summary Prescription   198
    Detailed Guidelines   199
    Conclusion   212

19. A Business-Based Community Currency   213
    Community Trading Coupons   214

20. Currency Alternatives for Impersonal Markets   220
    Grain Banks and a Commodity-Based Currency   221
    Comparison to Conventional Money   224

21. Good Money for Good Work   227
    Community Service Coupons   227
    Earth Rescue Receipts (ERRs)   232
    Sidebar: ERR Questions and Answers   234
    Funded Temporary Receipts (FTRs)   236
    Sidebar: FTR Questions and Answers   239

22. Youth Employment Scrip (YES)   241

   The Youth Problem   242

   The Money Problem   244

   How Does the YES Program Work?   245

   Benefits of the YES Project   247

   Involving Local Businesses   248

   Program Participants and Agreements   249

   Sidebar: YES Questions and Answers   252

Epilogue   255

Appendix A: Note on Banking as a Profession,
      and Its Reform   257

Appendix B: Note on the Proper Basis of
      Issue for Currency, and the Means of
      Financing Capital Investments and
      Consumer Durables   260

Acknowledgments   263

Notes   264

References   274

Sources and Resources   277

Index   289

ILLUSTRATIONS

4.1. The ideal money circuit 27

4.2. The bank credit money circuit, lending phase 30

4.3. The bank credit money circuit, redemption phase 31

8.1. Caslow scrip, face side 59

8.2. Caslow scrip, reverse side 59

8.3. A Larkin merchandise bond, face side 62

8.4. A Larkin merchandise bond, reverse side 62

8.5. A Wörgl note, face side 67

8.6. A Wörgl note, reverse side 67

8.7. A Constant note, face side 73

8.8. A Constant note, reverse side 73

9.1. News clip about Argentine provincial bonds 77

9.2. A circulating bond of Salta Province 83

10.1. The LETS trading circuit 93

10.2. A Deli Dollar $10 note 95

10.3. A Massachusetts Farmers' Market Coupon 95

10.4. An Ithaca HOUR 1-hour note, face side 97

10.5. An Ithaca HOUR 1-hour note, reverse side 97

11.1. A pencil and paper accounting system 102

11.2. A Tucson Traders 20-token note, face side 104

11.3. A Tucson Traders 20-token note, reverse side 104

11.4. Tucson Traders membership agreement 105

11.5. A Toronto Dollar $10 note, face side 108

11.6. A Toronto Dollar $10 note, reverse side 108

11.7. Various currency notes used within Argentina's
Red Global de Trueque network 119

13.1. The mutual credit trading circuit 139

13.2. A mutual credit system check 141

14.1. Basic classification of community currency types, with examples 149

14.2. Gift certificate issuance, transfer, and redemption 150

14.3. *Fund-raising scrip issuance, transfer, and redemption* 152

14.4. *Traveler's check issuance, transfer, and redemption* 154

14.5. *Toronto dollars issuance, circulation, and redemption* 157

14.6. *Historical examples of true community currencies and their basis of issue* 163

17.1. *HOURS issuance, circulation, and redemption—HOUR Town as issuer* 187

17.2. *HOURS issuance, circulation, and redemption—HOUR Town as agent* 188

17.3. *A community currency based on donations of excess business capacity* 194

19.1 *Conceptual rendering of a community trading coupon* 215

19.2. *The community trading coupon circuit* 217

19.3. *Currency circulation through the levels of economic production and distribution* 218

20.1. *A commodity-based currency circuit* 222

21.1 *The cooperative community service credit (SERV) circuit* 228

21.2. *Typical service credit announcement* 230

21.3. *Typical service credit agreement* 231

21.4. *Conceptual rendering of an Earth rescue receipt (ERR)* 232

21.5. *The Earth rescue receipt circuit* 233

21.6. *The funded temporary receipt (FTR) circuit* 238

22.1 *The youth employment scrip (YES) circuit* 246

22.2. *Youth employment scrip promotional announcement* 250

22.3. *Youth employment scrip agreement* 251

FOREWORD

SOME TRUTHS ARE HARDER TO TAKE THAN OTHERS. The really hard ones are turning points in our maturation, our understanding of this world we live in. Losing Santa but discovering that Mom and Dad are the ones bringing you presents might be a tolerable trade of fiction for reality. But learning that Mom and Dad don't love each other anymore and are getting a divorce is an earthquake that might rock your world for life. To use another analogy, learning that the earth is round was revolutionary 500 years ago but is apparently "ho-hum" now. Yet try looking "up" at the stars and thinking of them as being "down" (just as true) or "out" and see what your insides do. Try thinking about sunrises and sunsets as the earth rolling toward or away from the sun and see if everything changes. When truth—perhaps known but suppressed for survival—erupts, often rage, relief, sorrow, confusion, and liberation flow out like lava from our core. Tom Greco's revelations about the reality of money have this kind of power to change you forever.

In *Your Money or Your Life* we examined certain truths about money that could liberate people from consumer hypnosis. We asked, "What is the reality of money to you?" Without understanding our economic system, people could use the tools in the book to see whether or not their relationship with money was buying them the life they wanted. Without understanding markets and trade, people could see that money was something for which they traded their most precious good: their life energy. Without any political or scientific sophistication about how the world does—or should—work, people became naturally good resource managers, natural ecologists, natural builders of stronger communities of sharing. They did so because they had tools to evaluate the flow of money and stuff through their lives in terms of the amount of happiness and meaning that flow produced. It was, and still is for hundreds of thousands around the world, a transformative process. It didn't involve new knowledge, but a clearer way of seeing that more accurately tracked with reality. Stepping into alignment with the way things are gave people the capacity to invent, in their own life circumstances, ways to save money and liberate themselves from mindless consumption. Their behavior, from the old mindset, might have looked like sacrifice or deprivation—but they all reported being happier and more able to live the life of their dreams.

These dreams, however, happen in a larger context. Personal transformation merely enables the individual to ultimately encounter "the rules of the bigger game."

Tom Greco brings the force of years of study and practical application to explaining a lynchpin in this bigger game: how money is created and the consequences of that choice. Like Dorothy in the Wizard of Oz, he heals us by whisking back the curtain that reveals a small and very human device behind a grand illusion.

A wise person once said, "It is the sign of true intelligence to look at what everyone else thinks is normal and to find it very strange indeed." If this is the case, Tom Greco is truly intelligent.

Part 1 is where Greco turns our world upside down. He explains, clearly, that just as presents don't come from Santa, money isn't a simple, wholesome, and value-neutral artifact. It is no longer backed by real wealth, and it isn't created by the government or by people but rather by banks, when they make new loans and the interest on these loans requires the very growth economy that is transgressing the limits of human communities and the natural world. Fully 95 percent of money is based on interest-bearing bank loans. He says: "How money is brought into being has everything to do with the kind of society we bring into being and that society's impact on the natural systems we rely on."

How money is created, by whom, and on what terms actually creates an artificial world of winners and losers, a world where abundantly creative humans are pitted against one another for scarce money while all around them—and in them—is the real wealth to create a rich life. Again and again, Greco tells us: "By issuing money to unproductive or privileged clients of the money monopoly at more favorable terms, and by demanding higher interest rates from the rest, the banking system redistributes wealth from producers to privileged nonproducers."

From the foundations of money creation, Greco shows us how money, banking, and finance interlock with our institutionalized agreements about property ownership, corporate power, taxation, and the like. This perspective allows us to see how the seeming cacophony of issues being lifted up on the streets at every meeting of the World Bank, the World Trade Organization, the International Monetary Fund, and the World Economic Forum all spring from the same source. This protest isn't, as the media would have us think, just sour grapes on the part of underdogs with nothing better to do than bite the hand that feeds them miracles like antibiotics and telecommunications and the Green Revolution. It is making visible and audible the parts of the community of life on Earth that are getting the short end of the stick—a stick that could be a very different sort of artifact.

The hope *Money* holds out is that there are other ways to create money that support social justice, community self-reliance, economic democracy, and personal freedom. Money, it turns out, is not the root of all evil; nor is the love of it, though institutionalized greed as practiced among some of the privileged is surely a travesty. Money—in the form of complementary currency—can be a very creative and life-serving medium of exchange. Greco is not advocating a rupture with the past. While this book is revolutionary, he calls for a slow revolution. He suggests that we step out humbly by providing local communities with a way to buy and sell some goods and services using a self-created means of exchange that isn't based on debt, interest, and distant financial decisions made solely for economic gain. Make no mistake, however. The impact of this local trading ability, if developed in an intelligent and sophisticated way, could shift our society away from dependence upon unsustainable and ignoble ways of meeting our needs.

In Part 2 Greco teaches us the fascinating history of complementary currencies. It's a story filled with both surprise and a sense of familiarity. Trading stamps, store coupons, discount matinees, entertainment books, and air miles are all forms of complementary currency. You pay part of the price of an item in something other than dollars. Volunteering and "house work" (washing the dishes, cooking, shopping) are also activities that fulfill human needs with no exchange of money. Indeed, these are all strategies that individuals discover through doing the 9-step program in Your Money or Your Life. To maximize the value of each dollar, people quickly learn that developing do-it-yourself skills, creating sharing networks, being smart shoppers, and keeping possessions for a long time can yield a low-cost yet high-quality life. Greco shows that by making these choices systemic rather than individual, communities and the Earth can prosper.

Parts 3 and 4 are the recipe book for those who would relish giving the creation of a complementary currency a try. Will you be the one? Social innovations require champions to turn good ideas into living realities. Social innovators willingly buck systems, tinker, make adjustments, maintain the faith, solicit feedback, and—as a reward—have meaningful lives and even, sometimes, great success. While few readers will have the will or time to set up full-scale complementary currency systems, these sections round out the picture. No reader can henceforth blindly accept that there is no alternative to the sorry rules of the conventional money system.

Having new road maps for healthy money in a healthy world is as vital to our souls as food, air, and water are to our bodies. Tom Greco has given us a grounded, well-researched, comprehensive, and fascinating account of how money and commerce could work for our deeper values of justice, caring, community, and the Earth.

—VICKI ROBIN

PREFACE

F OR MORE THAN TWENTY years, I have been intrigued and engaged by "the money problem." Prior to that I didn't even know there *was* a money problem, despite the fact that my profession as an educator in business administration placed me in the midst of business, finance, money, economics, and the "science" of management. Like the vast majority of my colleagues, I had been schooled in the orthodox theories and views, but, more important, we had taken our monetary system as a given.

Our job was to teach students how to "play the game" within the context of the rules as they were defined for us, and the rules of money, banking, and finance were fundamental in defining that game. Who was I to question them? It was not until after I had experienced a personal crisis and emotional catharsis that my mind was opened and I began to look more deeply into the ways of the world. There was too much that did not make sense; too much that was unjust; too much inequity, violence, repression, hunger, disease, and needless suffering. Why, I asked, must it be like this?

I began an earnest inquiry as I attempted to discover the root causes of such pervasive problems. As I embarked on my self-directed program of reeducation, I realized that I first needed to prepare myself for the journey by working on my own faults, limitations, and inadequacies. I was fortunate to be living in a time when there was a burgeoning of activity related to "personal growth," "self-awareness," and "consciousness raising." I took advantage of many of the available opportunities.

About the same time, I began intensive exploration into a wide variety of subjects. Having had my values, attitudes, and core beliefs shaken, my mind was open to consider anew the foundations of our social, political, and economic institutions. As my quest for root causes progressed, I began to focus much of my attention on the institutions of money, banking, and finance. I soon came to realize that, despite all my education and degrees, my understanding of money was rudimentary at best. I came to understand that the kind of money we use today and the mechanisms by which it is created and controlled are fundamental determinants of the distribution of power and wealth in the world and are, in fact, among the major structural obstacles to peace, freedom, harmony, and a healthy environment.

My first book on the subject, *Money and Debt: A Solution to the Global Crisis,* explained the nature of money, identified fundamental flaws in the current monetary and financial system, and suggested an approach to resolving the problem of exploding debt and the social and environmental degradation that it causes. That book also laid out the foundation principles necessary for the creation of both a more rational means of value measurement and more humane and equitable forms of money (or other structures enabling the exchange of goods and services).

The second book, *New Money for Healthy Communities*, was written to complement that earlier work. While *Money and Debt* focused on highlighting the nature of the problem and outlining general principles and global prescriptions, *New Money for Healthy Communities* provided more specific details about exchange alternatives: their essential design elements, how they work, and how they are able to empower ordinary people and local communities. It described exchange mechanisms that have worked in the past as well as some of the contemporary local currency and exchange efforts. It was intended to serve as a how-to manual. It identified pitfalls to be avoided, and it proposed specific methods for transforming the exchange process—methods that are rational, equitable, and empowering and that can be easily implemented at the community level by small voluntary groups.

This present work continues those earlier efforts in a more complete and better way, focusing on what can and is being done, not only at the local grass-roots level, but also at the levels of business, government, and global trade. While the community currency and private exchange movement has continued to develop and mature, I have, through additional reading and experimentation, both broadened and deepened my understanding of the issues involved in the process of economic exchange. This book includes many new insights and understandings and describes several of the more important developments that have occurred in the intervening years since my other books were written. Chapters 1 and 4 provide a good example. These two chapters together comprise, I think, a clear and complete, yet concise exposition of money. They are a distillation of many volumes and reveal the simple essence of money. Another example is chapter 14. It provides a classification scheme for the basic types of currency that have been developed and tried. This is, to my knowledge, the only complete taxonomy of community currencies developed to date. Other sections of the book cover developments and innovations that have occurred over the past few years. Chapter 11 describes important community currencies that did not exist when my other books were written.

My hope is that the information contained in this book will be widely disseminated and applied. The implementation of private exchange mechanisms such as those described in this book will, I firmly believe, go a long way toward helping humanity create a more harmonious, equitable, and happy world.

INTRODUCTION

T HIS BOOK IS ABOUT FREEDOM and empowerment, about community and relationships, about fairness and prosperity, but most of all it is about money and exchange. Something extraordinary is happening to money. It is being reinvented. And this process of reinvention is sure to have far-reaching effects on every aspect of life for everyone living in the world today.

But what is money? Where does it come from? What roles does it play? And how does money fit into the greater scheme of things? These are questions this book will address. The social, political, economic, cultural, and ecological aspects of life cannot be isolated from one another. Whatever affects one of these must, in some way and measure, affect all the others. Therefore, whatever actions we humans contemplate taking must be subjected to comprehensive evaluation. Are they generally beneficial, and are the outcomes sustainable over the long term? Will they contribute to maintaining and improving the physical environment? Will they promote healthier relationships between individuals and among different sectors of society? Will they lead to the wider fulfillment of basic human needs? Will they promote responsible citizenship? Will they promote the fuller realization of the creative potential inherent in each person and community?

The much vaunted efforts toward globalization of "free trade," which have been pushed forward in the post–Cold War era, have failed to address these questions. They are mainly the result of an undemocratic process that gives voice only to a privileged few, who make far-reaching decisions based on questionable assumptions and limited perspectives. Those decisions, almost entirely, reflect an emphasis on the economic benefits that would accrue to the political and financial elites in the so-called developed world and their minions in developing countries. What is promoted as "free trade" is more often an attempt to dominate markets and exploit people and resources, as giant corporate players in the game of global economy seek to continue their expansion and avoid defaulting on their debts. The drive toward territorial expansion by national governments, which characterized the global conflicts of the past century, has given way to a drive toward market expansion and profit accumulation headed by corporate and financial elites.

One especially forceful reaction, called the "Battle of Seattle," occurred alongside the World Trade Organization (WTO) conference of November 1999. This was not just an emotional outburst by a few anticapitalist ideologues. It was a cry of pain by, and on behalf of, those who are suffering the adverse effects of globalization on their cultures, communities, and environments—working people and ordinary citizens who perceive its destructive impact on democratic governance and decision making, leadership accountability, consumer safety, and overall quality of life. As Vicki Robin, who was there, reported, "The people in the streets, by and large, were not against trade, but want the 'goods' of globalization to make room for 'goods' like clean water, fresh air, intact ecosystems, respect for non-human life, wholesome foods and sharing the benefits of prosperity more universally."[1]

But, apart from the "elitist agenda," there are positive globalizing phenomena, too. The development of computerized telecommunications technologies and the Internet have put into the hands of ordinary people an information matrix and ability to communicate that was undreamed of just a few years ago. Among other things, such tools have enabled the organization of grassroots communities of interest that transcend barriers of distance, language, and culture, and, as we shall see, they have also enabled the development of new nonmonetary, nonpolitical ways of exchanging goods and services. My prescription for a healthy, peaceful, and prosperous world is based on the belief that it must be built from the ground up. A healthy world requires that the focus of attention must be on fundamental socioeconomic entities: families, households, villages, bioregions,[2] and communities of all kinds. You cannot have a healthy body if your cells and organs are feeble or diseased. This book is both descriptive and prescriptive, and, like all prescriptive treatises, it is biased by my own values, attitudes, and beliefs. I must confess to a distinct bias in favor of social justice, economic equity, personal freedom, participatory government and decision making, local self-reliance, and community self-determination. All these considerations, combined with my understanding of the relationships among smaller socioeconomic units within the global hierarchy, lead me to propose particular approaches to improving the health of those units at each level of society. These approaches are broadly outlined as follows:

- Cultivate functional diversity and versatility.
- Strengthen social bonds and organize for mutual support.
- Set and adhere to standards for quality of life: environmental, social, economic, recreational, and so forth.
- Build on available local resources and capabilities.
- Create buffering structures between global, national, regional, and local economies, not to isolate, but to provide a placid "safe harbor" conducive to the overall realization of shared goals and a better quality of life.

- Maximize the amount of local value added in all economic activity.
- Give priority to fulfilling the needs that are closest to home: spend locally, save locally, invest locally.

Central to the entire approach is the need to transform money and to liberate markets. As civilization has evolved, the work of each individual has become more and more specialized, and, with the increasing specialization of labor, exchange has become the central necessity of economic activity. The response to this need for exchange has been the evolution of money and markets. With the development of low-cost, efficient transport and communications technologies, markets have become increasingly efficient. Money, on the other hand, remains clouded in mystery and the subject of political intrigue.

Money is a subject that very few people really understand. Most believe that it is something they are not even capable of understanding. This is not surprising given the shallowness with which the subject is treated by the mass media and the seemingly intentional mystification of the subject by bankers, economists, and politicians. Even within the academic realm there is a considerable amount of confusion of concepts and misunderstanding of terms, and little attention is paid to critical analysis of the dominant structures of money and banking.

My research into the areas of monetary theory and history has spanned more than two decades. It has encompassed the accumulated literature and contemporary debate as well as hands-on activism and experimentation. I have been involved in the design, development, and operation of several cashless community trading systems and local currencies, assuming a variety of roles including those of organizer, administrator, and consultant. My active, local involvement gave me many chances to observe and experiment with various exchange approaches, currency features, and system enhancements. My active correspondence, meanwhile, has been extensive and global in scope, including academics, activists, and business people. I have continued to monitor developments in mutual credit, in LETS, in HOURS, and in various other existing and emergent exchange and currency models. The following chapters will describe these systems and others.

The rise of the community currency movement in recent years has provided ample learning opportunities for a great many people. But these opportunities are still the exceptions rather than the rule. There remains a massive job of education to be done if the subjects of money, banking, and finance are to be generally understood and people are to have the tools they need to bring about their own economic liberation. Toward that end, it is useful to clarify at the outset some essential terminology and to sketch a general outline of the major themes.

My purpose in writing this book is threefold:

first, to begin to demystify the subjects of money, banking, and finance so
that the ordinary person can understand their workings and the profound effects they have on his or her everyday life and well-being;
second, to strengthen the ongoing monetary reform movement by sharing
what I have learned about monetary history and theory over more than
two decades of research;
and third, to help guide the contemporary wave of development of community currencies and private exchange systems.

WHAT THIS BOOK CONTAINS, AND HOW TO USE IT

This volume focuses particularly on the creation and control of money, money
substitutes, and alternative exchange mechanisms. It is actually four books in
one, divided into four parts. While all the objectives are addressed in each
and every part, the individual parts tend to emphasize the objectives in the
order stated above. I advise you to read the book in its entirety, but depending on your main interests, you may want to read the various parts in a different order from that presented.

Part 1 is titled, "Monetary Realities and Official Illusions." It explains what
money really is, how it is created and extinguished, how it malfunctions, and
how it works against the interests of most individuals and communities. It
continues with a description of how money has evolved, taking on different
forms over time. It explains how these forms have enabled the further concentration of money's power in fewer hands and the erosion of social cohe-
sion, community power, and democratic governance. This is background that
I consider important to gaining a proper understanding of the money problem and how communities might cope with it. While I believe that this part
should be read by everyone, it could be skipped temporarily by readers who
already have some understanding of the nature of the problem and are anx-
ious to get to "the solutions."

Part 2, "Complementary Currencies, Past and Present," describes both historical and contemporary currency and exchange alternatives. These descriptions highlight the fundamental features, and the strengths and weaknesses, of
each example. Parts 1 and 2 together show some of the processes by which
individuals and communities have been disempowered, and some local
responses that have been effective in restoring community control and economic vitality in the face of centralized power. They set the stage for the more
prescriptive community exchange material contained in the remainder of the
book. This part, too, might be passed over temporarily by those who already

have some familiarity with these topics and wish to get right to the details of community currency design, improvement, and implementation.

Part 3, "Monetary Transformation and Community Empowerment," is essentially a primer on community exchange, highlighting the basic design elements and describing various forms, features, procedures, and methodologies. It outlines gentle strategies by which communities can establish equitable, sustainable, and ecologically sound local economies using "homegrown" exchange media and participatory methods for the allocation of credit and capital. It also provides in-depth coverage of the why, what, and how-to details. Community activists, organizers, and social entrepreneurs will find in this section the meat of the book.

Part 4, "Currency Design, Improvement, and Innovation," continues to build on the material presented in Part 3. It contains a number of innovative proposals for currencies, coupons, and scrip that address specific community problems while enhancing community power and strengthening the entire local economy. These models can be adapted to suit local conditions and needs. Social entrepreneurs and community organizers will find much here to stimulate their imaginations.

Throughout this book I will use the term *community currency* to mean any mechanism, under popular control that provides a means of payment other than official currency.

In this context, the term *community* is used to describe any association of individuals, groups, or businesses that bind themselves together under an agreement to use an internal payment mechanism. Under this definition, it is clear that a community need not be defined by geographical proximity. It is possible to conceive of a community of traders who are widely dispersed geographically. Indeed, we are seeing the emergence of Internet-based communities in which the transactions take place in cyberspace and participants are scattered all over the world. It is not hard to imagine a payment system that is global in scope and beyond the control of any government or bank. There have already been some interesting experiments with so-called e-cash or cyber cash.

A community currency need not take the form of paper notes. It can be as simple as a set of account pages in a notebook in which the values of trades are recorded. Such a book is called a *ledger,* and the *currency,* in that case, consists of the numbers that comprise the members' account balances.

In essence, then, a community currency means that members of the group empower themselves to create their own "money," which they agree to use in paying for purchases made among themselves.

My hope is that readers will quickly grasp the enormous power inherent in these cooperative and democratic exchange arrangements and that the information and ideas contained in this book will prove useful to others who share my dream of a world that works for everyone.

PART I

MONETARY REALITIES AND OFFICIAL ILLUSIONS

~

Money is a topic that few people understand. Sure, we use it every day and it seems familiar; but like water to the fish, we take it for granted and seldom give its role any notice. Yet the quality of the water that the fish inhabit is crucial in determining the quality of their existence. If the water happens to be polluted, the fish sicken and die. Likewise, money is a primary element of the modern economy that we inhabit. The quality of the money we use determines, to a great extent, the quality of our lives.

This section of the book looks beneath the surface, describing the nature and functions of money and markets, how they have evolved, and how they have become problematic. It examines the relationship between communities and the larger national and global economies and outlines principles and strategies that can enable the emergence of healthier communities and a more equitable and harmonious society. It begins the process of building a foundation of knowledge and understanding needed to design better exchange systems, which are essential to bringing that about.

Chapter 1

~

What's the Matter
with Money?

The process by which banks create money is so simple that the mind is repelled.

—JOHN KENNETH GALBRAITH

MONEY IS THE VITAL MEDIUM within which we live our economic lives. It is the central element around which many of our interpersonal relationships are organized. It is no exaggeration to say that the quality and essence of our medium of exchange, our money, are crucial to the quality of our lives— our social interactions, our personal priorities, our relationship to the earth, and our very ability to satisfy basic human needs. As water is to the fish, so money is to people. Though we are largely unconscious of it, its *quality* (as opposed to quantity) is crucial. When the water is polluted, the fish sicken and die; when money is "polluted," our economy malfunctions, and people suffer as their material needs go unmet and social dynamics are distorted.

Although the existing systems of money, finance, and exchange are severely flawed, few people understand the structural nature of these flaws, much less how they might be remedied. Money is a human invention that has changed over the years, and if it does not perform the way we want it to, we can reinvent it. Most of us take money for granted. Oh, it occupies plenty of our attention as we try to get enough of it to make ends meet, but we don't normally stop to think about what it really is, where it originates, or how it comes into being. We pay a huge price for our ignorance. Money has become an urgent problem.

As chapter 4 will explain, money is an information system. Therefore, let me describe the fault in terms of the information that it conveys, and explain why that information is inaccurate, incomplete, or false. Indeed, the present official monetary system has become a *misinformation* system. As the tightly controlled news media in totalitarian states are the antithesis of a free and independent press and political democracy, so is our monopolized and political system of money and finance antithetical to free exchange and economic democracy. Just as the news industry can be perverted into a propaganda machine to serve the interests of a dictatorial government, so has the finance industry been perverted into a machine of privilege to serve the interests of a power elite.

Symptoms of Disease

The symptoms are readily apparent, and the news media are daily filled with reports that highlight them: inflation; unemployment; bankruptcies; farm, home, and business foreclosures; ever increasing indebtedness and impoverishment; homelessness; and widening gaps between the incomes and wealth of the various economic classes—the "haves," the "middle class," and the "have-nots." These economic problems, in turn, are largely responsible for social and environmental decay: violent crime, suicide, drug and alcohol abuse, theft, and embezzlement, along with pollution of the land, water, and air. Such frequently reported events are not accidents; they derive from the inadequacies and errors inherent in structures that humans have themselves created.

Three Ways in Which Conventional Money Malfunctions

Conventional money malfunctions in three basic ways:

1. It is kept artificially scarce; there is never enough of it to serve the purposes for which it is created.
2. It is misallocated at its source, going not to those who are most in need or who will use it most effectively but to political power centers (especially central governments), well-connected "insiders," and those who already control vast pools of wealth (such as large corporations).
3. It systematically pumps wealth from the poor and the middle class to the rich.

Why this is so, and how it can be remedied, will be explained in turn, but to do so we first need to know how money is created within the current monetary system.

How Money Is Created

When I try to explain to people the way in which conventional money is created these days, I am generally met with a blank stare. I think it is not that they don't understand what I am saying; they just can't believe it. In the words of renowned economist John Kenneth Galbraith, "The process by which banks create money is so simple that the mind is repelled."[1] It is generally believed that money is created by the government, but here is the simple truth. **Today, money takes the form of bank credit that must be borrowed into circulation.** In other words, conventional money commonly exists as bank deposits, that is, balances in checking or savings accounts that are secured by interest-bearing debt. Money is the product of a private banking cartel.

The familiar Federal Reserve notes, the cash that we use every day, are simply physical tokens of the money that was first created as bank credit. The use of checks and debit cards is simply a way of transferring bank credit (that is, money) from your account to someone else's account; the checks and debit cards are not themselves money. Neither are credit cards money, but they allow you to create money by going into debt to the issuing bank. The main point that needs to be understood is that **in order for money to come into circulation, someone must go into debt to a bank.** If there were no bank debt, there would be virtually no money—it's as simple as that. Since banks charge interest on all this debt, and since the money to pay the interest can come only from further debt, debt grows like a cancer within the global economic "body." This *debt imperative* creates a *growth imperative* that is forcing us to destroy the life-support systems of the planet.

Wealth creation and money creation are two entirely different things. Wealth is created by the application of human skills to natural resources in the myriad ways that produce useful goods and services. Planting crops, assembling computers, building houses, and publishing a newspaper are all examples of the production of wealth. Money, on the other hand, is a human contrivance; it is a symbol created by a deliberate process involving entities called banks.

The Federal Reserve is the entity responsible for the issuance and regulation of money in the United States. Here is the simple truth about money and its creation straight from the horse's mouth. This quote comes directly from an official Federal Reserve publication:

> The actual process of money creation takes place in the banks . . . checkable liabilities of banks are money. . . . These liabilities are customers' accounts. They increase when . . . the proceeds of loans made by the banks are credited to borrowers' accounts.[2]

Let's take that one piece at a time. *The actual process of money creation takes place in the banks.*

Yes, money is a human creation, and it is the banks that create it. People still dig gold and silver out of the ground, but we no longer use those metals as money. What, then, is the substance of money today? It is bank credit, that is, *checkable liabilities,* or *customers' accounts.* So the balance in your checking account and mine is a liability of the bank—something the bank owes you and me—and that is money.

How does that liability get created in the first place? These liabilities *increase when the proceeds of loans made by the banks are credited to borrowers' accounts.* In other words, the money is created when the bank makes a loan to someone. That person's account is credited (increased) when the loan is approved, and new money is thus created. That person then spends the money, and somehow, perhaps after changing hands many times, it ends up in your account or mine.

"What?" you say, "I thought banks loaned out other people's deposits." That's true enough. In their role as depositories banks do lend other people's deposits, but in their role as *banks of issue,* they actually create new money by making loans. So banks are the wellspring of money. They create it by making "loans," and they extinguish it when loans are repaid. Money has a beginning and an ending. It begins when the bank makes a loan, and it ends when the loan principal is repaid.

Now what makes this kind of money credible and generally acceptable as a payment medium? First, we know that everyone else is willing to accept it, but this begs the question, why? The answer is that anyone can go to their bank and draw out "cash" against their bank account balance. This cash is in the form of *Federal Reserve notes.* If you examine one of these notes carefully, you will see that they have been declared to be *legal tender*—"for all debts, public and private." This means that they must be accepted as payment by anyone to whom money is owed, be it an individual, a corporation, or a government agency. Further, Federal Reserve notes are backed by the *full faith and credit* of the federal government of the United States of America, which is credible because of the government's power to levy and collect taxes.

In the United States, it is mainly the *commercial* banks that create the bulk of the money supply in the form of bank deposits (or bank credit). Most of our money consists of deposits in checking accounts. About 30 percent of the money supply is in the form of coins or circulating paper currency. According to the Federal Reserve Bank of Chicago: "currency is a relatively small part of the money stock. About 69%, or $623 billion, of the $898 billion total money stock in December 1991, was in the form of transaction deposits, of which $290 billion were demand and $333 billion were other checkable deposits."[3]

But even this understates the matter, for Federal Reserve notes, while printed by the United States Treasury, are put into circulation by the banking system, which buys them from the Treasury for the cost of printing. These paper notes represent bank credit. Banks give it out whenever depositors prefer to have paper "cash" in their wallets. Whatever amount of paper money you withdraw from banks is debited against your bank account balance. Thus, even the part of the money supply that appears as paper currency begins as bank credit or "loans" on which the banks collect interest. So about 95 percent of the money supply is based on interest-bearing bank loans. Only about 5 percent of the money supply, which exists as coins spent into circulation by the Treasury, arises outside the banks. In sum, the bulk of our money gets created as bank credit.

The amount of credit money that the banking system as a whole can create is determined by the policies of the Federal Reserve Board. The Federal Reserve is a private corporation to which Congress has delegated power (some say unconstitutionally) over money in the United States. The "Fed" acts as a central bank that presides over a private banking cartel. The share of the money-creating power allocated to each individual bank is determined by the amount of deposits that a bank is able to attract from customers and use as "reserves."[4]

As pointed out above, banks act both as creators of money and as depositories for money. When you deposit your paycheck in a commercial bank, the bank is acting as a depository. This money is then available for you to use by writing checks against your account or using a debit card. But the money that you deposited had to begin somewhere. You got it from your employer; your employer got it from a customer; the customer got it from another employer or customer; and so on, back to the beginning. The important thing to understand is the nature of that beginning. Banks *create* money by making loans; they don't just reshuffle it. The money that you received in your paycheck was created at the point when a bank, acting as a bank of issue, granted a loan to someone and credited her or his account for the amount of the loan.

As the Federal Reserve itself describes it:

> Debt does more than simply transfer idle funds to where they can be put to use—merely reshuffling existing funds in the form of credit. *It also provides a means of creating entirely new funds.* . . . [emphasis added]
>
> . . . a depositor's balance also rises when the depository institution extends credit—either by granting a loan or buying securities from the depositor. In exchange for the note or security, the lending or investing institution credits the depositor's account or gives a check that can be deposited at yet another depository institution. In this case, no one else loses a deposit. The total of currency and checkable deposits—the money supply—is increased. New money has been brought into existence by expansion of depository institution credit. Such newly created funds are in addition to funds that all financial institutions provide in their operations as intermediaries between savers and users of savings."[5]
>
> [All bank deposits originally] come into existence as banks extend credit to customers by exchanging bank deposits for the various assets that banks acquire—promissory notes of businesses and consumers, mortgages on real estate, and government and other securities.[6]

This last paragraph is just a way of saying that the bank credits your account for the amount of a loan, and you, in return, give the bank your promissory note or a mortgage on your house. Those instruments—promissory notes, mortgages, and securities—are assets to the banks. They are claims that the banks have against the property of its customers, but to the customers they represent debts owed to the banks.

An Example of Money Creation

1. You go to a commercial bank and ask for money, let's say, to start a business.
2. The bank offers you a "home equity loan" of $100,000, which you accept. You are required to sign a note giving the bank a mortgage on your house. This note carries interest at an annual rate of, say, 8%, and requires you to make regular monthly payments of $836.44 for the next 20 years. (By that time you will have paid the bank a total of $200,745.60.)
3. The bank makes two entries on its books. One increases the amount of its assets, while the other is a corresponding increase to its liabilities. Specifically, it debits (increases) its asset account for $100,000, the asset being your mortgage note; and it credits (increases) deposit liabilities for the same amount, the liability being the $100,000 it credits to your checking account.
4. You are now free to spend $100,000. You typically do this by writing checks drawn on your account or by using your debit card to make purchases. As you do so, the supply of money circulating in the economy is increased.
5. As you make payments on your loan, the principal portion of your payment reduces your loan balance, and the supply of money circulating in the economy is decreased by that amount. The interest portion of your payment is added to the bank's equity and reserves, which allows the bank to make additional loans to others and further expand the money supply.

Why There Is Never Enough Money

Debtors are always required to pay interest on these loans. Thus, the commercial banks lend something that they create out of nothing and then require that the "borrower" pay interest for the privilege. Further, such bank loans are usually secured, that is, the banks usually require that the borrower pledge some "collateral," which they will confiscate if the borrower fails to repay the loan. Interest-bearing debts grow simply with the passage of time, but the supply of money with which to repay those loans, plus interest, can be expanded only by the banks making additional loans. The principal amount is created at the time the loan is made, but the money to pay the interest due in subsequent periods has not yet been created. Thus debtors, as a group, are in an impossible situation of always owing more money than there is in existence. They are forced to compete with one another for scarce money, in a futile attempt to avoid defaulting on their debts. Like the game of musical chairs, the system requires that some must eventually fail. Those borrowers who default on their loans, of course, end up losing their collateral.[7]

The Federal Reserve unabashedly admits that it purposely tries to maintain the scarcity of money. It clearly states in one of its official publications the misguided notion that **"money . . . derives its value from its scarcity in relation to its usefulness."**[8] This may indeed be true for politicized and improperly issued money, but it is decidedly not true of money that is properly issued and subject to the discipline of the free market. If the central government and the financial sector claim a disproportionate share of the country's wealth by emitting what may be regarded as legalized counterfeit, then, of course, they must limit the amount of money made available to everyone else. The current system is based on the "myth of scarcity," but the world needs systems and structures that affirm the truth of an abundant universe. This does not mean structures that allow inequity and waste, but structures that are efficient, self-regulating, democratic, and unbiased, structures that enhance the prospects that each person will able to satisfy his or her basic, real needs.

How Money Is Misallocated

Money, as it emerges from the banks that create it, is not distributed fairly, because the allocation decisions are not made democratically but rather by elite groups of corporate bankers who are not held properly accountable. They act in their own interests, pursuing goals that are typical of any corporate business—profit and growth. As Ralph Borsodi explained it:

> It is a sad but outrageous fact that banking is conducted today as a business by men who label themselves businessmen—which presumably means an enterprise conducted for profit. In its essential nature, banking is a profession, and like every profession should be conducted to render a service by men whose motivation is service first, last and all the time. They must, of course, be properly compensated for their work, but this, in its essence, should be a professional fee, not a business profit.[9]

The misallocation of credit is a problem that has gained some degree of official recognition, and government attempts to remedy it are evident in such laws as the Community Reinvestment Act, which requires banks to allocate a minimum percentage of their loans to local needs for business finance and housing. Such measures may give the appearance that the problem is being addressed, but their practical effect is minuscule. In recent years, locally owned banks have been increasingly acquired and merged into ever larger holding companies. Credit allocation policies and lending decisions have been increasingly shifted to remote home offices, and many communities are being starved for capital as the savings of the community have been sent to other regions and other countries in search of higher returns. Recent deregulation of banking, which allows banks to engage in a wider variety of financial activities, is likely to intensify this problem. Banking, always a flawed servant of the community, is today no longer a member of the community but a remotely controlled financial engine less concerned about local needs and more singly obsessed with the bottom line.

The greatest abuses, however, derive from the politicization of money, banking, and finance. Private banking interests and the central government have become intertwined and mutually dependent. In return for its privileged position, the banking cartel must assure that the central government is able to borrow and spend virtually any amount of money it wishes. The banking system, despite its public rhetoric about the importance of fiscal responsibility, will always "float" the necessary budget deficits of the central government, by "monetizing" the debt. What this means is that the banking system will create enough new money to allow the market to absorb the new government bonds that must be issued to finance the deficit. Thus, it allows the government to spend as much as it wishes without raising taxes directly. The most destructive aspect of this almost limitless power to spend is that, as E. C. Riegel has written, "it permits ambitious or designing or fanatical men who are in control of government to light the fires of war."[10] If governments were required first to come to the people to obtain the money to fight, there would be few if any wars.

The effect on the economy of monetizing government debt is that it causes a general increase in prices. This phenomenon is called "inflation," which has been called a "hidden tax." As the well-known economist Milton Friedman argues, "inflation is a monetary phenomenon." This means that the increase in prices is not due to goods and services being worth more but to the money being worth less.

Economists often argue that inflation is caused by *too much money in circulation*. This would seem to refute my contention that money is chronically in short supply. The answer to this is that inflation is *not* caused by the amount of money per se but by the fact that some of the money in circulation is improperly issued and misallocated. Such is the case when the banking system "monetizes" the government debt, as described above. We can think of that money as counterfeit, albeit legal counterfeit. It is spent into the economy without putting more goods and services into the marketplace; thus, as it is commonly put, "there is too much money chasing too few goods." Merchants, sensing this presence of excess (bogus) money, increase their prices to compensate. Other players in the economy (suppliers, workers, and so forth) follow suit to the extent that their market power allows. The phenomenon of inflation, along with that of deflation, will be discussed more thoroughly in chapter 9.

In our economy, the people have been cut out of the most important decision process, that of determining how the aggregate wealth of the nation, the fruits of everyone's labor, will be spent. Some of the abuses that result are massive expenditures for weapons; military interventions; "foreign aid" to support client governments; and bailouts of corporations and third-world governments, which benefit mainly the banks and the wealthy well-connected few while increasing the gap between rich and poor.

How Money Pumps Wealth from the Poor to the Rich

When I say that money pumps wealth from the poor to the rich, I speak not of the very poor, who have little or no wealth-producing capacity, but of the vast majority of people who work for a living but have little or no financial "net worth." The "debt trap" is the bane of that class of people. Debt within the current system is destructive in two ways, first because of the interest (usury) that must be paid for the use of money (bank credit), and second, because of the collateral that must be forfeited when the debtor is unable to make repayment.[11] The chronic insufficiency of money assures that there will inevitably be some forfeitures. It is interesting to note that the word *mortgage* derives from roots that mean "death pledge," a kind of gamble. It is almost impossible anymore for a family to acquire a home without undertaking the "death gamble." My grandfather, along with countless others, lost that gamble and his home during the Great Depression, when because of unemployment he was unable to make his mortgage payments to the bank.

If information is the essential quality of money, then the next logical question is, What kind of information does it, and should it, carry? The answer that immediately presents itself is that money should carry information about "merit." If money allows its possessor to claim wealth from the community, what is the basis for that claim? The possession of money should be evidence that the possessor has delivered value to the community (in the form of goods and services) and is therefore entitled to receive back a like amount of value.

If money is improperly issued, though, the information that it carries is polluted at the very source. By issuing money to unproductive or privileged clients of the money monopoly at more favorable terms, and by demanding higher interest rates from the rest, the banking system redistributes wealth from producers to privileged nonproducers. The consistent pattern of official action over the past several decades has been to concentrate economic power by centralizing control over the medium of exchange, limiting access to it, and charging exorbitant prices (in the form of interest/usury) for its use. Money carries information, but the present monetary system is dysfunctional because it carries flawed information.

For Whom the Debt Tolls

No debtor is an island, paying interest all alone. Everybody pays the cost of interest, even those who do not borrow directly. Interest costs are included in the price of everything we buy, whether the goods or services are provided by the business sector or the government. The production of whatever we buy must be financed in some way, and interest is the cost of using financial capital. Margrit Kennedy gives examples that show the percentage of the costs that go to pay interest on capital. Though her examples are drawn from her native Germany, it is clear that the pattern would be similar for all industrial nations, since their monetary and financial structures are all basically the same.

Kennedy shows that the costs of interest on capital in the 1980s, as a percentage of the fees paid by users, were 12% for garbage collection, 38% for water, 47% for sewers, and a whopping 77% of rents paid for public housing.[1] She also compares the interest paid and the interest gained (as income) for the population of what were then West German households divided into ten different income groups of equal size. This comparison indicates, as expected, that the lower income groups, because they tended to be net debtors, paid much more interest on their debts than they gained in interest on their investments. Indeed, the 80% of households having lower incomes, on average, paid more interest on their debts than they gained in interest on their investments. The highest 10% gained about twice as much interest as they paid, and the richest of those gained progressively more.[2]

Lending money at interest, either directly or through financial intermediaries, is one of the primary mechanisms by which the rich get richer and the poor get poorer.

Chapter 2

_~_

Community Currency and the New World Order

Money will decide the fate of mankind.

—JACQUES RUEFF

THE FOUNDATION OF POWER and centralized control in today's world is the power to create and manipulate the medium of exchange. Because money has the power to command resources, and because most of us take current monetary practices for granted, those few who control the creation of money are able to appropriate for their own purposes vast amounts of resources without being noticed. The entire machinery of money and finance has now been appropriated to serve the interests of centralized power.

The key element in any strategy to transform society must therefore be the liberation of money and the exchange process. If money is liberated, commerce will be liberated; if commerce is liberated, the people will be empowered to the full extent of their abilities to serve one another; the liberation of capital and land and the popular control of politics will follow as a matter of course. Once equitable exchange mechanisms have been established, it will no longer be possible for the privileged few to appropriate the major portion of the land, productive resources, and political power.

Why Community Currencies?

Community currencies are complementary to, and operate in parallel with, the dominant national money systems. They are intended to serve purely as a medium of exchange that circulates among a limited group of associated traders who may be geographically proximate or widely dispersed.

The need for community currencies stems from the fact that the mechanisms of money, banking, and finance in the dominant political-economic reality are designed to promote the accumulation of capital (wealth) in the hands of a few corporate entities that serve insider interests at the expense of the mass of society and the physical environment. As these entities become ever more powerful, the traditional countervailing forces of government and other organized societal groups (such as labor unions) are either neutralized or co-opted and become ineffective in asserting the interests of the majority of people.

Usually, within most community economies, there is plenty of demand for goods and services that remains unfulfilled, and there are plenty of skills and talents which go unused. Why can't the unused resources be employed to fill the unmet needs? Mainly, it is because there is a general lack of money circulating within the local economy, and what money there is does not reach those who are most in need. Official money can, and does, flow anywhere. But it does not remain in circulation for very long within the local economy. Rather, it provides a means by which absentee owners can extract their gains from the local economy and allocate them to more profitable investments elsewhere.

Everyone who works for a livelihood is thus forced to compete in markets that are increasingly global in scope and are dominated and controlled by the biggest players in the global monopoly game. With the increasing mobility of capital, workers are being driven to the lowest common denominator of wages, working conditions, and environmental quality, and communities are increasingly deprived of control over their own quality of life. The result is a "race to the bottom" that everyone is forced to enter.

Is there no escape? More and more creative thinkers are saying that there is, and that community money must be part of the solution. Humanizing globalization requires that money be reinvented, so that the new rules work in harmony with deeper values that most of us cherish.

The New World Order

It was a close friend and colleague who first impressed upon me more than thirty years ago the truth of the saying, "The chains that bind are in the mind." It is what we believe, or refuse to believe, that limits us, both individually and collectively. But it is not belief alone that limits us. We must also have the courage of our convictions. We must be willing to act on our beliefs if we are ever to realize our dreams. While it may appear that our liberation is mostly constrained by external forces and the material aspect of our being, we are actually more powerful than we are willing to admit.

Many of us have a sense that all is not right with the world, that maybe we can do something to make it better. My own struggle has taught me some important lessons, the most important of which is that I cannot change anything without first changing myself. Freedom is not free. It has to be earned. Freedom cannot be had without taking responsibility. When we seek to make change in the world, we must make it at every level, beginning with ourselves. Change at the personal level then enables change at the *inter*-personal level, then at the societal, structural, and institutional level, and maybe even at the biological level.

For me, the process has been one of opening up to a greater Spirit, of being vulnerable, of allowing even my cherished values, attitudes, and beliefs to be called into question. Taking greater guidance from within and letting go of erroneous and limiting beliefs has allowed me to better grasp my connectedness with my fellow humans, my environment, and the entire web of life.

When we have taken the "beam" out of our own eye, we can see more clearly to take the speck out of our brother's eye. Then we can begin to heal our relationships. We have to find a way to transcend disputes and differences, to be able to accept one another as we are and relate to one another in compassion and love. Healthy relationships in functional communities provide a stable platform from which we can examine the adequacy or inadequacy of the economic, political, and social structures we have inherited from the past and then start creating structures that are more consistent with our highest values, dreams, and visions. We can abandon those that are flawed, dysfunctional, and beyond repair, and we can build new ones that support greater realization of the human potential.

I believe that there is something beautiful trying to be born in the world. The new world order will not be dictated from the top down. It will not be something arranged in private by some global elite. It will emerge from the bottom up, revealed by a higher Spirit accessible to everyone. We humans, in our role as cocreators with the "higher power," have plenty of work to do. There is work to be done at the personal level, confronting our own fears and doubts and taking responsibility for resolving our dilemmas; at the community level, using inevitable conflicts as opportunities to transcend our petty selves and limited perceptions; and at the societal level, building new structures that support and nurture rather than coerce and brutalize.

Gaia Consciousness and Human Unity

The past four decades have brought a new period of enlightenment in which humans in increasing numbers have become aware of their oneness as a species and their place in nature, not as dominator or controller, but as an integral part of the whole web of life. Many cultures have held the view that Earth is a living being in which each living species plays a vital role. It is a view that is now becoming current in our own culture and that sees humans as the "global brain," the Earth's center of self-awareness.[1] This changing identity is beginning to have profound effects on the way we live our lives and, if we allow it, can change the course of history. Imagine a world in which war and abuse are only dimly remembered, in which everyone has enough to live a dignified life, in which harmony among the species prevails and the rape of the earth has ceased.

In order for us to realize that vision, we must believe that it is possible; then we will find a way to make it happen, for "faith is the substance of things hoped for."[2] Our actions emerge out of our visions and ideals. Yet they are also grounded in current realities. Economics drives politics, and money is the central mechanism through which economic power is exerted in the modern world. The history of the United States shows how power has progressively migrated from the people, local communities, counties, and states toward the federal government in general and the executive branch in particular. It is only through a study of monetary history, however, that a clear picture can be gained of how this has happened.

Humanizing globalization requires that money be reinvented, so that the new rules work in harmony with deeper values that most of us cherish.

Among the primary obstacles to the improvement of the human condition are the general reliance on the current structure of global finance and the nature of its primary element, money. The dominating nature of these institutions is akin to that of the monarchies and ecclesiastical hierarchies of past eras. Their time is quickly passing.

New, transformational structures based on different values and assumptions are being developed. These structures need to be more equitable, democratic, and "ethereal."[3] They must be established in ways that promote the expression of values such as service, fairness, fellowship, and cooperation rather than greed, privilege, and self-seeking. Thus, they will not compete with existing institutions but develop in parallel with them, providing operational alternatives that can better serve the needs of people and the earth as the old order continues to decline.

Correcting Past Errors

Many of our fundamental social contracts and conventions are based on notions that are erroneous and self-defeating. Among the most insidious of these are

1. The belief that the universe was created for humans and that we should dominate creation and manipulate it for our own ends; that humans are separate from the earth and that nature is an enemy to be subdued and controlled
2. the division of people into classes or castes—"us" and "them"; "nobles" and "peasants"; "aristocrats" and "commoners"; elites who are suited to govern and the masses who must be governed; clients who are defective and need to be "fixed" and professional fixers who are certified as competent to do the fixing
3. the belief that it is just for a majority, in the name of government, to coerce the conscription of either person or property for the use of the state
4. the belief that land and natural resources, which are the common heritage of all humans (and indeed, all life on Earth), can be treated in the same way as other property, to be bought and sold, to be used or abused, and to be held as an object for speculative gain
5. belief in the legitimacy and efficacy of the practice of granting to a few the privilege to create money based on debt and to charge interest for its use

While all these conventional notions require reexamination, the last of them is the main concern of this book.

The entire world is now in thrall to the central bankers who create and control the official exchange media. In almost every country, official money is kept intentionally scarce, much of it is improperly issued, it is expensive, and it is increasingly unavailable to those who cannot compete in the global economy or will not be drawn into the "race to the bottom." Communities that wish to preserve a higher quality of life need to find ways to protect themselves from the pernicious influences of conventional money and the machinations of global finance. Community currency and exchange systems can provide the foundation for revitalized and healthy community economies.

Chapter 3

❧

The Power and Place of Money

Money has become a ring we wear through the nose, which allows us to be lead around by those who control it.

—MARK KINNEY

THERE ARE THREE FUNDAMENTAL modes of economic interaction: *gift, involuntary transfer,* and *reciprocal exchange.* A gift, if it is truly a gift, is given freely without expectation that anything will be obtained in return. If there is such a thing as altruism, the gift is its visible expression. Involuntary transfers, on the other hand, are based on an entirely different sentiment. They can take a variety of forms, some of which may be considered to be legitimate and others not. Among the latter would be such criminal acts as robbery, theft, and embezzlement. Involuntary transfers also include taxation in its various forms. Opinions differ as to the legitimacy and fairness of the various kinds of taxes. The third mode, reciprocal exchange, is defined as a voluntary agreement between two parties, in which each one delivers to the other goods or services that the parties consider to be of equal value. Actually, since value is subjective, each party receives something that he or she considers to be more valuable than what she or he gave up.

Reciprocal exchange can take a variety of forms. The most fundamental form is the barter trade, about which the next chapter will have more to say. Money was invented to get around the barter limitation. More recently, we have seen the emergence of community currencies and mutual credit systems that are complementary to official monetary systems.

The Power Inherent in Money

The rise of the market economy has been the single most important element in defining the modern industrial society. With the increasing specialization of labor, exchange becomes an ever more important process. The power of money lies in the fact that it is readily accepted in the market in exchange for whatever one may need or want. This universal exchangeability is potentially liberating as it reinforces specialization, which, in turn, provides the potential for greater economic efficiency and personal satisfaction in one's work. When a person is able to do that work at which she or he is most skilled and most enjoys, both the individual and the community benefit. In the ideal, anything that facilitates exchange enhances productivity and the ability of everyone to meet their needs. In practice, however, exchange does not always distribute benefits in an equitable way. For some, livelihood is obtained from the income derived from investments or accumulated wealth; for most, livelihood depends on the ability to sell their labor in the market. To the extent that markets are dominated or distorted, the people who exchange their labor for money are at a disadvantage.

The use of money is so pervasive in our society that each individual becomes habituated to it very early in life. Even children of four or five know that their material desires can be satisfied by taking money to the shops, and they learn very quickly to value money. The dominant roles of money and markets have been exaggerated by our collective conditioning and mentality—our values, attitudes, and beliefs. Modern Western culture is preoccupied with the physical aspect of existence and man's domination over nature. We are, to a large extent, alienated from nature and from one another. Seeing ourselves as separate and apart, we have degraded both our physical and social environments. The personal portfolio takes on greater importance than the common good, and the short-term payoff takes precedence over long-term health and sustainability.

As money became a more powerful element of economic life, its creation and control became an object of political contention. Those who understood its power have been able to gain a monopoly over its creation and allocation, making it readily available to the favored few and scarce and expensive for everyone else.

To possess money is to possess power, for with money one may induce others to conform to one's will. So money has become, as Mark Kinney describes it, "a ring we wear through the nose, which allows us to be led around by those who control it." Our *collective* liberation will result from a common understanding of how we are controlled by money and how we can transcend the structures of money we have inherited from the past.

The Place of Money in Human Interaction

To say that money confers power is not to say that money or the use of money is inherently evil; on the contrary, the proper kind of money used in the right circumstances is a liberating tool. Money, properly conceived, can allow the fuller expression of human creativity and the fuller realization of a dignified

life for everyone. Those who like to quote the Bible on this subject usually
quote it incorrectly. The Bible does not say that money is the root of all evil. It
says, *"the love of money is the root of all evil."*[1] But the word *money* in this context actually is more accurately rendered as "riches" or "wealth," not money
as we understand it to be a medium of exchange. So the meaning of this verse
is to caution us against the extreme pursuit of material riches—greed and
acquisitiveness, and the bondage of materialism.

The power of money lies in the fact that it is readily accepted in
the market in exchange for whatever one may need or want.

Money, in its current form as the medium of exchange, has not lived up to
its potential as a liberator. This is largely because it has been politicized and
centrally controlled but also because money and markets have been extended
into realms that are better served by other exchange mechanisms. For example, within the family and clan, where relationships are close and personal and
nurturing is a central concern, needs are easily assessed, responsibilities are
readily assigned, and altruism is generally expressed. In these contexts, free
gift exchange and sharing, rather than buying and selling, are clearly seen to
work best. The use of money to mediate exchanges within the household, family, or clan would be destructive to the human relationships that are normal
and necessary to their health. Money is better suited to facilitating the more
impersonal exchanges that need to take place between social units, where
reciprocity and strict accounting are more important.

The Body Economic

The human body is an apt analogy through which economic processes can be
understood. As blood circulates throughout the body, bringing nutrients to
every cell and organ, we can think of money as the "lifeblood" of society,
enabling the distribution of goods and services to all sectors of the economy.
But blood is not the only distribution mechanism. Within cells and organs
there are other, more subtle processes by which nutrients are distributed and
allocated as needed, being transmitted and shared by those closest to the need.
So, too, do the basic socioeconomic units have internal processes that exclude
money but use it effectively for transfers between them. A primary economic
unit may consist of a single household or a cluster of households, a village, or
a tribe. It is an economic entity within which all processes of production,

exchange, and consumption take place. There is, of course, always a certain amount of importation and exportation of goods and services, the nature and amount of which vary according to the needs and resources of that economic unit.

A healthy society depends on the health of each of the units of which it is comprised. A primary aspect of that health is a high level of complexity of internal function, which implies, in this case, a high level of personal, household, and community self-reliance. As Jane Jacobs has so convincingly argued, it is not nation-states that are the salient entities for understanding the structure of economic life, it is cities; and the economies of cities grow and develop through import replacement, which is replacement of imported products by goods that are locally produced. Import replacement is the outcome of a dynamic tension between specialization and diversification that enables ever higher levels of achievement. It seems likely that smaller economic entities—towns, villages, and even households—might also develop and grow in a similar way. Thus, our efforts should be focused on promoting the health and vitality of local economies, and, as I shall argue throughout, community-based exchange mechanisms and a large measure of local self-determination are essential elements in any strategy designed to achieve that goal.[2]

In the remainder of part 1, we will narrow our focus to explore more deeply the true nature of money. The next four chapters will describe the impact of the intrusion of politics into money and the exchange process and will then outline broad strategies by which communities might protect and empower themselves.

Chapter 4

~

What Is Money?

Money is an information system we use to deploy human effort.

—Michael Linton

The question What is money? may at first seem trivial. After all, we in this modern day make constant use of it. But it is our confusion about the essence of money that has allowed it to be abused, misused, and misallocated. Like water to the fish, money is the primary medium within which we live our economic lives. As such, we take it for granted and rarely look at it objectively.

At the outset, it is necessary to make a clear distinction between *money* and *wealth*. It is quite common for us to use these terms interchangeably, but an understanding of the money problem requires that we be precise in our meanings and usage of terms. Have you ever heard someone make a statement to the effect that so-and-so "has a lot of money?" What do people mean by that? That so-and-so has stacks of United States currency notes stuffed in a mattress or closet? Or a huge balance in a checking account at the bank? Or owns lots of stocks, bonds, or real estate? Chances are that so-and-so actually has very little currency and only a small amount in the bank. What was probably meant, and what should have been said, is "so-and-so is very *wealthy*." People hold their wealth in various forms, but most of these forms are not money.

How did we come to be so careless in our usage of these words? It is understandable in light of the fact that we live in a culture in which market mechanisms are highly developed and very efficient. These markets allow for the easy conversion of one form of wealth into another by means of ordinary exchange processes of buying and selling, and borrowing and lending. Stock markets, bond markets, real-estate markets, and others make it relatively easy to convert "illiquid" assets into more liquid form: into money. It is no accident that we apply the term "liquidity" to distinguish various kinds of assets from one another on the basis of their acceptability as payment in the market for goods and services. As blood in the physical body is liquid and provides for the easy exchange and transport of nutrients and wastes throughout the body, money is also "liquid" in that it facilitates the exchange of goods and services and their allocation throughout the economy.

Definitions

So what *is* money?

There are three kinds of definitions we should consider.

A practical definition describes money's distinguishing feature in common practice.
A functional definition tells what money *does.*
An essential definition tells what money actually *is.*

The practical definition of money is this: Money is anything that is *generally accepted* as a means of payment. According to this definition, money is whatever people collectively say it is. Something is established as money by a general consensus among traders that they will accept that something as payment for the goods and services they sell.

The functional definition of money is the one typically found in the textbooks, which lists multiple functions as belonging to money. These include the following:

1. Money is a medium of exchange.
2. Money is a standard of value.
3. Money is a unit of account.
4. Money is a store of value.
5. Money is a standard of deferred payment.

There are many problems with these definitions, but their primary inadequacy is that they tell what money *does,* not what it *is.* We need to understand the basic *essence* of money. Once we have grasped its essence we can begin to design exchange systems that will more equitably serve the needs of people and avoid money's destructive impact on the earth.

The Essential Nature of Money

What, then, is the essential nature of money?

Michael Linton, the originator of an exchange system called "LETS" (Local Employment and Trading System), has provided us with an essential definition of money. Linton defines money as "an information system we use to deploy human effort." This is a profound revelation, and, if we think about his definition, it becomes clear that our **acceptance of money is based on its informational content.**

Think of the market economy as a game of put-and-take. Each player takes goods and services from the market, and each player puts goods and services into the market. Money is really just a way of keeping score. When you take something from the market (by buying), you offer money in payment. When you put something into the market (by selling), you receive money in payment. Other things being equal, those who put more value into the economy (by selling) receive, over time, more money. **Money, then, is an accounting system.**

Another problem with the traditional functional definitions given above is that they are mutually contradictory. Consider that *money as a medium of exchange* is diametrically opposed to *money as a store of value.* If money is to be used as a medium of exchange, it should be spent; if it is to be used as a store of value, it should be held. The ideal money, as I will show later, should be purely a medium of exchange, and that is what we will consider it to be. Storage of value is best accomplished in other ways, for instance by investment in real assets such as land, buildings, tools, equipment, and commodities or in financial assets such as stocks, bonds, or time deposits in a bank, to name a few. Similarly, the use of money (in its modern form) as a standard of value invites confusion and mismanagement. When money was in the form of gold or silver, it could effectively serve as a standard of value, but now, when money is simply an IOU of a government or central bank, its value is determined more by monetary management policies than by market forces. This issue has been more completely addressed elsewhere, and will be revisited in chapter 6.[1]

The Exchange Process and the Purpose of Money

The process of economic exchange always involves two parties. The fundamental exchange process is the barter exchange. When Smith delivers to Jones a sack of flour and Jones gives to Smith a bushel of apples in return, a complete barter transaction has occurred. Both parties are satisfied, and both have profited from the exchange. Smith values Jones's apples more than the flour he has to give for them, while Jones values Smith's flour more than the apples he must give. Thus, both parties are satisfied that they have gained something in the bargain. The problem with simple barter, of course, is that Jones may want Smith's flour, but he may have nothing that Smith wants. In that case no trade can be made. The fundamental purpose of money, experts have long agreed, is to transcend this limitation of barter. Bilgram and Levy, for instance, assert: "We should . . . define money as *any medium of exchange adapted or designed to meet the inadequacy of the method of exchanging things by simple barter.*"[2]

But what constitutes a medium of exchange, and how can one trading partner use it to get what she wants, even though she has nothing wanted by the other? Bilgram and Levy go on to explain: "The one quality which is peculiar to money alone is its general acceptability in the market and in the discharge of debts. How does money acquire this specific quality? It is manifestly due solely to *a consensus of the members of the community to accept certain valuable things, such as coin and certain forms of credit, as mediums of exchange.*"[8]

We can see then that **the essence of money is an agreement** (a consensus) **to accept something that in itself may have no fundamental utility to us, but that we are assured can be exchanged in the market for something that does.**

Whatever we use as money, then, carries information. The possession of money, in whatever form, gives the holder a claim against the community of traders who use that money. The amount of money informs us about the magnitude of that claim. But the *legitimacy* of that claim also needs to be assured in some way. The possession of money should also be evidence that the holder has delivered value to someone in the community and therefore has a right to receive like value in return, or that the holder has received it, by gift or other transfer, from someone else who has delivered value.

Unfortunately, throughout history, this ideal has been subverted in various ways depending on the kind of money used at the time.

Historical Forms of Money

Many different forms of money have been used. But the forms or kinds of money in common use have, over time, become progressively less substantial and more ethereal. There are three basic kinds of money:

  commodity money
  symbolic money
  credit money

In earlier times, certain useful *commodities* were used as money. These included such things as salt, cattle, and grain. Tobacco was commonly used as money in colonial America. Commodity money carries value within itself, making it easy for traders to evaluate its soundness. The use of commodities as a medium of exchange really amounts to *indirect barter*. Such commodities can serve the exchange function because they are useful in themselves and generally in demand. I may have no use for tobacco myself, but if I know that others want it and it can be easily traded, I may accept it in payment when I sell my goods or services.

The use of precious metals as money is no different in nature from the use of any other commodity. Gold and silver came to be widely used as money because they provided the advantages of greater convenience, portability, and durability, especially when stamped into coins of certified weight and fineness. The certifying entity was initially the king or the government of some nation or political subdivision, but private coinage also has historical precedent.

Later, it became more common to use paper notes and base metal coins, which were *symbolic* representations of commodity money, typically gold or silver, deposited with a goldsmith or a bank. The bank would give the depositor paper notes that were, in effect, receipts or "claim checks" for the metal deposited. These notes could then be used as money. They were accepted in the marketplace because everyone knew that they could be presented to the issuer, who would "redeem" them, that is, give the note holder the metal they represented. Modern banking developed on the basis of issuing paper currency against "fractional reserves," meaning that the banks issued more paper "claim checks" than they had gold to redeem them with.

Commodity money and redeemable paper have progressively given way to nonredeemable notes, bank credit, and computerized accounts, that while offering certain advantages, are easier for issuers to abuse and more difficult for traders to evaluate. Today, most of the money in use exists in the form of bank credit, with a small percentage also in the form of circulating paper notes of the central bank, which, in the United States, is the Federal Reserve Bank. These notes, however, are merely a physical representation of money that was first created as bank credit and later exchanged for paper.

Confusion often arises, as well, from the variety and proliferation of *monetary instruments*. These include what we commonly think of as money itself—precious metal coins, base metal coins, tokens, paper notes or bills—but also deposit account balances, smart cards, and now e-cash. In addition, we have checks, wire transfers, and debit cards, which are not money themselves but ways of ordering the transfer of money from one account to another.

The Money Circuit

Money flows in circular fashion. In order to apprehend the meaning of money, one must first recognize the essential fact that **money has a beginning and an ending; it is created and it is extinguished.** This is depicted in figure 4.1, which shows money in its basic and ideal form. Money is first created by a buyer who issues it to a seller as evidence of value received. The money issued may be thought of as an IOU that the buyer uses to pay for the goods and services he bought. That IOU might be passed along from hand to hand as each recipient, in turn, uses it to pay for his or her own purchase. Eventually, it must come back to the originator of the IOU, who redeems it by selling something of value and accepting the IOU as payment.

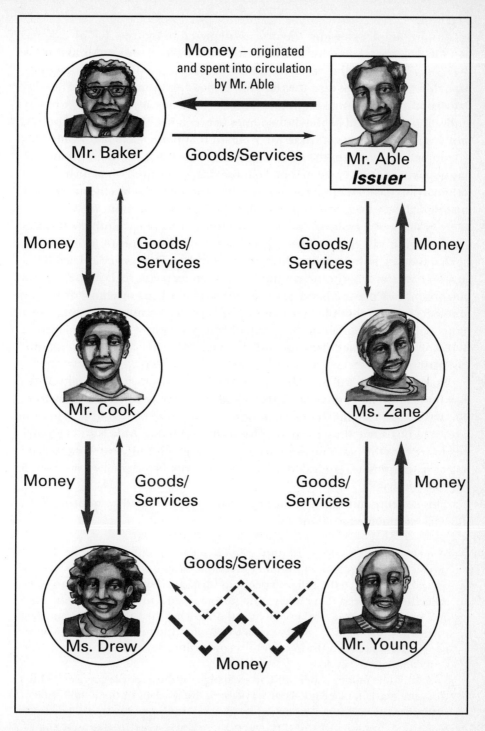

Figure 4.1. The ideal money circuit.

As an example, consider the process depicted in figure 4.1. The originator, Mr. Able, buys something of value from Mr. Baker. He gives Mr. Baker his IOU as evidence of value received. Baker then uses the IOU to buy something from Mr. Cook, who in turn uses it to buy something from Ms. Drew. The IOU may continue to change hands any number of times as others use it to buy and sell (as indicated by the dashed lines between Ms. Drew and Mr. Young), but eventually it must return to Mr. Able. At that point, Able has fulfilled his commitment to redeem the money he issued (the IOU). He does this by selling goods or services equal in value to those that he received when he made his original purchase, accepting as payment his own IOU, which is the money that he originally created. At that point, Able extinguishes the money.

Now think of a group of traders who agree to accept each other's IOUs as payment in trade. Suppose they design a standardized form for their IOUs so that they are indistinguishable from one another. These standardized IOUs can take whatever form the community of traders has agreed to use for this purpose. They may be paper certificates, metal tokens or coins, or simply numbers in an account ledger that can be kept in a computer or simply in a notebook. Each member of the group obtains a supply of these standardized IOUs or notes of fixed denomination, which she or he can now spend into circulation.

Now the originator, Mr. Able, instead of using his own personal IOU to pay for his purchase, gives Mr. Baker standardized notes or IOUs. As before, Mr. Baker then uses that money to buy something from Mr. Cook, who in turn uses it to buy something from Ms. Drew, and so on. Mr. Able is still committed to redeem the notes he issued and must eventually sell something, accepting as payment notes equivalent in amount to those he originally issued when he paid Mr. Baker.

This conceptualization of money is further elucidated by quoting E. C. Riegel's excellent exposition:

> Money simply does not exist until it has been accepted in exchange. Hence two factors are necessary for money creation: *a buyer, who issues it, and a seller, who accepts it.* Since the seller expects, in turn, to reissue the money to some seller, it will be seen that money springs from mutual interest and cooperative action among traders, and not from authority. That the Government can issue money for the people . . . is an utter fallacy. Money can be issued only by a buyer for himself, and he must in turn be a competitive seller to recapture it and thus complete the cycle.
>
> A would-be money issuer must, in exchange for the goods or services he buys from the market, place goods or services on the market. In this simple rule of equity lies the essence of money.[4]

Riegel conceived a "private enterprise money" that closely conforms to this ideal.[5] Most contemporary mutual credit systems, for example LETS, also conform to this ideal.

Bank Credit Money and the Interest Burden

In simple mutual credit systems, money springs easily into existence whenever it is needed for exchange. In the current official system of money and banking, however, an originator of money must first obtain authorization from a commercial bank before putting money into circulation. Typically, this is done by making an application for a "loan." Let us use our previous example as a staring point to explain how it works. Before Mr. Able can spend money into circulation, he must get a "loan" from a bank. After his application is submitted, the bank will evaluate Mr. Able's "credit-worthiness" and the value of his collateral. Let's say that Able offers his farm as collateral against the "loan." He signs an agreement known as a mortgage deed of trust, and, in turn, the bank credits his account for so many dollars representing the principal amount of the "loan." This is depicted in figure 4.2. In effect, Mr. Able gives the bank a legal claim (the mortgage) to his farm in return for standardized IOUs (bank credit or cash notes), which others will accept as payment for his purchases. In terms of the prevailing practice, Able has obtained authorization to write checks against or draw out cash from his bank account, up to the amount of his "loan."

Mr. Able, as before, has obligated himself to the community to *redeem, by selling*, the same amount of money he *issued by spending*. But, in addition, he has also obligated himself to return to the bank the amount of money he "borrowed," *plus interest*. Thus, he must make sales sufficient to recover not only the amount of money he issued ("borrowed") but also to obtain an additional amount in order to pay the interest. If he is successful in doing so, he can reclaim his mortgage note from the bank; if not, he loses his farm. When he repays the bank, the money he issued is extinguished. The redemption phase of the process is depicted in figure 4.3. Note that the diagram shows a dashed line labeled "interest" coming to Mr. Able from outside the circuit and going to the bank.

In this scenario, Mr. Able is still the issuer, not the bank. The bank has not really loaned him anything; it has simply converted the value of Mr. Able's farm into negotiable form. This process is called *monetization*. The bank has used its legal authority to "create" money by adding credit to Mr. Able's checking account or giving him the equivalent amount in the form of Federal Reserve notes in return for his mortgage or IOU. In other words, the bank has monetized part of the value of Able's farm. The problem here is that the extra amount of money required of Mr. Able to pay interest on the loan is not available within the circuit; it can come only from some other similar circuit,

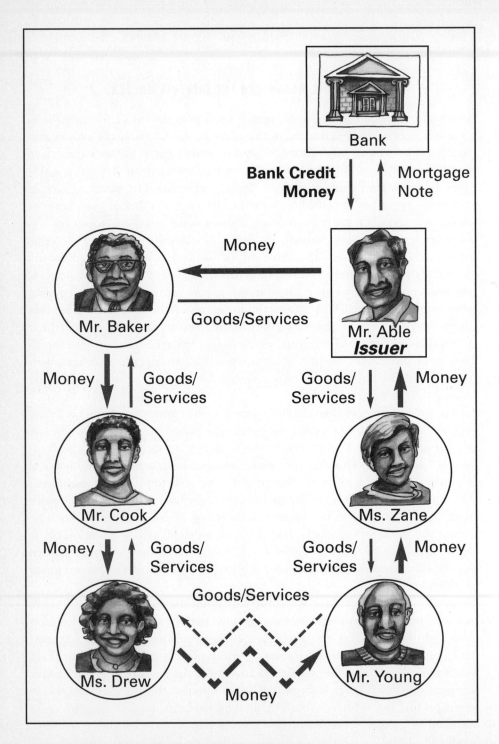

Figure 4.2. The bank credit money circuit — lending phase.

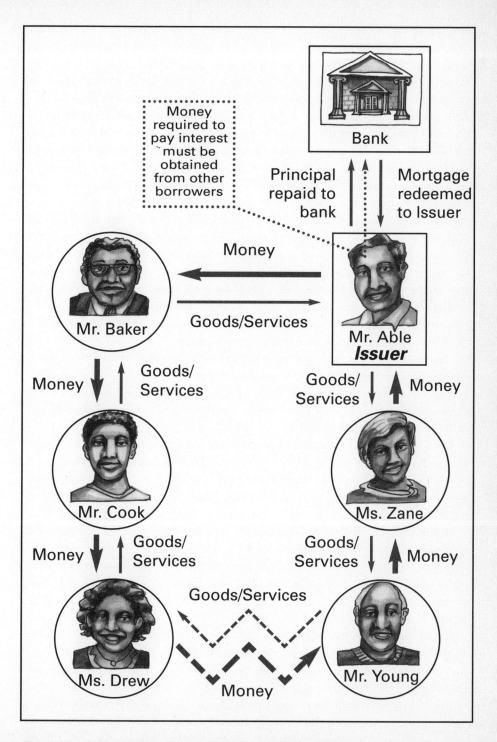

Figure 4.3. The bank credit money circuit — redemption phase.

which is to say, money "loaned" to some other trader ("borrower") who has also gone in debt to the bank. Now, if Able succeeds in earning some of *that* money, the second borrower will not be able to earn back enough money to redeem *his* mortgage. Thus, the charging of interest on the bank "loans" on which new money is based causes a deficiency of money in circulation, eventually preventing some debtors from earning back enough to redeem their collateral. **Thus, the prevailing system guarantees that there will be a steady parade of losers. This is the fundamental flaw in the present monetary system.**

The example above is simplified to illustrate the point. In the real world there are thousands of banks and millions of borrowers. The banks are continually making new loans and retiring old ones as they are repaid. In the aggregate, the debts owed to banks are increasing with the mere passage of time, because interest accrues over time. The money available to repay those debts, however, can be created only by the banks as they make additional loans. **The net requirement, then, is that banks must make new loans faster than they retire old loans, that is, there must be a continual expansion of bank credit money.** If there is not, the result is depression—increasing numbers of defaulted loans, greater numbers of bankruptcies, expanding unemployment—and all the human misery that comes with it.

The problem is not that we use bank credit as money but that there is an interest burden attached to it. In systems theory this is known as a "positive-feedback" mechanism, one that causes each subsequent state to be, in some way, bigger than the preceding state—in simplistic terms, an explosion, but in this case an explosion of debt.

Am I saying, then, that all interest is dysfunctional and must be avoided? Not necessarily. It is one thing for those who have *earned* money to expect a return for its use when they lend or otherwise invest it; it is quite another for banks to charge interest on newly created money that they authorize based on debt.

In the former case, we are talking about businesses and individuals who have earned money in the course of their business and exchange activities. They have produced and sold real goods or services, received money in return, and seek to make productive use of their current surplus through saving and investment. They are entitled to share in the gains resulting from the allocation of these surplus funds to others.[6]

In the latter case, however, the imposition of interest creates an unstable condition in which the money supply always lags behind the growing amount of debt owed to banks. Inevitably, a point is reached at which the private sector is unable or unwilling to assume any additional debt burden. Then, a way must be found to keep the money supply from lagging behind the growth of debt. Such was the case during the Great Depression of the 1930s (more about this later). From that time onward, the federal government has assumed the role of "borrower of last resort." Thus, when the monetization of private debt cannot be further pursued, the Federal Reserve will monetize part of the government budget deficits to prevent a shrinkage of the supply of money.

The prevailing monetary policies of the Fed determine whether money is "easy" or "tight," that is, whether the monetization of government debt will be sufficient to provide private "borrowers" with the amounts of money needed to pay what they owe to the banks, or whether it will fall short. These actions by the Fed are largely responsible for the "business cycle" and periodic rounds of inflation and recession. Through the various mechanisms under its control—interest rates on loans it makes to banks, purchase or sale of government securities, and setting bank reserve requirements—the Fed has the power to decide whose interests will be favored and whose will be harmed.

～

Chapter 5

The Disintegration of Local Economies

The way that a national economy preys on its internal colonies is by the destruction of community.

—WENDELL BERRY

CONTROL OVER HUMAN AFFAIRS is achieved primarily through the control of economic factors. Economics drives politics, and economic and political realities shape the structure of society. The long view of history shows a progression of control strategies that kings, emperors, and ruling elites have employed, applying their power in turn to each of the primary factors of economic production: labor, land, and capital.

Levers of Power, Then and Now

Conquest, plunder, domination, and enslavement remain to this day the prevailing mode in international affairs. Blatantly brutal and gross political subjugation has declined in popularity, at least among the nations of the "civilized" West. The favored methods have become increasingly subtle, shifting from political domination of nation over nation to economic and financial domination of peoples by supranational institutions. The "debt trap" is neater than direct force but no less tyrannical.

Slavery is the direct control of labor through physical coercion and threat of harm. It has been commonly practiced throughout history, even in so-called civilized countries, and was a prominent feature of our own "free" country until little more than a century ago. As "civilization" has progressed, overt slavery has become both less palatable and less practical. Typical of the transition from direct control of labor to control over land was the passage, starting in the late 15th century, of the "enclosure acts" in England. The elimination of the commons (fields and pastures upon which the vast majority of people depended for their livelihood), and the deeding of the land to the lords, deprived people of their means of living free and forced them to pay rent, usually in the form of crop shares. Restricted from using formerly open lands, and forced to pay onerous rents, people were increasingly driven from the countryside into urban centers.

Karl Polanyi paints a vivid picture:[1]

> Enclosures have appropriately been called a revolution of the rich against the poor. The lords and nobles were upsetting social order, breaking down ancient law and custom, sometimes by means of violence, often by pressure and intimidation. They were literally robbing the poor of their share in the common, tearing down houses which, by the hitherto unbreakable force of custom, the poor had long regarded as theirs and their heirs'. The fabric of society was being disrupted; desolate villages and the ruins of human dwellings testified to the fierceness with which the revolution raged, endangering the defenses of the country, wasting its towns, decimating its population, turning its overburdened soil into dust, harassing its people and turning them from decent husbandmen into a mob of beggars and thieves.

With the advent of industrialization, the bulk of production shifted from the cottage and village to factories and cities. Then the control of capital—the tools or means of production—increasingly became the method of social control. Separated from their land and lacking the tools of modern industrial production, individuals were forced to work for money as a means of earning their livelihood. For most, this meant migrating to the cities and selling their labor to the factory owners. These upheavals caused the evolution of what is commonly known as "wage slavery." Polanyi describes the conditions that ensued:

> Writers of all views and parties, conservatives and liberals, capitalists and socialists invariably referred to social conditions under the Industrial Revolution as a veritable abyss of human degradation.

While wage slavery yet remains, the mechanisms of privilege and control have become even more subtle still, so subtle that few people have even the slightest idea of what is happening. Besides the economic factors of labor, land, and capital, there is also a suprafactor that mediates and controls the process of exchange and the interchangeability among the other three economic factors. That suprafactor is *money*.

The Evolution of Money

As pointed out previously, money has, over time, become increasingly ethereal, (less substantial). For thousands of years, even up to the writing of the United States Constitution, the common substance of money was precious metals, mostly gold and silver. These commodities, typically in the form of coins, carried value within themselves. The only questions needing to be ascertained by traders in the marketplace were those relating to the weight and fineness of the metal tendered. The stamping of metal into coins provided a means of certifying these factors, thus further facilitating the process of market exchange.

For reasons of convenience and safety, paper notes began to be used to represent ownership of metal. The exchange of paper notes in the marketplace then provided an easy way of exchanging the value inherent in the metal, which was safely stored elsewhere. The paper had value because it could be exchanged for metal at the storage place. As paper money became more common and acceptable, and as the need for exchange media began to exceed the amount of metal available, the temptation grew stronger to issue more paper than there was metal to redeem it. This gave rise to what is known as "fractional reserve banking."

Fractional reserve banking is the practice of issuing paper notes in amounts that exceed the value of the stores of metal the notes represent. In the latter stages of redeemable currencies, the amounts of paper in circulation grew to many times the value of the gold or silver held. The abuses of paper money and fractional reserve banking soon created problems such as bank failures. Governments, naturally enough, began to intervene to regulate and centralize banking, eventually themselves becoming the greatest abusers. They either began to issue paper money themselves or, as in the case of the United States, allowed the formation of a banking cartel (the Federal Reserve system), through which their profligate spending could be financed.

When the monetary abuses became apparent, people increasingly exercised their option to redeem their paper notes for metal, causing "bank runs" and "panics." Occasional runs on isolated banks, while disastrous for their depositors and investors, were not of great consequence to the general economy. The centralization of money and banking, however, did not end the abuses but rather has institutionalized them to the point where the entire economy is adversely affected.

As their reserves of metal began to run low, governments and central banks had no other choices but to stop their abusive issuance of paper money or to rescind the redeemability feature. They have invariably chosen the latter.[2]

Through the development of a medium of exchange that can be created virtually out of nothing and allocated according to the values and objectives of those who have the "money power," it is now possible for a small elite group, both in and out of government, to quietly and imperceptibly control the entire realm of human affairs. As Nobel Prize–winner Frederick Soddy has put it, "Money now is the NOTHING you get for SOMETHING before you can get ANYTHING."[3]

Social Control through Control of Money and Finance

At the same time that money was becoming more etherealized, centralized, and politicized, market mechanisms were becoming a more dominant feature of economies at all levels. From the individual level to the community level to the region and on up, economies have become increasingly specialized and therefore dependent on market exchange. This predominant condition contrasts sharply with many historical (and a few current) examples of local and regional economies characterized by high levels of versatility and self-reliance. Versatility derives from a diversity of skills and resources; self-reliance is based largely on production for use as opposed to production for market and on the use of less formal internal exchange mechanisms.

Specialization of function is beneficial up to a point, and so is the market. The well-known economic concept of "comparative advantage," which provides the fundamental argument in favor of free trade, cannot be denied. Yet the advantages of self-reliance and versatility at every level must also be acknowledged for both individuals and communities. If they are to avoid complete loss of control over their quality of life, they must also avoid becoming overly dependent on existing markets in which the exchange media are monopolized and abused, and in which the mechanisms of finance are political and undemocratic.

For people living in industrialized countries, everything has become increasingly commodified. Even babies, human blood, and body parts have become objects of commerce. We have become increasingly dependent on external and remote sources of supply for the most basic necessities of life. Most of us, when separated from our highly developed technology and intricate mechanisms of finance and transportation, lack even the most basic skills required to keep ourselves warm, dry, and well fed. Our alienation from the land, the basic tools of production, and each other manifests itself in increasing environmental and social degradation.

Social Disintegration

Along with our increasing dependence on remote and impersonal political and economic entities has come the disintegration of traditional social structures: the family, the clan, the tribe, the village, and the bioregional community. All these have paled into economic insignificance, and, lacking economic power, they have become politically and socially impotent as well. Now, in this atomistic society, the wage earner's allegiance must be to his or her employer: the corporation or the government bureaucracy. The majority of those who are not wage earners depend on some form of government-granted privilege or transfer payment, such as mining rights, grazing and timber leases, farm price supports, and Social Security payments.

The social disintegration that we see seems somehow related to both the loss of freedom and the inability to participate effectively in the process of making the decisions that affect our lives. All the rhetoric about democracy and "government by the people" notwithstanding, freedom and citizen participation are today constrained in many subtle ways, both politically and economically.

PAC (Political action committee) money, professional lobbying, and the so-called free speech rights for corporations have utterly corrupted our representative system and deflected our government from the democratic ideals that we supposedly espouse.

Lord Acton is famous for having said that "power corrupts, and absolute power corrupts absolutely." Thus, the concentration of power in the hands of so-called representatives makes it possible for the few to have their way by co-opting or intimidating the lawmakers. Our forefathers lived in a much different world from that of today. With the primitive communication and transportation technologies available at the time, it made sense to vest power in the hands of representatives. But it no longer makes sense to delegate such power. PAC (Political action committee) money, professional lobbying, and the so-called free speech rights for corporations have utterly corrupted our representative system and deflected our government from the democratic ideals that we supposedly espouse. A more direct form of democracy seems more appropriate to today's conditions.

A further defect in this representative system is the obvious gerrymandering of congressional and legislative districts. The drawing of the lines of these districts seems to be aimed, not so much at gaining advantage for one or the other of the two major parties, but at limiting the ability of various ethnic, economic, and social classes to gain effective representation in government. This political homogenization limits the ability of legitimate interests to organize effective political power or even to have their issues and concerns debated in the political arena. The consequence is that only the corporate and monied interests are able to get their voices heard and influence the process of government.

Although good models of government are hard to find, there are some obvious steps that could be taken toward improvement. Many countries in Europe and elsewhere have parliamentary governments that provide for "proportional representation." They have numerous political parties representing particular interests. A party is able to gain representation in parliament in proportion to the percentage of the votes it receives in an election. Thus, even a small minority party can gain representation with as little as 5 percent of the votes. Far from being divisive, this assures that various points of view will be heard.[4]

A basic factor that seems to underlie the limits both to freedom and to effective participation is that of scale. As Chilean economist Manfred Max-Neef explains,

> It is absolutely impossible to have participation in a gigantic system; it can only occur at the human scale—in other words where people have a face and a name, where they mean something to each other and are not simply statistical abstractions.

He goes on to say that the critical size of a participatory group will depend on its function but, "in any case, . . . will never be very large."[5]

If we are to reverse the trend of ever increasing alienation, we must begin to organize ourselves into small functional social groupings that empower their members and provide a meaningful level of mutual support. Democracy needs to be economic as well as political. Actions taken to extend it in the one realm will have implications for the other.

The End of Empires

Although the dominant trend of civilization over the past several millennia has been toward increasing centralization of power in the hands of fewer and fewer people, there are signs that civilization may now be starting to move toward decentralization and local control. Even as the shadow of "Big Brother" looms ever larger and the prospect of global tyranny appears increasingly probable, we can see a major turn approaching.

Diverse networks of communication and mutual support are beginning to emerge. The village, neighborhood, household, farm, and community are now becoming more significant as centers of education and economic activity. Manufacturing operations, while they are largely being shifted to lesser developed countries (LDCs) are at the same time being decentralized. Many large companies are forming work teams that are given broad decision-making power over their own work methods. Information handling is increasingly becoming the substance of work, both inside and outside the formal economy. Work styles are changing. More and more people are moving toward diversification of skills and self-employment. As cities grow larger and transportation channels become clogged, people are finding ways of working that are less stressful and more efficient. "Telecommuting" and home-based employment and business are becoming ever more common, especially among highly skilled workers and professionals.

Centralized political institutions, even while appearing to consolidate their power, are disintegrating from within. The world has been startled with the suddenness of the collapse of the Eastern European bloc and the Soviet Union, which once seemed monolithic and indestructible. Old ethnic identities are reasserting themselves as the seeds around which a new order is beginning to crystallize. But even this degree of centralization around ethnic identities, with all their historic rivalries and animosities, will probably be transitory. With the emerging global consciousness and person-to-person communications, it seems likely that the nation-state as the dominant political institution is in its last days. Its power seems to have been supplanted by that of the transnational corporations, which bodes ill for democratic government. But corporations are creatures of the state. How will the power dynamics play out in the 21st century?[6]

It is important to recognize that economic, political, and social structures are interdependent and mutually determining. They compromise the fabric of "culture." In our highly mobile and atomistic society we have grown dependent on structures that are inimical to humane and liberationist values. Any attempt to address the "megacrisis," or to transform socioeconomic realities, must come from a holistic perspective. Undoing the damage caused by centuries of subtle plunder and domination will require a thorough understanding of the interconnections among money, banking, and finance; land tenure and property ownership; government and law; taxation and public finance; corporate power and the concentration of wealth; and the technological infrastructure and physical environment.[7] Transformation will require not only a deeper understanding of the mechanisms of land speculation, money creation, and coercive wealth redistribution but also a change in our basic assumptions and attitudes.[8] Above all, the establishment of our own democratically controlled, interest-free complementary exchange media should be a basic element in 21st century community empowerment.

Chapter 6

〜

Money, Power, and the U.S. Constitution

No State shall . . . make any thing but gold and silver coin a tender in payment of debts. . . .

—ARTICLE I, SECTION 10, U.S. CONSTITUTION

THE ORIGINAL ARTICLES OF CONFEDERATION of the United States of America provided for a loose federation of thirteen sovereign states. This was seen by some to be inadequate for the destiny of the new nation as they envisioned it. The adoption of the Constitution was an attempt to strengthen the position of the federated states relative to foreign nations by delegating certain powers to the federal government, in particular, the power to declare war and the power to enter into treaties. The Constitution carefully spelled out the limits of federal authority and sought to preserve the power of the states and of the people. Despite the care with which the powers of the federal government were enumerated, various interpretations by the courts over the years have allowed power to be increasingly concentrated at the federal level and have given the federal government permission to engage in activities that seem contrary to the intentions of the Founding Fathers when they drafted the Constitution. One of the founders, John Marshall, often stated that "the powers of the federal government are enumerated and few." It is unfortunate that subsequent generations of judges have ruled differently. The ambitions of empire require ever greater concentration of power, and that is what has evolved.

Of special note are the agreements of the states with respect to money, which were written into the Constitution. Article I, Section 8, enumerates the various powers of the Congress. Among these is the power to "coin money, regulate the value thereof, and of foreign coin, and fix the standard of weights and measures."

In order to understand the meaning of this section, one must understand the prevailing situation and the parlance of that time. The form of money that we use now was not the form used back then. At the time of the writing of the Constitution, the substance of money was gold and silver coin, but now almost all the money is in the form of bank credit, with the remainder in paper bills and base metal coins. The power given to Congress by Article I, Section 8, was simply this: to stamp precious metals into coins of measured weight and fineness and to decide how much metal was to be contained in the monetary unit, that is, to "regulate the value of" the dollar. Congress was not given the power to print paper money nor to create some other form of "legal tender."

The intent of the Founding Fathers is further clarified when we consider another part of the Constitution, which listed certain limitations on the powers of the states. Article I, Section 10, provides that "no State shall enter into any treaty, alliance, or confederation; grant letters of marque and reprisal; *coin money; emit bills of credit; make any thing but gold and silver coin a tender in payment of debts . . .*" [emphasis added].

The clear intention was to standardize coinage by placing such monetary power in the hands of Congress. The *required* form of payment for debts was to be limited to gold and silver coins. Other forms of payment might be accepted by the payee but could not legally be required of the debtor, that is, be made "legal tender."

Bills of credit were promissory notes such as those which were issued by the colonies (which later became states), and which commonly circulated as money prior to the Constitution. The colonies spent these notes into circulation in quantities that were typically excessive in relation to the tax revenues available for their redemption. The eventual consequence of such abuse was that colonial currencies in the hands of the people lost much of their value, causing economic distress. During the Revolutionary period, the Continental Congress issued paper money, called "continentals," which were similarly abused. To make matters worse, the British government, as part of its strategy to defeat the Americans in their war for independence, worked to debase the colonial money by printing counterfeit continentals and giving them to anyone who would spend them into circulation. Thus derived the saying "not worth a continental."

By writing these coinage provisions into the Constitution, the Founding Fathers sought to prevent a recurrence of the earlier monetary disasters. Although the federal government was not specifically prohibited from issuing bills of credit, this power was not specifically given to it either. In fact, an earlier draft of Article I, Section 8, included the power "to emit bills of credit" (paper notes), but it was deleted in the final version, an obvious indication that the founders were wary of granting such power. In the end they voted to neither grant it nor explicitly withhold such power.

Measuring Value and Defining the Dollar

The final clause in that same section speaks of "fixing a standard of weights and measures." This may seem to us moderns to be out of place and unrelated to the rest of the section, but actually *regulating the value of money* and *fixing a standard of weights and measures* were matters of the same sort. We all know what weights are. In the United States, we measure weights in units called *pounds;* most of the rest of the world, uses a unit called the *kilogram*. Each of these is defined in concrete physical terms by a "standard." A standard is simply a lump of metal, which serves as a reference against which all other measuring devices can be compared. Similarly, units of length are defined by a standard metal rod of *fixed* length.

Defining the monetary unit was simply a matter of specifying the weight and fineness of the metal composing the coins that Congress was supposed to mint. The word *regulate* means to "keep constant," not to manipulate up and down, as some seem to think. This is exactly what the founders proceeded to do when they appointed a committee to define the monetary unit for the United States, the *dollar*.

In colonial America, Spanish milled silver coins, called *dollars,* circulated widely as money. The Constitutional Congress, in adopting these coins as the basis for the monetary system of the newly formed United States of America, was simply recognizing what was already common practice. Since the Spanish coins varied in their silver content, the main work of the committee was to determine the average silver content of the coins in circulation and to specify what should be the silver content of the new American dollar coins. This they did, and eventually settled on a figure of "371.25 grains of silver, .999 fine."[1]

The Consolidation of Money Power

It is probably unconstitutional for Congress to do directly what is done through the Federal Reserve, which is to issue money based on the government's promise to pay. The issuance of "greenbacks" by the United States Treasury under Abraham Lincoln during the Civil War was just such a case in point. Lincoln, instead of borrowing from the banks at exorbitant rates of interest to finance the war, had the Treasury issue paper currency by spending it directly into circulation. These "greenbacks" were controversial throughout their entire life. While Lincoln managed to save the taxpayers the enormous cost of interest by printing money instead of borrowing it, he usurped a power that the Founding Fathers had intended to withhold.

Subsequent to the end of the Civil War, the banking interests saw to it that such a costly (for them) move would not be repeated. They found a way for the federal government to get what it wanted, namely, the power to spend without limit, while enhancing their own wealth and power. Thus, the constitutional limitation on the federal government with respect to monetization of its debt has been circumvented by its collusion with international banking interests to redefine and manipulate the exchange media (money) and their allocation within the economy.

This cozy relationship began with the National Bank Act of 1863, which required each bank to purchase a dollar amount of government bonds equal to one-third of its capital and surplus.[2] The collusion between bankers and politicians became more formalized with the establishment of the Federal Reserve system in 1913, and was legitimized by the subsequent entry of the United States into World War II. The Federal Reserve at that point announced a policy of providing the Treasury with the money needed to finance the war. It agreed to buy *any* amount of Treasury bills at the posted rate and to resell them at the same rate.[3] In the postwar era, the use of monetary mechanisms to handle fiscal (budgetary) indiscretions came to be taken for granted. This, more than anything else, has undermined the democratic process in America and allowed the emergence of the American empire under elite control.

The single most important element needed to assure a future of freedom, dignity, health, and realization of the human potential is the creation of nonpolitical, equitable exchange media and the dispersal of financial power.

Over the years, the monetary authorities have managed to quietly redefine the dollar, from a specified weight of silver or gold to a unit of bank credit with no defined value. While the federal government ostensibly controls the central bank (the Federal Reserve system) and regulates the banking industry, the reality is probably more the other way around. Those who pay the piper call the tune. It is naive to think that political campaign contributions made by wealthy individuals and corporations do not buy influence. Not only has power migrated from the local and state levels to the federal level; it has been privatized and appropriated by a monetary and financial ruling class, which respects no borders.

Western civilization has reached a crisis point. The imperial stage of civilization is approaching its zenith. To permit its continued development to its ultimate maturity would be to permit a global tyranny far beyond Orwell's imagining and to sell the soul of humanity into a new feudalism of material excess for some, comfort for a few, and meager subsistence and drudgery for most. But the worst of the consequences for most is not material inequity but the poverty of spirit that accompanies the abridgment of freedom.

The single most important element needed to assure a future of freedom, dignity, health, and realization of the human potential is the creation of non-political, equitable exchange media and the dispersal of financial power. The only feasible way to achieve this, I believe, is through the establishment, by private initiative, of community-based complementary exchange mechanisms that are democratically and locally controlled. Such exchange mechanisms need not be limited to *geographical* communities. The emergence of computerized telecommunications and the Internet have enabled the development of *virtual* communities whose members are scattered around the globe.

Chapter 7

～

Restoring Local Economies

Wage slavery will exist so long as there is a man or an institution that is the master of men; it will be ended when the workers learn to set freedom before comfort.

—G. D. H. COLE

SOLUTIONS TO GLOBAL PROBLEMS require a global perspective and transglobal interaction, but it does not necessarily follow that we need to have a centralized global authority with coercive power to carry out the resulting policies. Indeed, we have ample evidence to demonstrate that such centralized authorities lack sensitivity to local needs. The more remote the government, the less responsive it is, and, indeed, the more oppressive it becomes. Competition among nation-states has generally compounded human misery through war. What seems more appropriate for the 21st century is a pyramid of communication and cooperation with power vested in the small societal units that comprise its base—families, households, affinity groups, neighborhoods, and villages—and with higher-level representative bodies commissioned not to make decisions but to investigate, deliberate, propose, and inform, thus helping to harmonize and coordinate local actions.

Manfred Max-Neef, in discussing a new paradigm for economics, enumerates nine fundamental human needs, which fall into two categories: "having" needs and "being" needs. They are the needs "for permanence or subsistence; for protection; for affection or love; for understanding; for participation; the need for leisure; for creation; for identity; and for freedom." He points out that industrialized countries are better at providing for the "having" needs than they are at satisfying the "being" needs, while the lesser developed countries (LDCs) often do the opposite. He argues that it is possible to organize economic systems that can satisfy the entire range of human needs.[1] I agree, but the question is how to achieve that goal.

Healthy Communities, Healthy World

The direction that needs to be taken is toward structures and mechanisms that provide greater personal freedom and wider, more effective participation. Since adequate participation is possible only within small groups, the emphasis must be on the strengthening of local communities and voluntary associations. These will, in my opinion, form the foundation of a new order that will be both *sustainable* and *humane*.

Mechanistic models are based on abstraction of reality. Computers perform some of the same functions that our brains do, but, being creations of human intelligence, they are in most respects inferior to the human brain. Organic living-system models provide a better guide for us in structuring our social, economic, and political systems. The human body, for example, is composed of cells, which make up organs, which function for the benefit of the whole body. The health of the body is determined by the health of the organs and cells, which, in turn, is determined by the health of the body. There is something that tells each cell and each organ what to do and how to do it. A cell that lacks this whole-body consciousness is a cancerous cell, working not toward the health of the body but toward its destruction. Health is vitally dependent on receipt of such information and on action in accordance with it. The cells of the body are not centrally controlled by the brain or any other organ but, in fact, seem to be highly autonomous, with the information coming from "someplace else." This may be, perhaps, the realm we call spirit, the level at which the interests of the cell are harmonized with the interests of the whole body.

Healthy local economies, like healthy individuals, are characterized by a diversity of skills and resources and by effective and efficient transport and exchange mechanisms. If any part of the body is starved for nourishment, the whole body suffers. The brain does not tell the liver or the heart what to do; the cells that comprise those organs seem already to know. Likewise, each person has a way of knowing what his or her role is, although sometimes that message may be suppressed. America was founded on the ideals of personal freedom, self-reliance, and self-determination, and, it seems to me, those ideals are still appropriate. But much ground has been lost over the past two centuries, particularly in the economic realm. The institutions that have evolved have created tremendous disparities of power and wealth. Economic empowerment will require some degree of decoupling from the present global exchange system and the implementation of exchange media that are locally and democratically controlled.

The vogue in economic development strategies for the past several decades has been for local communities to recruit major corporations to move into the area, bringing new investment funds to the community and creating jobs. On the surface, this strategy seems perfectly reasonable, but in many cases there has been insufficient attention paid to the cost side of the equation. This is true especially when the costs come as social and ecological degradation, rather than in direct financial terms. But even in financial terms, the benefits for many communities have been less than expected. With communities bidding against one another, tax abatements and other concessions needed to lure companies often negate most if not all of the benefits. Recognition of these costs, coupled with the costs of providing additional public services needed to support the new businesses, is causing many communities to take another look at the efficacy of this "recruitment strategy."

Two Fundamental Strategies

If not recruitment, then what? I believe that the emerging trend in community economic development activity will be for communities to rely more on their own resources, to support businesses already there, to place greater emphasis on quality of life, and to begin restructuring in areas that presently make them vulnerable to external factors such as the supply of money and bank credit, prevailing interest rates, and levels of state and federal government spending in their area.

What practical steps can be taken to protect local economies from the distorting effects of external monetary and financial machinations and to restore some measure of local autonomy? Two general approaches are most evident:

1. reduce reliance on conventional money and markets, and/or
2. bring money and markets under local, democratic control

An effective strategy will probably require some combination of the two. Reducing reliance on money and markets implies a number of adjustments. On the personal level, it means becoming free of the consumerist mentality, distinguishing real needs from conditioned wants, eliminating expenditures that are induced by fear, becoming more diversified in one's skills and abilities, learning to do it yourself, make do, or do without, and, above all, developing mutual support relationships with others of like mind and with complementary needs and abilities. Communities must likewise take stock of their own resources and take steps to reduce the amount of value imported into the community, substituting local production for imports and thus reducing their need to earn cash by selling exports in markets where the terms of exchange are tilted against them.

Small (and Local) Is Beautiful

Even the poorest among us are able to exert some power through purchase decisions made every day. Every dollar spent is a vote cast. It is important to recognize that however much or little money one might have, the choices one makes in spending that money carry a great deal of weight in determining not only the products and services that the market offers but also the very quality of community life. Although price is one of the primary criteria to be considered, it should not be the most important one.

Consideration should also be given to the question of where and with whom one should do business. The familiar aphorism that "charity begins at home" contains much wisdom. An appropriate corollary might be that "prosperity begins at home." The first might be interpreted as "deal with the problems closest at hand," and the second as "support the business efforts of your friends and neighbors."

Local businesses spend most of their revenues in the local area, while chain stores and absentee owners withdraw most of their revenues to other places, building up ever greater pools of capital that can distort economic relationships everywhere. Chain stores, for example, may be able to offer lower prices for a time, but it is often a false economy. We must ask, At what price do they offer lower prices? It is often at the expense of the environment, poorer working conditions for employees, and depersonalization of human interactions.

Because they control so many jobs and so much revenue, large corporations and chain stores can make a community dependent on them. They can dominate a community by their lopsided economic power, which allows them to wield political power as well. They can buy political influence, negotiate tax breaks, and extort concessions on zoning, safety, and environmental regulations. Further, large companies, after they have driven out the smaller local competitors, have a clear field to raise prices and reduce wages.

It is also becoming more apparent that continual growth and construction, while it may benefit some privileged sectors of the community such as landowners, builders, real-estate brokers, and mortgage lenders, can often be detrimental to the community as a whole. There are several negative effects that need to be considered. First, there are the added costs for services and infrastructure—fire, police, water, sewer, road construction and maintenance—which may exceed any additional tax revenues. Second is the cost of living, which may increase because of "gentrification" and the increased demand for housing and other limited local resources. Third are the quality of life costs: increased traffic congestion; noise, air, land, and water pollution;

loss of farm, forest, meadow, and marsh land; and increasing anonymity and depersonalization.

Locally owned businesses are more likely to use local suppliers, saving on transportation costs, reducing the environmental costs of transport, and stimulating local production. They are more likely to employ local people, and they contribute to the culture and uniqueness of a community. These are the qualities that make European and third-world cities so interesting and charming.

How to Bring Money under Local Control

Later chapters offer a number of concrete proposals for bringing money and markets under local, democratic control. These proposals, which can be implemented at the local level by voluntary groups, attempt to incorporate the principles and ideals outlined previously. Some of the ideas have already been tried in some form and to some degree, while others, to my knowledge, are original.

The kinds of exchange systems implied by the above considerations are both self-regulating and independent of outside control by government or any other centralized power. To use an organic metaphor, they function autonomically. This implies a decentralized approach in which the creation and extinction of money (the symbol) is directly linked to the creation, transfer, and consumption of value (the reality that money represents). In such systems the quantity of money (symbols) should adjust automatically to increases and decreases in the value and quantity of goods and services being traded. The process of money creation should be open and accessible, or, to use Ivan Illich's term, "convivial." It must also be interest-free. If money were to become a symbol of merit from the very point of its creation, the producer of economic value would be properly rewarded for his or her effort and skill, and production would be encouraged. At the same time, production would be ecologically sound, since money, in a convivial system, is more readily available and has less power to induce people to act in self-destructive ways. Money would be the product of cooperation among individuals and groups within integral communities.

Community Banking and the Liberation of Money

We can perhaps envision two distinct types of exchange systems emerging concurrently, one from the grass roots and another from the realm of mainstream business. These will be complementary to one another. One type will be limited, local, "soft" and "personal" systems—along the lines of Michael Linton's LETS (Local Employment and Trading System), which, in effect, monetizes the credit of community members. These are generically referred to as "mutual credit" (MC) systems, which are intended to facilitate exchanges that are intermediate between the informal exchange processes of the family, clan, or affinity group, on the one hand, and the formal, impersonal marketplace on the other. Mutual credit systems are by nature "personal" systems, in that they operate within relatively small affinity groups in which there is easy access to information about each member and in which interactions are more regular and broader in scope than purely economic.

The other type of system will be an extended, "hard" and "impersonal" system, necessary for exchanges between individuals in different social units and in trades between relative strangers and corporate organizations. While these latter characteristics are also those of the present global monopolistic system, the transformed system that I envision will differ from it in significant ways, which will enable the realization of human values.

At some point, it should be possible to "network" community exchange (currency and mutual credit) systems together into a web extending over a wide geographic area and including a very large total population. It could conceivably be a global network. This might then obviate the need for impersonal systems entirely. In fact, there has been some experimentation with "intertrading" between different LETSystems, particularly in Australia and New Zealand. Intertrading is one way of allowing two people who belong to different community trading systems to trade with each other.

It has been the stated goal of centrally controlled monetary systems to match the money supply to the needs of the economy, but the "needs" have never been well defined in monetary terms, and, as pointed out above, the mechanisms of control have never worked to benefit more than a relatively small privileged class. A fundamental principle of sound money management is that **the supply of money or credit available at any given time should accurately reflect the wealth of material wares and services available in the market for purchase in the near term.** This is a principle that has been disregarded in modern money and banking but must be heeded in establishing healthy community exchange systems.

The Role of Community Currencies

Community currencies empower people by shifting some degree of economic control from remote external agencies to people within the community. When properly designed and managed, they can provide a strong component in building economic equity and participatory democracy. A greater degree of economic independence allows a community to set its own quality-of-life standards.

Three fundamental advantages distinguish community currencies or mutual credit systems:

1. They provide an abundant medium of exchange that is created locally in accordance with the needs of the local economy.

Community currencies supplement the available supply of conventional money, which is kept artificially scarce and expensive (because interest is charged). The amount of community currency can be expanded as needed to enable whatever amount of trading the local economy requires. Since official money is controlled by outside entities, which manipulate it for their own purposes and ends, there is a need for complementary exchange media that can buffer communities from the more adverse effects of actions by the government and central banks. Community currencies serve this purpose.

2. They are low in cost, being created interest-free.

Community currencies enable participants to, in effect, create their own "money" by monetizing the value of their own labor and material resources. Unlike conventional money, which originates as "loans" made by banks and requires the payment of interest, community currencies can provide an interest-free line of credit for all authorized participants. The members of a community exchange system form an open, mutually supportive community in which almost everyone can be authorized to create some amount of community currency.

3. They stimulate the local economy and promote local self-reliance.

Community currencies favor local production for local use, reducing dependence on imports and production for export. Because such currencies are recognized and accepted only within the community, they have a built-in propensity to give local providers preference as sources of supply for goods and services, thus promoting the health of the local economy. The purchase of imports requires a more generally accepted currency or some mechanism of exchanging one currency for another. While some degree of trading between communities and regions is necessary and desirable, the health of any economy requires that it be able to resist the imposition by outside entities of exploitative trade relationships and capital arrangements. Local production for local use and "import replacement" also reduce the need for long-distance transport, thus reducing the environmental impact and transportation costs.

When people have needs that remain unfulfilled, the first question that ought to be asked is this: Is it for lack of skills, resources, or motivation, or is it because they lack money? Much "good work" is left undone because those who have the will to see it done lack the money. Much "bad work" is done because it is in the narrow self-interest of those with money to do it and because others, who need the money to live, can be persuaded to do it, too. How often do we hear that child care cannot be provided, that streets cannot be repaired, that parks cannot be beautified, that schools cannot be properly maintained **because there is not enough money?** How often do we see workers accepting conditions that they know are damaging to their health or doing jobs that are clearly harmful to their neighbors or the environment **because they need the money?**

Official currency is created by entities external to the community that have little sensitivity to or concern for the needs of the local population, and its supply is artificially limited. This intentional scarcity of official money is in large part responsible for such destructive effects, and **that scarcity can be alleviated by the creation of supplemental community currencies.**

Furthermore, the scarcity of money in the local economy is aggravated by the fact that official currency can, and does, circulate far and wide. It can easily be spent to buy goods and services from remote regions. Money spent outside the local community is no longer available to facilitate trading within the local community. It must be replaced by attracting more money from outside, by either exporting products or receiving government transfer payments or attracting tourists and businesses to come and spend.

The universality of national currency, its greatest advantage from the standpoint of flexibility and spendability, is also its greatest disadvantage from the standpoint of local self-reliance and integrity of the local economy. Rather than resulting from the lack of skills or physical resources, local unemployment and business stagnation more often result from the fact that the money necessary to connect needs with supplies has gone elsewhere.

A local currency is, by its nature, limited in scope. It is recognized only within a limited area, and therefore can be created, earned, and spent only within that area. This fact tends to favor local producers who have agreed to accept it, and its narrow range of circulation makes it more likely that the spender will be able to earn it back. Local currencies, thus, stimulate local production and employment.

Just as a breakwater protects a harbor from the extreme effects of the open sea, so does a local currency protect the local economy from the extreme effects of the global market and the manipulations of centralized banking and finance. Complete reliance on national currencies and the competitive conditions of the global market tend to force all communities to the lowest common denominator of environmental quality and working conditions. Local currencies, however, provide a buffer that allows local communities to set their own standards and maintain a higher quality of life.

There need never be any scarcity of community currency, since it is created by members of the community themselves in the course of trade. Any time two parties wish to make a trade, they can do so even if they have no money. Local currency or credits can easily be created to enable the exchange to take place.

With greater equity, economic security, and general prosperity comes the capacity of ordinary people not only to make better choices about the work they do but also to be more philanthropic and involved in volunteer efforts. People also can afford to make better choices in their spending, choosing in favor of better quality or durability over lower price, and choosing products made in ways that are consistent with their values. Furthermore, community currencies promote community culture and identity and thus social solidarity.

Individual businesses also stand to gain. Their acceptance of community currency can benefit them in many ways:

by enhancing their image and gaining the goodwill of people in the community,

by developing customer loyalty, and

by increasing their cash business, as community currency users change their shopping patterns in favor of local suppliers.

Succeeding chapters will address more fully the crucial role played by local business in assuring the success of local currency systems and will explore more fully the benefits that they derive from their participation. See especially chapters 11, 17, 19, 20, and 22.

Part 1 has described the nature of the dominant system of money and explained how and why it is dysfunctional; outlined its political and social implications, its historical manipulation, and its use as an instrument of power; defined what money really is and how its primary role as a medium of exchange can be served by nonpolitical, democratic community currencies; and shown how community currencies fit into an overall strategy for restoring and maintaining the health of communities. Having that foundation, the reader should now be prepared to comprehend the significance of historical examples and draw useful insights from the case studies presented in part 2.

PART II

COMPLEMENTARY CURRENCIES, PAST AND PRESENT

This section provides a historical overview of some of the more significant private and community exchange systems and currencies. You may have heard of *scrip* from your grandparents who lived through the Great Depression, or you may have seen one of the many news stories that have appeared in recent years describing *LETS, Ithaca HOURS, Time Dollars,* or one of their many related offshoots, or you may be one of the pioneers who have actually participated. These and other local money systems are described here, but the material is not solely descriptive. As we try to learn from the experience of both the distant and recent past, we also begin in part 2 an evaluation and critique that will be continued and elaborated in part 4.

Chapter 8

⤏

A Brief History of Community Currencies and Private Exchange Systems

It seems axiomatic that whenever a government fails to provide an adequate supply of currency or coin to maintain commercial trade, the people will step in to provide their own to fill the vacuum.

—RALPH A. MITCHELL AND NEIL SHAFER

THE GREAT DEPRESSION OF THE 1930S was a very important chapter in history. It provided a great many important lessons for civilization, many of which are yet to be fully grasped. Much has been written about the nature and causes of the Depression, which need not be repeated here, but for those for whom the event is too remote in time to have much meaning, I will attempt a brief summary.

The Great Depression is generally considered to have begun with the stock market crash in October of 1929, but it took a year or two before the economic distress became widespread and general. The Great Depression, although worldwide in scope, was particularly severe and long-lasting in the United States.[1] It was characterized by several concurrent financial and economic symptoms, which the United States Department of Commerce listed as follows:

an unemployed population estimated at over 12 million,
a serious agricultural situation resulting from excessive production, ruinous (low) prices, and large debts,
a financial and credit system in grave danger of collapse,
a large internal debt,
almost insurmountable barriers to foreign trade,

a perplexing foreign debt situation,

an unbalanced federal budget,

disorganized state and municipal finances,

increasing disorder and an almost complete lack of confidence on the part
   of the people.[2]

Most important, however, was the fact that there was little money in the hands of
the people, and, given their uncertainty about their prospects of getting more
of it, people tended to hoard what little money they did have. Hoarding slowed
the velocity of circulation, which further reduced the volume of business being
transacted. Serious human needs went unmet—until people began to organize.

Scrip of the Great Depression

Besides learning how to "make do, or do without," people began to establish
mutual support structures such as workers' cooperatives, many of which would
recycle and repair donated or broken items. People learned to share what they
had and to bypass the market and financial systems. Most of these measures
were considered stopgaps to be utilized until the economy "got back to normal," but in some of them there seemed to be the promise of more permanent
improvements. One of these "stopgaps," which was intended to address the
problem of the dearth of currency in circulation, was the issuance of *scrip*.

History is full of examples of successful local initiatives aimed at providing
exchange media, but the Great Depression of the 1930s saw this done on an
unprecedented scale. There were literally thousands of scrip issues put into circulation by a variety of agencies, including state governments, municipalities,
school districts, clearinghouse associations, manufacturers, merchants, chambers of commerce, business associations, local relief committees, cooperatives, and even individuals. These issues went by different names, depending
on who issued them and the circumstances of their issuance. Common scrip
types were *certificates of indebtedness, tax anticipation warrants, payroll warrants,
trade scrip, clearinghouse certificates, credit vouchers, moratorium certificates,* and
merchandise bonds. All these were intended to supplement the supply of scarce
official money and to give people a means of paying for the goods and services they needed.

Caslow Recovery Certificates

Among these scrip issues were many failures but also many impressive successes. There is much to be learned from both the failures and the successes.
One interesting case was the issuance, beginning in 1933, of "recovery certificates" by a Chicago newspaperman named W. H. Caslow. There are some
important lessons to be learned from this case. I would not recommend that

Figure 8.1.
Caslow Recovery
Certificate—front
side.

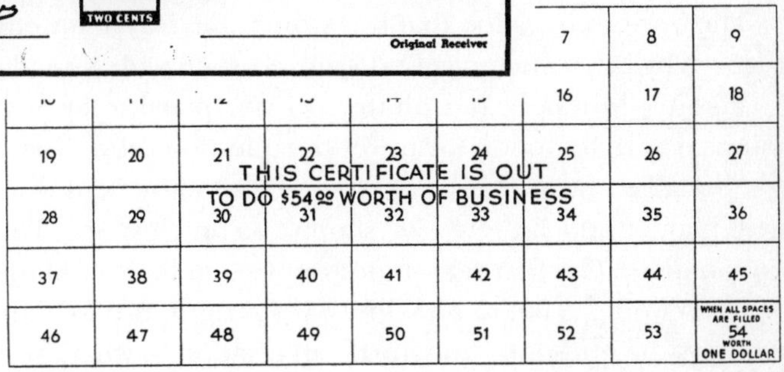

Figure 8.2.
Caslow Recovery
Certificate—
reverse side.

this model be emulated; in fact, it could be held up as a model of how not to do it. Figures 8.1 and 8.2 show the front and reverse sides, respectively, of a *Caslow Recovery Certificate.*

As can be seen from figure 8.2, these notes were of a variety known as "stamp scrip" and were supposed to be "self-liquidating." The inscription on the face of the notes describes the basic terms of their circulation. A two-cent "Redemption" stamp, available from scrip distributors, was supposed to be affixed on the back and signed by the buyer each time the note changed hands in a transaction. This, in effect, amounted to a 2 percent "tax" on each transaction. When all the stamp spaces had been filled, a one-dollar note of this scrip would have changed hands fifty-four times and facilitated $54 worth of business. The fifty-four stamps that had been sold and affixed would have provided $1.08 in official money, $1.00 of which would presumably be used to redeem the note and the remaining eight cents going to cover the expense of operating the plan.

While Caslow managed to gain wide acceptance of his scrip idea, it does not seem to have worked out quite as planned. Ralph Mitchell and Neil Shafer relate the story as follows:

> At first a small amount, it [the scrip] was manageable and fully accepted by a number of merchants. At one time over 500 stores were participating. Through his newspaper, *The Caslow Weekly,* Caslow was able to form a large organization of self-styled "scrippers." The plan kept growing, and clubs, local clearing houses,

etc., sprang up to take care of the scrip. The bulk of the scrip placed into circulation came through Caslow's using it to pay his workers. As for himself, he demanded cash for advertisements in his newspaper. As the scrip idea spread, as much as $30,000 might be issued in a single week. The plan failed, largely because there were too many field workers promoting the scrip plan and simply too much scrip. Around $1,000,000 was issued, and very little redeemed. After about two years, Caslow suspended publication of his newspaper and closed up shop.[3]

The obvious question that this story raises is, What went wrong with Caslow scrip? Why did a currency that enjoyed such widespread and strong support turn sour? Mitchell and Shafer do not provide enough details about its issuance or redemption to answer the question fully. They do, however, suggest two possible reasons: (1) "there were too many field workers promoting the scrip plan," and (2) there was "simply too much scrip." This is too simplistic an explanation. The first reason does not seem logical. Many people promoting the plan would seem to have given it strength, not weakness. The second reason begs the question, "too much" in relation to what? and does not even consider the nature of the scrip and its basis of issue, which are the more important considerations.

Examination of the inscription on the face of the scrip makes several aspects of the procedure apparent:

1. Caslow was the "sole distributor."
2. Stamps were "procurable from Distributor [Caslow] or contracted agents."
3. There is no mention of how the funds obtained from the sale of stamps were to be administered. It must, therefore, be presumed they simply went into the general fund of Caslow's business.

The eventual redemption of the scrip, therefore, seems to have depended entirely on the integrity of Caslow and the solvency of his business. We also note that the "original disbursement hereof" was "limited to Relief, Employment on Public Works, Public Purposes, and administration thereof." This basis of issue is rather vague and seems to be somewhat at variance with Mitchell and Shafer's report that "the bulk of the scrip placed into circulation came through Caslow's using it to pay his workers."

In this case, the self-liquidating feature would work only if the note changed hands enough times to generate sufficient stamp revenue to allow the scrip to be redeemed for cash. **Far more important are the conditions under which scrip is first placed in circulation and the commitment of the original issuer himself to accept it in trade.** These are the questions that the reader should keep foremost in mind as we proceed to examine historic, contemporary, and proposed currency systems.

It appears that the key to the failure of Caslow's scrip might be found in his refusal to accept it in payment for his own services (advertising). One of the fundamental rules of currency issuance is that the issuer be willing to redeem his or her own currency at face value (par), and that she or he be able to generate enough value (sales) in goods and/or services to redeem the currency at the rate of about 1 percent per day, which is equivalent to being able to redeem the entire issue in about three months time. This rate of redemption is called the *reflux rate*. It provides a gauge as to whether or not the amount of currency issued is excessive. Caslow's reflux rate was apparently zero. He spent his scrip into circulation but was apparently unwilling to redeem it. Failure of the scrip was then just a matter of time. He received something (the services of his employees) for nothing. The success of the currency then depended on the purchase of the stamps by the subsequent users of the scrip, and the deposit of the proceeds into a liquid redemption fund. Caslow scrip seems to have fallen short on both fronts. Mistakes like this should not be repeated.

LARKIN MERCHANDISE BONDS

Another example, which was fairly typical of Depression scrip, was the "merchandise bond" offered in 1933 by Larkin and Company of Buffalo, New York. Larkin was a large company with diverse operations including wholesale merchandising, a chain of retail stores, and a chain of gasoline stations. When President Franklin D. Roosevelt declared his famous "bank holiday," the Larkin Company issued $36,000 worth of "merchandise bonds" that it used to pay its employees.

As shown in figures 8.3 and 8.4, these "bonds" consisted of certificates that bore the image of the company's founder and a guarantee that they would be accepted in payment for services or merchandise at any Larkin outlet in the United States. The "bonds" were endorsed on their reverse side and spent into circulation by the company. They were subsequently accepted by many Larkin customers and even other businesses. As the shortage of official currency eased, Larkin gradually redeemed and retired its bonds. Company accountants estimated, however, that while the bonds circulated, the original $36,000 issue had turned over enough times to allow the sale of $250,000 worth of merchandise, providing a significant boost to the company's business.[4] There is no telling how much additional business was facilitated by other merchants and individuals who used the Larkin bonds to trade among themselves, but it must have been substantial.

This is one of the scrip success stories. It was spent into circulation by a financially strong company that was ready, willing, and able to redeem it in the normal course of trade.

Scrip such as the Larkin bond was generally accepted and used to do business within a limited local area. The farther it got from home, the more

Figure 8.3. Larkin Merchandise Bond—front side.

Figure 8.4. Larkin Merchandise Bond—reverse side.

uncertainty there was about its origin and value, and the less confidence people had in it. For this reason scrip tended to remain within the local economy and had the effect of stimulating local development and community self-reliance. This limited range of acceptance might seem at first to be a disadvantage of scrip, but, from the standpoint of strengthening the local economy, it is a great advantage. A currency that can only be spent locally gives local suppliers a natural advantage over distant suppliers. Toward the end of the Depression, however, as official government and central bank currencies became more widely available, scrip disappeared.

SILVIO GESELL, DEMURRAGE, AND STAMP SCRIP

Some of the most notable examples of successful scrip issues were instigated by Silvio Gesell, a successful German businessman who lived much of his life in South America and who, at one point between the First and Second World Wars, served briefly in the Bavarian government. Gesell, in his once famous book, *The Natural Economic Order*,[5] explained his views on the nature of money and how it functions in the economy and outlined his ideas on how it should be reformed. He originated the plan for issuing a type of currency that would not be hoarded. Gesell believed that the value of money should depreciate with time, like the value of the goods that it is supposed to represent. In his words, "If money is not to hold sway over goods, it must deteriorate as they do."[6]

But how could this depreciation be made to happen when money took the form of paper notes? Gesell thought to impose a fee called "demurrage" on all paper notes. The term *demurrage* is actually derived from the shipping industry. It means "the detention of a ship, freight car, or other cargo conveyance . . . beyond its scheduled time of departure," or the *compensation paid for this deten-*

tion.[7] As applied to currency, then, demurrage could be thought of in the second sense, as a user fee or a negative rate of interest charged for holding onto money in paper form. This fee would be collected by selling stamps, which would have to be attached to the note at periodic intervals in order for the note to retain its face value. Gesell thought that a 1 percent fee, applied monthly, would be sufficient to cause the notes to circulate more rapidly; thus they would enable a much greater volume of trading than conventional currency.

During economic depressions, money is scarce, and, with unemployment rising, businesses going broke, and banks failing, people are inclined to hoard cash, reducing the velocity of circulation of the outstanding money stock and causing business to slacken even further. In such circumstances, substituting another currency that has a demurrage feature can help to stimulate trading. The Great Depression of the 1930s was a problem that seemed tailor-made for such a solution. There were many issues of "stamp scrip" put into circulation during this period, though many were an extreme departure from Gesell's original idea. Later, the great American economist Irving Fisher became a proponent of scrip and wrote a book about it. His book, titled *Stamp Scrip,* described some of the subsequent scrip experiments and outlined his recommendations for the proper issuance of scrip.[8] His is one of the few handbooks available on the subject.

The Story of *Wära*

Gesell's ideas were widely discussed, but there was initially no attempt to implement them. Shortly after the end of the First World War, a currency inflation in Germany of astronomical proportions caused severe hardships for the people. This inflation, like all inflations, was the result of improper and excessive issuance of official currency. It was part of a deliberate government policy to surreptitiously eliminate its debts by printing more paper money. This policy was probably a large factor in the eventual collapse of the German Republic and helped set the stage for Hitler's rise to power, as he was one who exposed the government's duplicity and promised to remedy the situation.

At about the same time, the so-called free money movement was emerging in Germany and elsewhere. Gesell's friend Hans Timm had formed an association for the purpose of implementing the scrip idea, but it had languished. Timm actually had printed a demurrage scrip, which he called *Wära,* a name derived by combining two words: *Ware,* the German word for "goods," and *Währung,* the German word for "currency." Timm's association was called the Wära Exchange Association. *Wära* became fairly well known in Germany, but it was never widely used. With the coming of the Depression, the nature of the problem shifted from inflation to deflation. Money was then in short supply and its rate of circulation had slowed, causing general economic distress. This was a problem for which *Wära* seemed to offer a solution.

This scrip, according to Fisher, was intended to circulate indefinitely. It was "not intended to be redeemed," and "the scrip bore stamps . . . at the rate of 1 percent attachable monthly." The proceeds "were to be used in the propagation of the scrip idea."

In order for the scrip to maintain its face value, a stamp, costing 1 percent of the face value of the note, had to be affixed each month. The stamps could be bought at the bank representing the association. This stamp device was supposed to keep the scrip from being hoarded, as people would try to spend it prior to the day the stamp had to be affixed and thus avoid the cost of the stamp.[9]

STAMP SCRIP IN GERMANY AND AUSTRIA

Among the most successful and famous applications of Gesell's stamp scrip idea were the ones that took place in the small Bavarian town of Schwanenkirchen and the Austrian town of Wörgl.[10] The scrip would consist of pieces of paper of uniform size (about 8 inches x 3½ inches) to be issued by a voluntary association of factories, merchants, a bank, and any others. It would be issued in denominations of convenient amounts and be used in payment of wages and for trade. The shops who were members of the association would, of course, get all the trade. This would provide an incentive for other businesses to join, and business generally would improve.

Schwanenkirchen   The village of Schwanenkirchen had a population of about five hundred, and its only industry was a coal mine that had been closed for two years because of the Depression. The village had barely existed by means of the government dole, and almost everyone was in debt. Deflation throughout Germany led to bankruptcies, suicides, and overcrowded jails. The coal mine owner had heard about *Wära* stamp scrip and decided to try it. He got a loan of official currency (reichsmarks) and with it bought *Wära* stamp scrip from the Wära Exchange Association.[11] Then, according to a report in *The New Republic* for August 10, 1932:

> Herr Hebecker assembled his workers. He told them that he had succeeded in getting a loan of 40,000 Reichsmarks, that he wished to resume operations but that he wanted to pay wages not in Marks but in *Wära*. The miners agreed to the proposal when they learned that the village store would accept *Wära* in exchange for goods.
>
> When, after two years of complete stagnation, the workers for the first time brought home their pay envelopes, no one was interested in hoarding a cent of it; all the money went to the stores to pay off debts or for the purchase of necessities. The shopkeepers, too, were happy. Although at first they had felt a little hesitant about *Wära*, they had no choice, as no one had any other kind of money. The shopkeepers then forced it on the wholesalers, the wholesalers

forced it on the manufacturers, who in turn tried to pass it on to those who carried their notes, or they exchanged it at Herr Hebecker's mine for coal.

No one who received *Wära* wished to hold it; the workers, storekeepers, wholesalers and manufacturers all strove to get rid of it as quickly as possible, for any person who held it was obliged to pay the 2 cent stamp tax.[12] So *Wära* kept circulating, a large part of it returning to the coal mine, where it provided work, profits and better conditions for the entire community. Indeed, one could not have recognized Schwanenkirchen a few months after work had resumed at the mine. The village was on a prosperity basis, workers and merchants were free from debts and a new spirit of freedom and life pervaded the town.[13]

Continuing the account in Fisher's words:

> The news of the town's prosperity in the midst of depression-ridden Germany spread quickly. From all over the country reporters came to see and write about the "Miracle of Schwanenkirchen." Even in the United States one read about it in the financial sections of most big papers. But no explanation was given as to the real cause of the miracle—that nonhoardable money was being tried out and that it was working marvelously.[14]

Acceptance of *Wära* subsequently spread to various parts of Germany. About two thousand shops and one or two entire communities recovered by means of it. Finally, in November 1931, the German government passed an emergency law ending the circulation of *Wära*. The "miracle" of Schwanenkirchen then ended, and the town went back on the dole.

The success of the Schwanenkirchen case seems to have stemmed primarily from two factors: (1) a loan of 40,000 reichsmarks to reopen the mine, and (2) the payment of workers in a supplemental currency, which, because of its nature, had a circulation restricted primarily to the local community. The limited circulation had the effect of stimulating the local economy relative to the rest of the country, and this is a major advantage of any local currency or mutual credit system: local suppliers are favored over distant ones.

The demurrage factor may also have played a role through its acknowledged effect of increasing the velocity of circulation. If official currency is being hoarded, as it seems that it was, substituting a currency that is sound but not widely recognized and perceived as possibly inferior will stimulate spending.

In any case, when people are generally empowered to create their own exchange media, for instance through a local currency association or a mutual credit system, the scarcity of currency is alleviated. If people have the power to create their own currency as needed, there is no incentive to hoard it, and if a few do hoard it, that will not create a major problem. Still, I like the use of negative interest or demurrage as a way of keeping exchange media separate and distinct from savings media, and as a way of promoting greater economic equity. Money circulating within the economy is analogous to blood in the body: it carries nutrients to the cells and organs. The organs store nutrients, but not by engorging themselves with blood. They use a different storage medium. Similarly, money provides the liquidity for exchange, facilitating the process of getting value to where it is needed. Once there, surplus value should be saved as either real assets or financial (ownership or creditor) claims against real assets and productive enterprises.

Wörgl   Another place where *Wära* succeeded was in the Austrian town of Wörgl, which, by 1932, was in dire straits. In this town of about four thousand people many factories had closed, and almost everyone in town had lost their jobs. A large amount of local taxes were unpaid. The mayor of the town had heard about *Wära* and decided to try it. In this case, the *Wära* were issued by the town, in conjunction with a number of merchants and the local savings bank. The town paid its employees half in *Wära* and half in official currency.

Initially, some of the local merchants refused to accept *Wära*, but when they saw the trade going to the other shops, they too had to climb on the bandwagon. The *Wära* issue was a great success. Professor Fisher describes the situation this way:

> After the scrip was issued not only were current taxes paid (as well as other debts owing to the town), but many arrears of taxes were collected. During the first month alone 4,542 schillings were thus received in arrears. Accordingly, the city not only met its own obligations but, in the second half of 1932, executed new public works to the value of 100,000 schillings. Seven streets aggregating four miles were rebuilt and asphalted; twelve roads were improved; the sewer system was extended over two more streets; trees were planted and forests improved.[15]

Unfortunately, this successful experiment was also ended under pressure exerted on the Austrian government by the central bank. Figures 8.5 and 8.6, respectively, show the face and reverse sides of one of the Wörgl notes. These show the spaces where the stamps were supposed to be attached. The "1g," which appears in the spaces for the months of September and October, means one *groschen*, which is one hundredth of a schilling. A loose translation of the writing on the reverse side is as follows:

> Everybody! The sluggish circulation of money has triggered a worldwide recession and completely ruined millions of working people. Therefore the exchange of labor and services must be improved and the living space for the already evicted must be regained. The Wörgl Labor Certificates shall serve this purpose. They alleviate misery and provide work and food."[16]

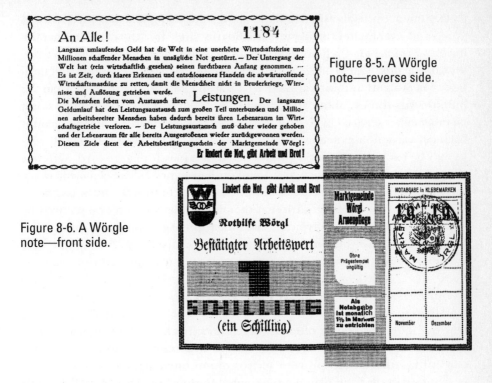

Figure 8-5. A Wörgle note—reverse side.

Figure 8-6. A Wörgle note—front side.

WIR: The Swiss *Wirtschaftsring*

Motivated mainly by the severe economic situation of the Depression, the WIR business group cooperative was founded in October 1934 in Zurich, Switzerland. The idea was to actively combat the economic crisis with the help of a "ring exchange system" modeled after a Scandinavian and Baltic organization. WIR is the first syllable of the word *Wirtschaftsring,* which means "business circle." WIR is also the German word for "we," which implies community. This term embodies the Swiss ideal: "to hold together and, together as a community, protect the interests of the individual" (from a speech by Werner Zimmermann, Fall Conference, 1954).

At the beginning, membership in the WIR business circle was open. Farmers, civil servants, and white-collar workers became participants. Each member paid cash into his or her account. A bonus of 5 percent was added, and members could then go shopping with WIR. Interest-free WIR credit provided extra buying power that served to stimulate the slow turnover of goods and services. Lacking any opportunity to earn interest, the WIR clearing credits were readily spent rather than hoarded. The benefits of WIR quickly became apparent, and information offices, staffed by volunteers, were established in many communities.

Despite many trials and tribulations over the years, WIR has survived and prospered, eventually evolving into a solidarity circle for "the commercial middle class" *(Mittelstand)* who operate small to medium-size businesses. By 1993, WIR had almost 77,000 participants, which amounted to 17 percent of all businesses in Switzerland, with annual WIR trading amounting to more than 2.5 billion Swiss francs (about 1.5 billion U.S. dollars). This large and growing membership is serviced by six offices scattered throughout the country. Account balances are denominated in WIR units equivalent to the Swiss franc. WIR credits may be exchanged by using WIR checks or a plastic charge card. WIR has adopted the latest technology, and members have, since 1995, been using transaction cards that enable the point-of-sale transfer of both WIR and Swiss francs.

Current procedures require that members' lines of credit be secured by adequate collateral, which typically takes the form of a second mortgage on the member's home or business real estate. Many consider WIR to be the best available model for bringing community exchange into the mainstream.

Legal Considerations

One question that people often ask when they first hear about alternatives to official money is, Is it legal? While laws vary from country to country, there is no current law that would prevent scrip, community currencies, and private exchange systems from being implemented in the United States. In fact, both commercial "barter" systems and community-based trade exchanges have been proliferating around the world for the past two or three decades. While history shows repeated official suppression of unofficial paper currencies, the well-established rights of contract and freedom of association will tend to protect nonmonetary exchange circles from government interference. The question of legality has been well researched by law professor Lewis Solomon. His findings are contained in his book *Rethinking Our Centralized Monetary System.*[17] He shares the opinion that, in the United States at least, there is no legal prohibition.

Lessons Learned

I believe that the application of community exchange media in our communities today could provide results every bit as dramatic as those obtained in Schwanenkirchen and Wörgl. The present-day community currency movement has much to learn from these historic precedents. In this regard, it is important that we take a critical look at stamp scrip. The whole matter of stamp scrip seems to have gotten confused by those who reported on it during the 1930s. A clear distinction needs to be made between the "self-liquidating" type of stamp scrip that was popular in the United States and the Gesellian-style demurrage stamp scrip that was used in Europe. In the former, the stamp was intended to provide a "tax" that would accumulate in a redemption fund so that after a year the fully stamped note could be redeemed for official money. In the case of *Wära,* the stamp was intended to serve an entirely different function. As Fisher points out, there was no intention to redeem the *Wära* scrip for cash; it was intended to circulate indefinitely. The purpose of the *Wära* stamp "tax" was to discourage hoarding of it and to stimulate its frequent transfer from hand to hand. The proceeds from the sale of the stamps, in the case of Schwanenkirchen, "were to be used in the propagation of the scrip idea,"[18] and, in the case of Wörgl, were to be used "for the enlargement of the town's welfare work."[19]

In the United States there were, it seems, two basic styles of the self-liquidating type of stamp scrip. One, the "weekly tax" style, required the stamp to be affixed on a particular day of each week; the other, the "transfer tax" style, required the stamp to be affixed prior to each transfer. With the former style, the tax could be avoided by spending the scrip prior to the next stamp date; with the latter style, anyone who accepted the scrip would have to pay the tax, including any arrears, before he or she could spend it. Of course, traders could accept the scrip at the depreciated rate instead of buying the stamp, and I expect that this was probably common practice.

The promise of being able to redeem the scrip for cash would have had, I think, a significant impact on the acceptability of self-liquidating scrip in the marketplace. It would be very instructive to know how these various designs worked out in practice, but my research has not turned up any good sources of information detailing the results.

Many of the scrip issues of the Depression era were defective in some way and should not be directly emulated, but the main thing to be learned from this chapter in the history of money is that it is possible for effective media of exchange to be issued at the local level and that the centralized control of money and finance need not limit the ability of a local economy to preserve its own health and quality of life.

Some scrip issues, of course, are more credible than others. The power, productive capacity, and good faith of the issuer all affect the credibility and market acceptance of a local scrip issue. The soundness and continued acceptability of a scrip issue depend on its basis of issue, the amount issued in relation to the issuer's willingness and ability to redeem it, and the means by which the issuance is regulated.

Currency or scrip issued by municipal and state governments will have a high level of credibility if those governments accept it as payment for taxes and fees, and if it is accepted at par with federal money. Such scrip is said to have a "tax foundation." Scrip issued by corporations, based on their own productive capacity, will have credibility to the extent that there is a demand for their products and their current assets are sufficient to "cover" the amount of scrip issued. Scrip issued by retailers in payment for their inventories of goods will have credibility because the goods are already there in the shops waiting to be bought. This is known as the "goods foundation" or "shop foundation" of scrip. Scrip issued by individuals is theoretically possible, but its acceptability will depend on the backing provided, usually in the form of real assets "pledged" or held as security by some third party.

The Deflation Dilemma

Economic depressions are typified by a scarcity of ordinary money. Indeed, most depressions are *caused* by restriction of the money supply by the monetary authorities. The subsequent felt lack of adequate payment media causes people to become fearful and to hoard what money they do have. This hoarding slows its velocity of circulation, which further reduces the volume of business being conducted. Thus, the depression deepens until money becomes plentiful again and people feel confident about spending it. Replenishment of the supply of official (debt) money requires not only an increased willingness of the banks to lend but also a willingness of individuals and businesses to borrow. People's experience of monetary stringency and slack business demand during a depression, however, makes them loathe to incur new indebtedness.

The prescription for addressing this dilemma put forth by Lord John Maynard Keynes was for government to intervene by borrowing money from the central bank and spending it into circulation. It was said that the temporary budget deficit thus incurred could be made up later by surplus revenues once the depression was over. The experience of more than sixty years has made it clear that the Keynesian prescription is flawed, that "later" never comes. As already explained, government budget deficits become chronic because of the very nature of the debt-money system, which requires an explosive creation of new debt to pay off the interest on the older debts.

The original intent of using scrip, at least in America, was to provide a temporary supplement to scarce official currency. But the permanent use of a locally issued and controlled exchange medium, such as scrip, has clear advantages for protecting local economies from the distorting effects of global finance and banking. The idea is not to *isolate* communities but to *insulate* them.

Railway Notes

There have been numerous instances of public service companies issuing circulating notes and tokens. The familiar bus and subway tokens used in various places provide some idea of what might be possible. The present-day use of tokens is, for the most part, intended only to provide a measure of convenience in regulating access to services and collecting fares. There have been instances, however, in which tokens or notes issued by railway companies have circulated as money, being used as a means of payment not only for railway services but also for a wide variety of goods and services in the marketplace. According to Dr. Walter Zander, in his paper, "Railway Money and Unemployment,"[20] the Leipzig-Dresden Railway, sometime in the early 1800s, was authorized to issue one-third of its capital in the form of "railway money certificates." These certificates, he says, remained in circulation for about forty years. Zander also indicates that during the 1920s the German Railway issued a considerable amount of its own money.

Zander's own proposal for a modern version of railway money, although apparently never implemented, was based on sound principles and makes good sense. My proposals, which are outlined in later chapters, draw much of their inspiration from Zander's work and are consistent with it. While his proposal was aimed specifically at the German Railway, there is no reason why the same rationale cannot be applied in proposing that any economic entity— such as airlines, or electric, gas, or communications utilities, or a consortium of producers—be empowered to issue circulating currency. Many corporations already utilize "commercial paper" to obtain working capital. It is not hard to imagine that, if such paper were to be issued in small-denomination notes, it might circulate as money.

The official monetary system puts the cart before the horse in that money must be obtained *before* a purchase can be made. Whether that money be in the form of paper, coins, or bank credit, its creation is beyond the control of the producers of real wealth. In other words, *the creation of goods and services depends on money changing hands.* Zander's proposal is much more rational. It puts the horse properly before the cart, in that producers can create a form of money themselves with which to enable others to purchase their products. In this instance *the creation of money depends on goods or services changing hands.*

When an economic entity such as a railway must pay for what it needs in official currency, it must first acquire the currency to get what it needs. Alternatively it might purchase what it needs on credit in anticipation of having the cash it needs to pay at the time the bill comes due. However, in doing this, it commits itself to deliver something (money) that it only hopes to obtain. As Zander points out:

> Whether its hope will materialize is uncertain. The undertaking to pay at maturity contains, therefore a speculative element, which is particularly hazardous in times of depression. But the railway can promise to pay something else, namely, to transport commodities and persons; that is to fulfill its function as a railway. There is nothing speculative about that. The means required for this, rolling stock and other plant, are available. This is therefore fundamentally different from a promise to pay cash at a future date, for in the latter case the means of payment have yet to be secured, and this by having transported passengers and goods. The capacity of the railway to act as a carrier is, on the contrary, unquestionable.

The Zander plan includes the following essential features:

1. The railway makes payment for the goods and services it buys, not in legal tender (central bank notes), but in transport certificates.
2. The railway certifies that it will accept the certificates at their face value like ready money, in payment for its services.
3. The certificates are made out to the bearer.
4. They are issued in convenient denominations.
5. No one is forced to accept them.
6. They have no legal value.
7. The market rate of the certificates in relation to official currency is freely determined by the market.

The primary feature assuring that the certificates will maintain their value is the commitment of the railway to accept them at any time *at their face value,* regardless of their market rate.

To further illustrate the workings of such a currency, consider the following example. Suppose the Intercity Railway Company decided to finance its operations, in part, by issuing railway certificates in small denominations of, say, $5, $10, and $20. It might put them into circulation by using them to pay employees and/or suppliers. These initial recipients need not be the ones who ultimately redeem the certificates. They might use them as currency to obtain other goods and services they need. Those in the community who use the railway's services will readily accept the certificates, and, because of this established demand, others in the community will accept them in trade as well.

The crucial question is, What amount of certificates can the railway issue? Prudence dictates that the railway not issue more certificates than it can comfortably redeem by providing the services promised. Furthermore, since ticket sales provide the main source of revenue for the railway, it must be careful to assure that its cash revenue remains sufficient to cover its cash expenses, and must therefore avoid having too much of ticket sales being taken up by coupon redemption. If the market becomes flooded with railway certificates in excess of the current demand for railway services, this will be felt by the market. Doubts will be raised as to the long-term ability of the railway to redeem all its certificates. Since the railway certificates are not legal tender, traders in the market are free to refuse them or to accept them at a discount from their face value. A certificate with a face value of $10 might now be accepted by merchants for only $9 worth of goods. The railway, on the other hand, is still obliged to accept it at full value for $10 worth of railway services.

In such a circumstance, a railway patron, instead of paying cash for his or her ticket, could pay for it using a certificate that he could buy in the marketplace at a 10 percent discount from face value. Thus she or he could buy a $10 ticket

The "Constant" Currency of Ralph Borsodi

In the early 1970s, Dr. Ralph Borsodi, political economist, social philosopher, and founder of the School of Living,[1] together with a few associates, developed and launched a currency experiment called the "Constant." Concerned about the chronic inflation resulting from official debasement of the dollar, Borsodi conceived a privately issued currency that would hold its value.

Borsodi's basic strategy for making his currency inflation-proof was to make it redeemable for a "market basket" assortment of basic commodities. The development of the Constant never progressed that far, but the Constants that were issued were backed by bank deposits of dollars. Constants circulated successfully for almost two years and enjoyed wide acceptance by the public. At its peak, the equivalent of about $160,000 in Constants was circulating throughout southern New Hampshire and elsewhere, both in the form of paper currency and as checking account balances at several area banks. News of the Constant was reported in several popular publications, such as *Forbes* and *Business Week*, in addition to numerous New England dailies.

Why Borsodi did not complete his plan for backing the Constant with commodities is not entirely clear. His advancing age and failing health may have been factors, along with possible organizational problems and lack of sufficient capital.[2] Figures 8.7 and 8.8 show the front and reverse sides, respectively, of a twenty-five Constant note.

Actually, the problem that Borsodi sought to solve by inventing the Constant was quite different from the one that gave rise to Depression-era scrip. The Constant was intended to preserve purchasing power in the face of official currency debasement (inflation), while scrip was intended to supplement the supply of scarce official currency (deflation). In either case, however, there was a stimulating effect on the local economy.

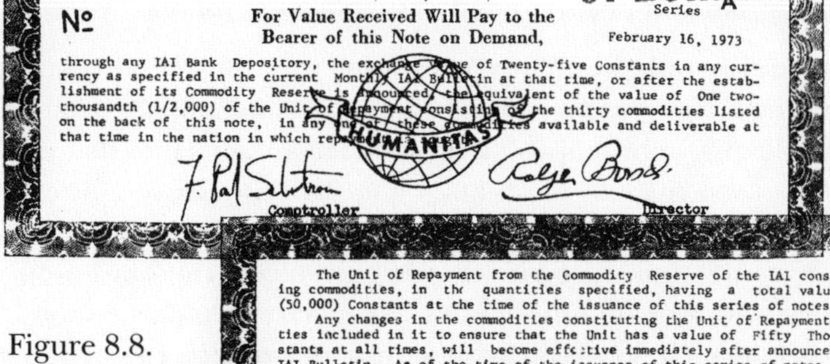

Figure 8.7. Constant Note —front side.

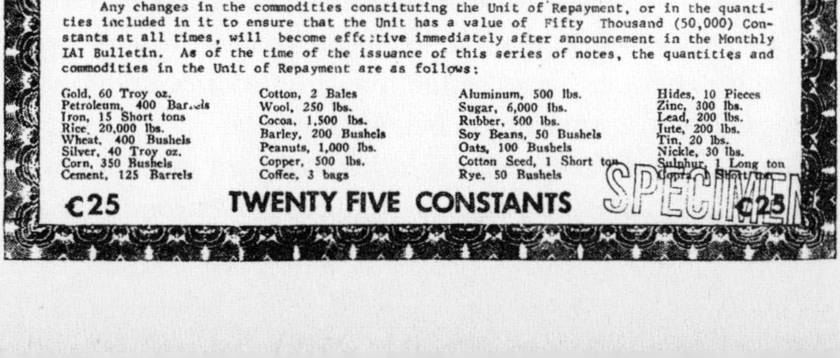

Figure 8.8. Constant Note —reverse side.

by using a certificate that cost only $9. Further, the suppliers and employees of the railway will no longer be willing to accept new certificates from the railway at face value. The railway will have two options: either it can cut back on its issuance of certificates until the supply of outstanding certificates and demand for railway services come back into balance, or it can continue its profligate ways and see its certificates suffer further loss of value in the marketplace. If it does the latter, its suppliers and employees, who were formerly willing to accept certificates from the railway at face value, will no longer be willing to do so. They too will discount them, or they might not accept them at all.

A persistent excess of certificates in circulation relative to the demand for railway services will sow increasing doubts about the financial strength and long-term viability of the railway and its ability to deliver the services that the certificates promise. Because their circulation cannot be legally compelled, private, nonpolitical currency issues tend to be self-correcting. Any established public utility or productive enterprise could, likewise, issue certificates that could serve as an effective medium of exchange.

An Early Proposal for a Credit Clearing System

As early as 1914, Hugo Bilgram and L. E. Levy proposed a "credit clearing" system.[21] They introduced their plan with the following statement:

> Were a number of businessmen to combine for the purpose of organizing a system of exchange, effective among themselves, they could clearly demonstrate how simple the money system can really be made. The greater the number of businessmen that would thus cooperate, the more complete would be their own emancipation from the obstruction to commerce and industry which existing currency laws impose.

The plan that Bilgram and Levy outlined was basically as follows:

1. A group of businesspeople would agree to settle their business accounts through a "clearing system," using their own credit as a medium of exchange.
2. The method of clearing accounts would be, in the main, similar to that used by depository banks to clear accounts among its depositors. Each business association would open an account for each of its members.
3. Each member would then furnish "thoroughly acceptable and amply adequate" security for the amount of credit he or she wished to establish.
4. The security would be held by the association as a pledge to cover the "credit cheques" that the member might draw in excess of deposits, that is, to secure his or her debit balance.
5. Such "credit cheques" would be accepted by all members of the association in payment of business accounts. The amount of the check would be

credited to the payee's account (causing it to increase), and the same amount would be debited to the payer's account (causing it to decrease).
6. Official currency and checks would be deposited to the account also, with the stipulation that only system credits, not official money, could be paid out or withdrawn from the account.
7. Members with net credits would be allowed to redeem a certain portion of them, say 20 percent each month, for official currency. This, of course, would require those with debits to provide the official currency for such redemptions.
8. Such associations in various localities could be federated to provide for interregional clearing of credits.

The WIR association, described earlier, in fact conforms closely to this prescription. It has proven itself in more than sixty-five years of successful operation. The path toward wider implementation seems obvious. Most businesses have accounts payable and accounts receivable. This plan provides a means of clearing the major part of these balances without the use of official money.

Mutual Credit and LETSystems, which will be described in chapter 10, are in concept much like Bilgram and Levy's credit clearing (B&L) plan. The B&L plan, however, required that members deposit "security" in the form that conventional banks require, for example, bonds, stocks, or mortgages. Mutual credit and LETS consider this to be an unnecessary burden and require only the member's verbal or written commitment to accept credits in payment. The rationale is that the privilege of continuing participation in the system will be sufficient inducement for members to honor their commitments. In the case of mutual credit systems, debit balances are usually limited to some amount determined by a member's trading volume, while LETS, as originally conceived, imposes no formal debit limits.

Further, neither mutual credit nor LETS require debtors to deposit official money, nor do they allow creditors to withdraw official money, except that mutual credit, as conceived, requires a member, on withdrawing from the system, to clear any remaining debit balance with cash if she or he cannot clear it by selling goods and services. Given such sources of cash income, there may be circumstances in which it would be advantageous to allow some limited redemption of system credits for cash.

I have also seen reports that similar credit clearance systems were in operation in some of the American colonies prior to the Revolutionary War. So despite the seeming novelty of current local money efforts, the basic ideas embodied in all these systems are not totally new.

Chapter 9

—

Global Finance, Inflation, and Local Currencies

Future students of history will be shocked and angered by the fact that in 1945 the same monetary system that had driven the world to despair and disaster [in the 1930s], and had almost destroyed the civilization it was supposed to stand for, was revived on a much wider scope.

—JACQUES RUEFF

A HEADLINE IN A MAJOR daily newspaper reads, "Cash-Starved Argentine Provinces Turning Out Their Own Money" (see figure 9.1).[1] The story tells of two remote provinces that were printing their own money in the form of small-denomination provincial bonds (basically, IOUs of the provincial governments) and paying their employees with it. This "to the chagrin of national and international banking authorities."

Two things are interesting about this story. The first is the fact that money was, and is, being issued by governments below the national level, while the second is that both the national and international banking authorities disapproved of it.

Why Central Governments and Central Banks Don't Like Local Currencies

Now, one might ask, Why shouldn't a provincial government, or a municipal government for that matter, issue its own money? Governments at these levels have tax revenues too, and any IOU of any level of government is ultimately supported by nothing more than its power to tax. So why, in the case of the

Argentine provinces, should the national and international authorities (namely, the International Monetary Fund) have been chagrined over provincial measures to provide their own exchange media? The stated reason, according to the article, was worry that the consequent expansion of the money supply would undermine the central government's efforts to reduce the inflation rate. This may seem rather odd considering that central governments and central banks themselves are the cause of inflation.

In order to get to the bottom of the inflation problem, we need to address several questions. What is inflation, anyway? What's wrong with it? What causes it? And, finally, does the issuance of provincial currency really contribute to it? Let's consider these in turn.

WHAT IS INFLATION?

Much of the difficulty in understanding inflation stems from the confused definition that economists use. A dictionary provides a good illustration of this confusion. Here is what it says: "Inflation 2. *Economics.* An abnormal increase in available currency and credit beyond the proportion of available goods, resulting in a sharp and continuing rise in price levels."[2]

In this definition we see the conventional "wisdom" reflected. We see a presumed cause, "an abnormal increase in available currency and credit," coupled with an observed effect, "a sharp and continuing rise in price levels."

Cash-Starved Argentine Provinces Turning Out Their Own Money

50A THE CHARLOTTE OBSERVER Thursday, November 24, 1985

By ANDRES OPPENHEIMER
Knight-Ridder Newspapers

MIAMI — Two remote Argentine provinces, short of cash to pay public employees, have come up with an easy solution.

They're printing their own money, to the chagrin of national and international banking authorities.

"We are paying all our public employees with provincial bonds," Roberto Romero, governor of the northern Argentina province of Salta, said in a telephone interview. He said Salta started printing its own IOUs because it wasn't getting federal currency fast enough.

"People can change these bonds for money at any bank," Romero said. "They can use them to shop at supermarkets and to buy cars or any other products."

The Argentine government is not smiling, and world bankers are worried that other cash-starved states will copy Salta's financial extravaganza and jeopardize Latin efforts to curb inflation and pay huge foreign debts.

The International Monetary Fund (IMF), the world's main financial inspector for debt-ridden countries, was concerned enough to bring up the issue in recent talks with the Argentine government, said sources in Argentina and Washington. The IMF does not comment on negotiations with individual countries.

After Salta started quietly issuing its IOUs in September last year, the nearby province of La Rioja started printing its own bonds, too. Four other Argentine provinces have either begun adopting similar programs or are preparing to do so.

In all cases, the bonds are good only within the province where they're issued.

But the government of President Raul Alfonsin says the provincial bonds are expanding the country's money supply and are undermining efforts to remove Argentina from the list of world inflation leaders. Earlier this year, Argentina had a 1,000% annual inflation rate.

Alfonsin made headlines worldwide in June when he launched an austerity program built around a commitment to stop his government from printing money. Since then, inflation has dropped to 3% a month, a record low in recent history.

The bonds printed in Salta come in denominations of 10, 100 and 1,000 australes, the same as ordinary Argentine currency bills. They pay no interest and can be either exchanged for Argentine currency or used to buy goods.

Romero, of the opposition Peronist party, and officials of other provinces claim their bonds are not really new currencies, because they are no good outside their provinces.

Figure 9.1. News clip about Argentine provincial bonds.

But even if this presumed cause is correct, it begs a further question: What gives rise to this abnormal increase in currency and credit? Let us hold in abeyance the question of cause and define inflation as the effect: it is a rise in the *general* level of prices of goods and services. This is the essence of the problem. Inflation hurts people who must live on a fixed income—pensioners and retirees, and workers who lack bargaining power—because they must pay more for the things they need while their money incomes go up very little or not at all.

Since the price of something is an expression of its value relative to the money being used to value it, an increase can result in two ways. First, it can be due to people valuing the item more, or second, it can be due to people valuing the money less. Changing conditions of supply and demand can cause price adjustments of particular goods or commodities. But when the prices of *most* goods and services are rising simultaneously, that general increase must arise from some systemic phenomenon.

WHAT CAUSES INFLATION?

Almost invariably, general increases in the price level reflect a debasement of the currency in terms of which the prices are stated. Sellers demand more money because each unit of money is worth less than it was before. Milton Friedman, the well-known economist, has stated the matter succinctly in saying that "inflation is a monetary phenomenon." History is replete with examples of inflation and hyperinflation—all caused by some form of currency debasement. Economists disagree about how to prevent or remedy inflation, but as Ralph Borsodi argued, inflation is dishonest, deliberate, and unnecessary.[3]

The standard approach to combating inflation employed by the Federal Reserve, which is charged with management of our money and consequently the economy, is to raise interest rates or to force a contraction in the money supply. This policy has been labeled by some as a "meat-ax" approach to the problem, while others have compared it to the archaic medical practice of bloodletting.[4] In any case, most economists seem to have given up on the idea of ending inflation and seek only to limit its rate.

If inflation is a monetary phenomenon, how exactly does it come about? I argue that it is not the amount of money in circulation per se that causes inflation but the basis on which the money is issued. Money that is improperly issued can be viewed as counterfeit, albeit *legal* counterfeit. It is counterfeit, not because its issuance is unauthorized, but because its issuance violates sound principles of money and banking. The mixture of such legal counterfeit with legitimate money, since each is indistinguishable from the other, causes the debasement of the entire money supply.

We have already seen how the issuance of money on the basis of interest-bearing debt causes a chronic insufficiency of money in general circulation.

The primary cause of inflation is the issuance of money on the basis of ever increasing debts of central governments, which they are unable to repay. (The total debt increases every time the government runs a budget deficit.) This is called "monetizing the debt," and it is the cause of the "abnormal increase" in currency referred to by the dictionary definition. It is an abuse of power that is almost universal today among governments and central banks.

In some countries the government issues money directly, through a central bank that it controls, by spending the money into circulation. In the United States, the federal government does not issue money directly. It is the private banking cartel, headed by the Federal Reserve, that issues United States money as bank credit. The Federal Reserve is *not* under the control of the government. Indeed, it can be reasonably argued that it is the other way around. But the evidence shows that the Federal Reserve will do whatever is necessary to accommodate any level of government spending, no matter how profligate.[5]

Other improper bases of issue include capital investments, such as tools and machinery; speculation in land, real estate, stocks, and other securities; and consumer credit. Surely, capital investments, construction, and consumer durables need to be financed, but they ought to be financed out of savings of money already in existence. New money that is created on the basis of anything except the exchange of goods and services coming to market represents a debasement of the currency and will cause inflation of prices in the market.[6] The banking principle that ought to be observed in issuing money is that new money placed into circulation should be matched by equivalent value being offered for sale in the marketplace.

The irresponsible and unsound banking practices that give rise to inflation can be compared to a dairy farmer adding water to milk. The farmer who takes a milk bucket to the well can increase the volume of fluid (milk mixed with water), but the volume of real milk remains the same. The total amount of nutrients in the bucket does not change. If the farmer tries to sell the mixture as pure milk, he or she is defrauding customers.

Real value comes from the efforts of producers, not from debt that is never intended to be repaid. Money issued to finance goods in (or on the way to) market is legitimate; it represents the milk of the economy. Money issued to finance government debt is valueless; it is like water, diluting the value of every legitimate dollar in circulation. Such monetized debt allows the government to take more value from the economy than it ever will put into it. It is for this reason that inflation has been called a "hidden tax."

It is astonishing that even the most respected economists still prescribe "massive government spending" as the medicine required to end an economic recession. Implicit in this prescription is the intention that this massive spending will be financed, not out of increased tax revenues, but by the creation of new money. This is like telling the farmer that the way to end the malnutrition among his customers is to add still more water to the milk.

And What about Deflation?

To completely understand the monetary problem, we should look not only at inflation but also at its opposite, deflation. The dictionary definition is: "Deflation 2. *Economics*. A reduction in the general price level, brought on by a decrease in the amount of money in circulation or by a decrease in the total volume of spending."[7] This time the dictionary correctly defines deflation as "a reduction in the general price level," but the definition again includes a presumed relationship with the amount of money in circulation.

But again, it is not just a matter of the *amount* of money in circulation; it is more a matter of banks not lending for things they should. When banks lend for purposes they should not, while neglecting to lend for purposes they should, the result is simultaneous inflation of prices, due to debasement of the currency, along with decline of economic activity (recession), due to inadequate amounts of money being issued to the private sector for productive purposes. When the Fed raises interest rates or restricts the money supply, legitimate business borrowers are squeezed. Not only does it cost them more to finance their operations, but the banks may "call" some loans, forcing perfectly viable business to default on their loans.

Which is worse, inflation or deflation? Given a choice between inflation and deflation, inflation is considered by many to be the lesser of evils. But that depends on your point of view and the source from which you derive your livelihood. When there is more money sloshing around (even if some of it is counterfeit), the "little guy" may be more likely to get a bit of it from within the private sector. Also, rising prices create optimism about the future, while falling prices bring gloom. On the other hand, when banks are unwilling or unable to lend enough new money into the productive sector in a mistaken attempt to control inflation, they bring about defaults and bankruptcies, which in turn cause greater unemployment and reduced production. Thus, many people have their incomes cut off completely, while those who are able to maintain some source of income fare well because of falling prices.

Another means of keeping the prices of basic commodities low is by use of military intervention or threat of intervention to keep weaker countries from restricting or closing off access to raw materials and export products. Thus, the Gulf War of 1991, the 1970s CIA-engineered coup in Chile, and innumerable interventions around the world by the United States government have made it possible for the United States to "export its inflation" to a large extent. The so-called free trade agreements, such as the North American Free Trade Agreement (NAFTA) and the General Agreement on Tariffs and Trade (GATT), are diplomatic attempts to do the same thing.

Those who lose their jobs, farms, or businesses can only hope for direct government payments in the form of welfare and unemployment benefits. In either case, when government appropriates more of the nation's wealth by deficit spending, it is able to dictate the direction of economic activity. Greater numbers of citizens are required to do its bidding, either in the military, as employees in the government's bureaucracy, or by working for its corporate and academic minions (engaging in such activities as designing and building weapons, space and scientific boondoggles, and infrastructure development to benefit favored interests). Others, who lack the requisite skills, have little choice but to suffer the indignities of being "on the dole." The central economic planning for which socialist and communist countries have been so roundly criticized has, unfortunately, become the modus operandi of the "capitalist" West, but in a disguised form.

To sum up, then, when the government covertly takes value out of the economy (which is evident from budget deficits and ever increasing government debt), the people pay for it in either of two ways: recession or inflation. In a recession, some people are deprived of their share of the total product as a result of losing their jobs, their businesses, or their homes, or having social programs cut. When the debasement of money causes inflation, the dollars people get do not buy as much as they did before.

A recession is like the farmer refusing to deliver milk to some customers, even though they have already paid for it, so that he or she can keep more milk for personal uses. Currency debasement is like the farmer adding water to the remaining quantity of milk so that, while she or he may continue to deliver the same amount of liquid to each customer, that inferior liquid (milk mixed with water) will provide them less nourishment and satisfaction.

Of course, it is possible for governments and central banks to use both strategies simultaneously, doing some of each.

DOES THE ISSUANCE OF PROVINCIAL BONDS CAUSE INFLATION?

Both national currencies and regional currencies are subject to possible abusive issuance and debasement. But the effects of the former are quite different from the effects of the latter. When a national currency is improperly issued, that causes a falsification of the monetary unit itself. Traders in the market have only one way of protecting themselves, which is to raise their prices (stated in terms of the official currency unit). On the other hand, when a regional or provincial currency is improperly issued, that has no effect on the official unit. Traders can protect themselves by discounting that currency from face value or refusing it entirely. For this reason, a regional or provincial currency cannot cause inflation.

This story about the Argentine provincial bonds is another instance of the conflict between exploiter and exploited. We see, on the one hand, the central government, supported by the international financial hierarchy, attempting to maintain its control over the entire national economy via its control over money creation and circulation. On the other hand, we also see the provincial authorities implementing measures to ameliorate the effects of central government and central bank policies that have been damaging to their local economies. By supplementing scarce official money with their own money issues, the provincial governments counter the stifling effects of the central government's and central bank's policies. These policies include alternating monetary expansion and contraction, misallocation of credit to finance privilege and to increase central power, compliance with the demands of international finance capital, and domestic "austerity" imposed on the people to pay for it.

The Argentine Experience

With that foundation laid, let us return to our story of the Argentine provincial currencies. It is a story I have been following ever since I saw that first newspaper headline. A subsequent article by Argentine native José Reissig, which appeared in the British journal *New Economics* in 1991, provided some details.[8]

The province of Salta, in 1985, was the first Argentine province to issue bonds in small denominations and to spend them into circulation. One such bond in the denomination of one hundred australes is shown in figure 9.2. By 1986, according to Reissig's article, three neighboring provinces, La Rioja, Jujuy, and Tucumán, had followed Salta's lead in issuing bonds into circulation. As of the end of 1991, they remained in circulation and comprised an important component of the money supply in those regions. "The bonds have become an intrinsic feature of the economy of Salta. Today they are more in evidence than the national australes, amounting perhaps to 60 percent of all currency in circulation."[9] Reissig stated further that in the province of Tucumán, provincial bonds at that time provided about 43 percent of the exchange media.

It may seem surprising to find that these bonds were still circulating and that the central government had not been willing (or able) to suppress them. Reissig speculates that the reason may simply have been because the provincial bonds, while providing a large portion of the exchange media in the provinces that issued them, constituted a relatively insignificant portion of the total money supply nationally.

This case provides an opportunity to consider two of the critical questions that relate to local and regional currencies. First is the question of what happens to a local currency denominated in the same units as the national currency that is being debased (causing inflation). A second question is what factors make a local currency credible enough to be accepted. Let's consider these in turn.

The bonds were denominated in terms of the official unit of account, which was the official currency unit, the austral.[10] The bonds typically matured in about

Figure 9.2. A circulating bond of Salta Province.

four years from the time of issuance. As the official currency was debased (inflated), the official unit of account would lose more of its value. Since the provincial bonds were denominated in the official units, their purchasing power would also depreciate along with the official currency. At the inflation rates typical of the recent past in Argentina (ranging from 95 percent to several hundred percent per year, except for a couple brief periods of stability), this would be enough to make the bonds almost worthless in terms of purchasing power over the period of their maturity. This factor was taken into account by those accepting them. As with the official currency, no one intended to hold on to them for very long.

As Reissig says, "The bonds make it possible for the provincial government to share in the revenues of the inflationary tax." That is true enough, but it was clearly not the primary intention of a provincial government in issuing them. The dependence on an exchange medium that must be imported from outside the region (official currency) makes the local economy dependent, to a large extent, on the central government and/or central bank. In order to acquire official money, it must subordinate regional priorities to the demands of the central government in order to obtain a share of government spending, or it must compete for loans from the banking system, or it must earn official currency by exporting products and services out of the region. If local needs are to take priority in the local economy, the local economy must be able of itself to mediate internal exchanges; it can do this only by using an exchange medium that is not controlled by outside agencies.

According to Reissig, who still travels frequently to Argentina, prices in that country are now widely quoted in terms of United States dollars, and "many firms are doing their accounting in U.S. units." While the United States dollar has also been subject to debasement (inflation), it has provided a relatively stable unit of account compared to the austral and the currencies of other less developed countries.

As for the factors that may have provided credibility and acceptability of the provincial bonds, Reissig mentions the following:

1. The time factor—the provincial government was willing to pay its employees in either its provincial bonds or official Argentine currency; however, they could receive the bonds immediately, while they would have to wait a few days for the official currency.
2. The provincial bonds could be exchanged at the local banks for official currency at par.
3. For a period of time the provincial government used the bonds as the basis for a lottery, making the bonds serve also as lottery tickets (the lottery was discontinued in 1987).
4. People in the region soon realized that the circulation of a limited, local currency had the effect of stimulating local businesses.
5. The provincial government agreed to accept its bonds in payment for provincial taxes and services.
6. The chamber of commerce agreed to accept the bonds.[11]

It is possible that provincial authorities might, like the central government, abuse their power by overissuing bonds/currency, but they would pay a high price in doing so. Since there is no forced circulation of the bonds, and since they must compete in the market with the official currency, overissuance would cause the bonds to trade below par relative to the official currency. This would cause a loss of revenue for the provincial governments, since they would still have to redeem the bonds at par. According to Reissig, there had been some abuse of this sort in the province of Salta. During one period in 1987, the Salta bonds were being discounted by as much as 20 percent with respect to the official Argentine currency. This situation was properly remedied, as one might expect, by a temporary suspension or slowing down of the rate of issuance of the bonds.[12]

As of March 31, 1992, there were reports that the provincial government of Salta was planning to redeem its bonds for official currency, using a loan obtained from the central government. Just prior to this time the bonds were again being debased, as indicated by the fact that they were being traded at an approximately 15 percent discount from face value.

A more recent article in the *Financial Times* (London, February 13, 1996, page 4) titled "Funny Money Fills Argentine Pockets" discusses Tucumani dollars, a currency issued by the government of Tucumán province in northwestern Argentina. The article gives a description and history of this currency, noting that it was first issued in the mid-1980s owing to "the province's inability to pay its bloated civil service which absorbs four-fifths of expenditures." The provincial government used these "bonds," in one- and five-peso denominations, to pay their employees.[13]

Roy Davies, in an e-mail message dated February 13, 1996, gave this summary of the article:

> The author of the article, David Pilling, says that although Tucumanis mostly accept the bonds at face value they tend to spend them first, keeping their real pesos in reserve. Although he does not say so, this is an illustration of Gresham's Law—that bad money drives out good. Given a choice between two forms of money most people will make payments in the one in which they have less confidence, keeping the other form for themselves. In consequence the more valued form tends to disappear from circulation.
>
> Pilling goes on to say that officially the value of Tucumani dollars in circulation is US $53 million—about one third of all Tucumán's paper money. However he quotes an economist as saying that the statistics are so terrible that nobody really has any idea what the true figures are. Pilling also points out that the legal status of Tucamani dollars and similar notes circulating in several other Argentine provinces, is uncertain. In the neighboring province of Jujuy the provincial government issued far too many notes with the result that their local currency was rendered worthless by hyperinflation.
>
> Although Tucumani dollars have escaped that fate, Tucumán's newly elected governor inherited such a mess that he has resorted to paying six weeks of public-sector wages in post-dated cheques and these cheques are already circulating as "money," although shopkeepers discount them by 10 to 30 percent.
>
> The *Financial Times* article ends by quoting Adolfo Martinez, vice president of Hamilton Bank, as saying "if Cavallo [Argentina's minister for the economy] really wants to straighten out provincial financial systems, he will eventually have to make all this funny money disappear for good.

The lesson in this is that provincial governments are just as susceptible to abusing the issuance of their currencies as central governments are. However, since the provincial currencies must compete with other currencies in the market, traders are more able to protect themselves since they are free to discount or refuse them.

Chapter 10

~

New Wave Pioneers

*I like the idea of local people putting money directly into each others'
pockets. Big industry is nothing to depend on; they're closing down and
moving out. I prefer to support people I know and trust.*

—JENNY

T HE NEW WAVE OF NONGOVERNMENTAL CURRENCIES and exchange
mechanisms began in the commercial sector in the late 1960s or early
1970s with the introduction of the first commercial "barter" exchanges, and
at the grassroots level in the early 1980s with the introduction of the first LET-
System in Canada. From that time, there has been a rapid growth and proliferation in both realms, accompanied by much experimentation with new
approaches and designs. The sections that follow, we will describe the more significant of these pioneering private exchange models, including the well-
publicized Ithaca HOURS currency and the Time Dollars service credit system.

Barter, Reciprocal Trade, and Mutual Credit

In recent years there has been a rapid proliferation of so-called barter clubs,
barter exchanges, and trade exchanges, including both nonprofit clubs that
serve individuals and communities and for-profit commercial trade exchanges
established to service business clients. For the most part, the activities of these
groups do not involve barter transactions at all but rather some form of what
has come to be known as "reciprocal trade."

In common usage, the word *barter* is frequently used to describe any
exchange that does not utilize official money, but this is grossly inaccurate
and misleading. An actual barter transaction involves only two parties, each of

whom has something the other wants. When party A gives item X to party B, and receives item Y from party B in return, then a complete barter transaction has taken place. If, however, one of the parties has nothing desired by the other, there can be no barter transaction. The primary role of money is to transcend the barter limitation by serving as an intermediary exchange medium.

But something other than official money may be offered as an intermediary. This can be a personal IOU that must be "made good" or redeemed at some later time. More commonly, the intermediary will be a generalized IOU that a group of associated traders have agreed to honor. Such arrangements are more accurately referred to as "reciprocal trade" or "mutual credit."

Commercial "Barter" or Trade Exchanges

Reciprocal trade or commercial "barter" has become big business in North America, and around the world. In the United States alone, there are presently several hundred "barter" or trade exchanges in operation. These exchanges generally operate as private incorporated businesses that collectively cater to the needs of hundreds of thousands of clients, mostly small and medium-size businesses but also including many large, well-known companies. Billions of dollars of sales are mediated each year by commercial trade exchanges.[1]

A trade association known as the International Reciprocal Trade Association, or IRTA, was founded in 1979 "to foster the common interests of the commercial barter industry in the United States and worldwide, and to uphold high standards of ethical business practice."[2]

According to IRTA, the rapid expansion of the barter industry is due to several factors, including:

1. the availability of computers, which facilitate the accounting and tracking of barter transactions, and
2. the growing appeal of cashless trading among business owners and professionals, because it allows them to
   a. generate extra sales, thus reducing unit costs,
   b. open up new outlets for disposing of excess inventory, and
   c. conserve their cash for essential expenditures.[3]

How Trade Exchanges Operate

Trade exchanges generally charge their members several hundred dollars to join, plus an annual membership fee. In addition, they charge a commission, often 10 percent to 15percent, on the gross value of each transaction. Membership fees are generally payable in official currency, but commissions may sometimes be payable in trade credits.

Trade exchanges perform two basic functions for their members. They act first of all as a clearinghouse, keeping accounts of members' transactions and trade balances, and second they actively stimulate trading by brokering merchandise, either finding buyers for members' merchandise or buying it for their own account for later sale to others.

The accounting unit used in exchange transactions is the *trade dollar*. When a member sells services or merchandise to another member, his or her account is credited for the fair market value, in dollars, of the merchandise, while the buying member's account is debited (reduced) by a corresponding amount plus any commission charges that may be levied by the trade exchange.

The contract between the trade exchange and its members specifies the respective responsibilities of each party. As part of the agreement, trade dollars are issued by a trade exchange by making loans to its members. Each member will have a particular "line of credit" (in trade dollars), which defines the maximum negative (debit) balance that member is allowed to carry. Thus, a trade or "barter" exchange, in effect, issues its own currency, not in the form of circulating notes, but as accounting debits and credits. The amount loaned to each member must, of course, be based on his or her creditworthiness, which is largely dependent on the demand for the member's goods or services. This process is very similar to the way in which banks create conventional money.

In general, trade exchange operators have the power to borrow trade credits for their own accounts. In the past, some trade exchange operators have abused this power, spending credits in amounts well beyond their capacity to earn them back through fees charged to members. The result in such cases is a reduced willingness of their members to sell merchandise and services for trade credits, a depreciation in the value of trade credits, and ultimately the failure of the exchange. IRTA has assumed a self-regulatory function for the industry to try to alleviate such abuses and protect the industry's reputation.

Tax Implications of Commercial Barter Trade

Trade exchange members doing business in the United States are required to provide the exchange with their taxpayer identification number (TIN). In accordance with the Tax Equity Act of 1982, all "barter" transactions are recorded, and the barter income of each client is reported to the Internal Revenue Service for tax purposes at the end of each year (using form 1099B). Income received in the form of trade credits is considered by the IRS to be taxable, on the basis of one trade credit being valued at one dollar. Standard rules for deductions also apply: "Each barter taxpayer must include in gross income the amount of his barter income. However, the taxpayer is entitled to include barter purchases made for business purposes with his cash deductions for business expenses."[4]

LETS: Local Employment and Trading System

LETS is an acronym that represents a community exchange system originally called "Local Exchange Trading System." That system is now often referred to as "Local Employment and Trading System." It is the best-known example of a type of system that can be generically referred to as "mutual credit" or "community credit."[5] LETS was originated in the early 1980s in British Columbia, Canada, by Michael Linton, a Scottish engineer. From that point on, LETS groups quickly proliferated, initially within the English-speaking countries, then later around the world. The success of this particular current in the community credit movement has been most notable in Australia, New Zealand, and the United Kingdom, where it has become widely recognized and has received considerable support in both academic and government circles.

Living in a place where the economy was depressed, Linton came to realize that the only thing missing was sufficient money to bring buyers and sellers together. The natural resources were there, the skills and talents were there, the needs were there, but the money wasn't there, at least not in sufficient amounts. Recognizing the limitations and dysfunctions of the dominant national currency systems, Linton devised an approach to facilitating trade without the need for scarce official money. He realized that the fundamental characteristic of money, which allows it to facilitate exchange, is the information that it carries. He envisioned another information system that would be locally controlled and operated in parallel with the official monetary system. He designed LETS as a not-for-profit association run by and for its members. It was never intended to replace the official currency but only to supplement it. By its nature, a LETS, like most community-based mutual credit systems, is limited, local, and personal, and these are the characteristics that give it its strength.

A LETS group operates very much like a commercial "barter" system, but it has several notable differences in its philosophy, intent, and practice:

1. A LETS is a not-for-profit cooperative arrangement, usually unincorporated and operated by volunteers, whereas commercial "barter" exchanges are for-profit businesses.
2. A LETS caters to individual traders, although business members are also welcome and desired, while commercial exchanges favor large-volume business clients.
3. In a LETS, the initiation and membership fees are nominal, sufficient only to cover the modest operating expenses of the system. Commercial exchanges charge large cash fees for membership and take a substantial percentage, usually in cash, on each transaction.

4. In a LETS, there is generally no interest charged or paid on either debit or credit balances.
5. Commercial exchanges often require that their members' lines of credit be secured by the pledge of some collateral. In LETS there is no such requirement.
6. While commercial exchanges actively broker trades among their members, a LETS functions only as a clearinghouse and information service; there is generally no brokering of goods or services by the LETS staff.[6]

Since a LETS is a membership organization, LETS credits can be spent only within the membership group. This stimulates the local LETS members to produce for their own needs and to import less from outside. Reducing imports from outside reduces the need to earn official currency. Because it is small and personal, a LETS also builds community and encourages members to support one another in a variety of ways.

How Does LETS Work?

A LETS arrangement typically consists of a set of accounts, usually kept on a personal computer.[7] It is like a bank in that each member has an account to which transactions are credited or debited. Like a checking account, your LETS account is credited (increased) when you sell something and debited (reduced) when you buy something. The two parties to the trade negotiate the price as they ordinarily would for a cash transaction, but, instead of using cash, the seller receives credits and the buyer is "charged" a corresponding amount as a debit.

The unit of account in the original LETS was the "green dollar," and LETS credits are still often referred to simply as "green," but each local LETS, being independent, is free to choose any name it wants for its accounting unit. Since we are all accustomed to evaluating transactions in terms of the official currency, LETS uses that same value concept (dollars in the United States, pounds in Britain, francs in France, and so forth) for accounting. Thus, members tend to equate the value of a "green dollar" with the value of a Federal Reserve dollar in the United States or a Bank of Canada dollar in Canada. Unlike official dollar-denominated bank credits or cash, however, which can be created only by the banking system, LETS dollars or green dollar credits are created by LETS members themselves, as needed, to execute a trade. This is the crucial element that makes LETS and other mutual credit systems so empowering.

Every account begins with a balance of zero. Sales of goods or services add to one's account balance, while purchases reduce one's balance. Account balances may be negative, and normally there is no interest charged on either negative or positive balances, though the members may agree to limit the amount of debit that a member may carry. A member with a negative or debit balance, however, is "committed" to supply that much value to others in the system at some time in the future. Having a negative balance in a LETS is not a problem. In fact, positive balances can exist only if there are negative balances. The total of positive balances in a LETS is always equal to the total of negative balances. Besides not charging interest on balances, there is no repayment schedule for debit balances in a LETS. There is, however, the expectation that members with debit balances will actively offer their services to prevent their accounts being permanently in debit. Members' balances are not secret but may be made known to any other member on request. Some LETS groups routinely publish all account balances periodically to give members a sense of the state of the system. It is still a matter of debate as to whether the published list of account balances should include members' names.

Transactions are reported to the LETS registrar or record keeper by either telephone or mail. Account balances are updated periodically, and each member is sent a statement of account showing his or her transactions for the period along with beginning and ending balances. In addition to the account statement, members usually receive a "noticeboard" or listing of goods and services currently being offered and requested. This noticeboard is actually a form of classified advertising by which members can advertise what they want and what they have to sell. Some LETS groups also publish a directory that gives more details about each members' interests, skills, and needs.

As with any system, there are costs involved in the operation of a LETS. Some of these are cash costs for such things as copying, postage, and telephone service. These are usually covered by charging an annual membership fee and/or setup fee in cash. Other costs, such as recordkeeping, publication, management, and other services provided by LETS members are typically paid in LETS credits. These are covered by charging members, in LETS credits or green dollars, for recording transactions, printing account statements, and noticeboard advertising.

AN EXAMPLE

To illustrate how LETS works, let us trace the steps one might take from becoming a member to receiving his or her first statement of account. Suppose Amy wishes to join the Happy Valley LETS. She fills out a membership agreement and pays an initial setup fee of five dollars, plus her first year's membership fee of fifteen dollars. She is given a copy of the current noticeboard and directory and an instruction sheet telling how to report transactions, as well as other system procedures. Amy's account balance begins at zero.

Amy sees from the noticeboard listings that Sarah is offering automobile tune-ups and that John is offering deep massage and acupressure treatments. She also notes that Harold wants fresh-baked, wholewheat bread and fresh vegetables. Amy sees in each of these a potential trade. She negotiates with Sarah to have her car tuned up. They agree on a price of 30 green dollars, plus $20 in cash to cover the cost of ignition points and spark plugs. She also negotiates with John to get two acupressure treatments for a total of 40 green dollars plus $10 cash. Next, Amy sells to Harold two loaves of her fresh-baked bread for 5 green dollars; she also sells him an assortment of vegetables from her garden for 10 green dollars.

The cash portion of the transactions is handled by the parties to the trades. Only the green dollar amounts are reported to the LETS registrar. On the tune-up, Amy is debited 30, on the acupressure treatments she is debited 40, and on her sales to Harold she is credited 15. If this is the extent of her trading for the period, her account statement at the end of the period will show a negative or debit balance of 55 green dollars (−30 −40 +15). There might also be system charges (additional debits) of 2 green dollars for her own notice-board advertising and statement fee, making her ending balance a minus 57. Meanwhile, Sarah's account has been credited 30, John's has been credited 40, and Harold's has been debited 15.

There is no particular time within which Amy must clear her debit balance. She understands, however, that her debit represents her promise to the community of members. She will, in all probability, try to keep her debit balance from becoming chronic or excessive. A primary reason for making account balances public within the system is to encourage self-regulation. In such a situation, a member with a chronic or excessive debit balance may find it increasingly difficult to find members willing to sell to her or him. By using the LETS, Amy has "saved" $55 of hard-to-get cash on services that she needed, has employed her friends and neighbors, and has, in effect, employed herself by providing others with the means to purchase her own goods and services.[8]

Figure 10.1 shows the creation and circulation of LETS credits. The LETS credit-trading circuit conforms closely to the ideal money circuit described in chapter 4. As in the ideal money circuit, Mr. Able creates a LETS credit when he buys something from Mr. Baker. Baker, in turn, uses that credit to buy something from Mr. Cook. The credit continues to circulate until Ms. Zane uses it to buy something from Mr. Able, who created it in the first place. When Mr. Able accepts it, the credit has returned to its source and ceases to exist. Of course, Mr. Able can begin the process anew by buying something else for LETS credits, which he can create just as he did before. Any other LETS member can do the same.

LETS ACTIVITY WORLDWIDE

Since Michael Linton introduced it in 1983, LETS has attracted considerable attention, and local systems have sprung up around the world. Articles about it have appeared in magazines and major daily newspapers, and LETS has been featured on national television programs in several countries.

While LETS has barely taken root in the United States, and it has been only a modest success in Canada, it has really taken off in other parts of the world. Its early success was primarily in Australia and New Zealand. A bit later it proliferated throughout Britain, and more recently it has been spreading

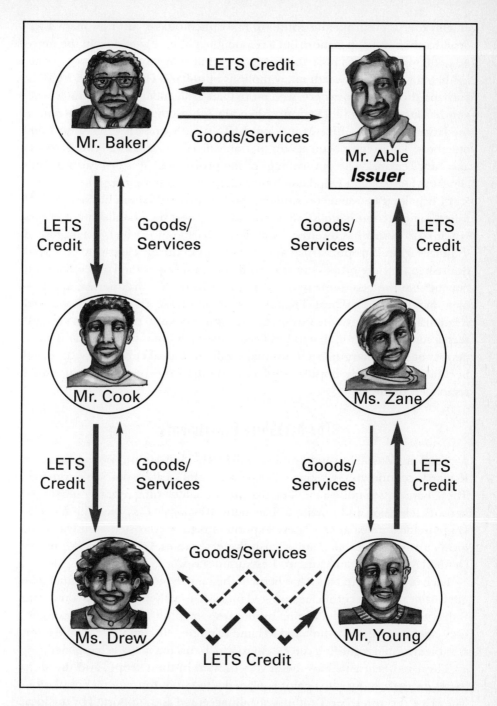

Figure 10.1. The LETS credit trading circuit.

quickly over the European continent. It is difficult to say just how many LET-Systems are now in operation, but a reasonable estimate would be in the range of 1,800 to 2,000. It is probably safe to say that they have, in the aggregate, mediated total trades worth many millions of dollars. The Auckland LETS is, perhaps, the largest anywhere, with more than 2,000 members.[9] Australia probably has more viable LETS groups than any other country, 120 at last count, the largest being the Blue Mountains LETS near Sydney, with close to 1,500 members. There have been several nationwide conferences in both Australia and New Zealand. The government of the province of Western Australia has allocated $A50,000 to help launch new LETS groups in that region.[10]

In Britain, a national coordinating body called LETSLink has been established to help coordinate LETS activity and support the establishment of new systems. LETSLink has received favorable media attention which has prompted inquiries from Europe, Africa, and Asia. It isn't entirely clear why LETS has flourished in these other countries while languishing in the United States. It may be that the economic need is greater outside North America, and perhaps the social and political climates are more favorable. Differing attitudes and relationships relative to the various taxing authorities also seem to be a factor. It seems certain, however, that as local economies continue to decline and more people become marginalized, mutual credit and local currency systems will become increasingly popular and important to the restoration of sound regional economies.

The Berkshire Experiments

A group in Massachusetts known as SHARE (Self-Help Association for a Regional Economy) has instigated some successful local currency experiments. These have gotten quite a bit of media attention, including reports on national network television and a major article in the *Washington Post,* in addition to coverage in local newspapers. These experiments have consisted of at least four local currency issues: Berkshire Farm Preserve Notes, Deli Dollars, Monterey General Store scrip, and Kintaro Restaurant scrip.[11]

Each of these scrip issues has been of the same type, functioning much like gift certificates. The certificates are sold for cash, usually at a small discount, and redeemed in trade by the issuing businesses sometime later. In the meantime, they can be circulated from hand to hand as money, though there is little information available regarding the extent to which this has actually happened.

These experiments have been very limited in their scope, and the scrip issues, by their nature, have not provided a medium for general circulation. They have, however, been enthusiastically accepted and supported by the local community, proving the practicability of local currencies. The Farm Preserve Notes, furthermore, have received official sanction by the Massachusetts State Agriculture Department, which is eager to support the state's few remaining

Figure 10.2. A Deli Dollar $10 note.

Figure 10.3. A Massachusetts Farmer's Market Coupon.

farms. The main effect of such notes has been to provide the farmer issuers with working capital in the off-season.

SHARE has been working for some years on the development of a more comprehensive scrip issue, called the "Berkshare," which will not be sold for dollars but will be spent into circulation by members of a consortium of local businesses, each on the basis of its capacity to provide value to the community. Figures 10.2 and 10.3, respectively, show a Deli Dollar and a Massachusetts Farmers' Market Coupon.

Ithaca HOURS

Probably the most successful present-day local currency program in the United States is the Ithaca HOUR initiated by Paul Glover in Ithaca, New York. Located in the Finger Lakes region of upper New York state, Ithaca is a city with a population of about 28,000. According to Glover, an additional 15,000 live in the surrounding towns and a total of about 120,000 live within a twenty-mile radius. "Most trading is among city people," he says, "but there are many active and avid traders in rural areas. They need money and don't care what it looks like."[12]

According to Glover, HOURS are accepted by more than four hundred local businesses, including fifty-five vendors at the farmers' market. "People pay rent with HOURS. The best restaurants in town take them, as do movie theaters, bowling alleys, two large locally owned grocery stores, our local hospital, many garage sales, the Chamber of Commerce. . . . Hundreds more have earned and spent HOURS who are not in the *HOUR Town* directory." Presently, the local credit union accepts HOURS for all fees, in addition to up to two HOURS per month on loan payments.

Since the project was launched in November 1991, there has been rapid growth in the number of traders using the local currency, and the volume of trading has grown steadily. By the end of 1997, 6,300 HOURS (equivalent to about $63,000) had been issued into circulation, thousands of individuals had used HOURS, and more than four hundred businesses had been enrolled. Glover claims that millions of dollars of trading has been facilitated by Ithaca HOURS since the plan was launched.

Ithaca HOUR notes have been issued in denominations of one-eighth, one-fourth, one-half, one, and two HOURS. The two sides of the one-HOUR denomination are shown in figures 10.4 and 10.5.

The Ithaca HOURS project has attracted a considerable amount of media attention. It was the subject of a cover article in *Mother Earth News* (Aug./Sept. 1993) and has been written up in many mainstream publications, including the *Wall Street Journal.* It was featured in a major Japanese television broadcast seen by an estimated 35 million viewers and was the subject of a 1999 half-hour documentary produced by a Syracuse PBS affiliate.

The foundation for the HOURS plan is a two-color tabloid newspaper, originally called *Ithaca MONEY,* which Glover published and distributed free of charge. The newspaper, now called *HOUR Town,* contains information about the local economy, community self-help initiatives, and the benefits of local currencies, but its primary purpose is to publicize the individuals and businesses that have agreed to accept the local currency in payment for their goods and services. Each issue of the newspaper contains classified-type ad listings of both offers and requests for goods and services, as well as display ads. Ads can be paid for with either dollars or HOURS.

The means of issuance of HOURS was initially very simple. Each advertiser who agreed to accept HOURS in either full or partial payment was issued notes worth four HOURS *as a premium* for participation. The advertisers were then free to spend their HOURS on purchases from anyone willing to accept them. *Ithaca MONEY* gave additional HOURS to those who repeated their listings over several issues and to those who signed up or renewed at one of the monthly barter potlucks.

Glover never claimed to be the issuer of a local currency but merely the publisher of a newspaper. The HOUR notes that advertisers receive have no foundation other than the agreement of advertisers to accept them in trade. For the first several years, decisions regarding operations were made collectively on an ad hoc basis by those who attend the monthly barter potlucks, but in 1998 a nonprofit corporation was formed and a board of directors was elected to manage the HOURS program.

Figure 10.4. An Ithaca HOUR one HOUR note — front side.

Figure 10.5. An Ithaca HOUR one HOUR note—reverse side.

The Ithaca HOUR plan includes a novel form of "tithing." Those who attended the barter potlucks decided to support community organizations by making grants of HOURS, which the organizations could then spend for needed goods and services. The allocation of HOUR grants among the organizational applicants is now made by the governing board.

Over the years, the pattern of issuance of HOURS has changed. Currently, HOURS are issued in a variety of ways:

1. They are issued as payment to those who agree to be listed in *HOUR Town:* one or two HOURS per person/business.
2. Every eight months participants may receive a small bonus payment of HOURS for reaffirming their participation.
3. Those who sign up or renew at a barter potluck receive an additional one HOUR bonus.
4. As well, 14% of HOURS are issued as grants to community organizations. Thus far, 46 such groups have received HOUR grants.
5. Presently, 10% of HOURS otherwise issued may be outstanding as loans. Our largest loan so far is 120 HOURS ($1,200). 25% of the value of loans repaid are added to the grant capacity.
6. Finally, 5% of HOURS may be issued to the system itself, as for printing *HOUR Town*, HOURS, bumper stickers, office supplies, etc. No HOURS are issued for staff time.[13]

By the end of the year 2000, grants totaling more than one thousand HOURS (worth $10,000) had been made to fifty-seven different community groups. On the lending side, the HOURS board agreed to make the largest local currency loan yet as a way of helping the Alternatives Federal Credit Union to pay for work on its new headquarters building. The loan of three thousand Ithaca HOURS (equivalent to $30,000) will be paid to several contractors for plumbing, carpentry, electrical, and various other services. The loan is to be repaid over a period of ten years, half in HOURS and half in United States dollars.

The success of the Ithaca HOUR community currency project can probably be attributed mainly to the dedication, energy, and persistence of its founder, core supporters, and governing board, as well as the elegant simplicity of its approach. Other probable contributing factors are Ithaca's compact size, its remoteness from any large city, and its highly educated, skilled, and progressive population. Ithaca also has the advantage of being located in the center of a richly productive agricultural region populated by small diversified family farms.

HOUR Town has been a big factor in promoting the community currency movement generally. It offers a "Home Town Money Starter Kit," which has been distributed to hundreds of interested people in dozens of countries around the world. The kit includes a copy of the book *Home Town Money: How to Enrich Your Community,* plus "all start-up and maintenance procedures, forms, laws, news articles, computer programs, updates and an *HOUR Town* subscription" (see the Sources and Resources section for the address and ordering information). Numerous other community groups have been inspired by the Ithaca HOUR experience and have started local currencies that resemble the Ithaca model. In chapter 17 we will have occasion to examine the operational details of Ithaca HOURS and its offspring and to offer some constructive suggestions for their improvement.

Service Credits and Time Dollars

Another interesting development in cashless exchange is the service credit plan originated by Edgar Cahn. Cahn, a prominent Washington, D.C., lawyer, conceived the plan as a way of addressing the inadequacy of government programs intended to deal with social problems. He set out to create "a new kind of money," independent of government and central banks, which could be created by people themselves in the process of helping one another.

The basic idea is that a person can get credit for helping someone else now and use those credits later to get similar services for him- or herself or a family member. The object is to empower people by allowing them to create purchasing power for themselves in the process of helping others. The plan was started with the exchange of a narrow range of services, primarily care of the elderly, education, and child care, but, as interest in the idea has spread, the range of services included has expanded.

The unit of credit in Cahn's service credit scheme is the Time Dollar, equivalent to one hour of service. The intention is to exchange services on the basis of an hour for an hour. For example, when Mr. Green spends two hours of his time to help the elderly Mrs. Brown do her grocery shopping, he receives two Time Dollars credit to his account. Later, when Mr. Green is himself in need of help, he can claim two hours of service from someone else in the system.

Cahn, presumably because of his prominence and mainstream political contacts, has been able to gain a great deal of official support at both the state and federal levels. He states: "[I] got it enacted into law, first in two states and the District of Columbia. I got the IRS to rule that it was tax-exempt and not barter in the conventional sense—in the commercial sense."[14] The IRS ruling that service credits are tax-exempt is a major milestone and has probably been a major factor in the rapid proliferation of Time Dollar programs around the country.

As of mid-1995, there were about 20,000 people participating in more than 150 service credit programs operating in thirty-eight states. In Miami, more than 1,600 volunteer participants are earning about twelve thousand Time Dollars a month by helping others. The Miami program, called Friend To Friend, connects individuals, nonprofit organizations, and government agencies in a network that provides a variety of services including job training and child care. In Wisconsin, welfare recipients who volunteer are allowed to accrue nontaxable Time Dollar credits without losing benefits.[15]

The state of Missouri alone has thirty-seven service credit programs.[16] The Missouri state government has been so enthusiastic about the plan that it has guaranteed the value of service credits. It will go into the market to buy services for those who have earned credits if there is no one willing to provide services for Time Dollars when needed.

Time Dollars provide recognition for services that would ordinarily be done by volunteers. One of the program's main advantages is that it allows participants, such as the elderly, teenagers, and the unemployed to "redefine themselves as producers and contributors rather than recipients of charity."[17]

Cahn also cites some other important outcomes of a service credit system: the social, community-building aspect. As he puts it:

> the very process of earning credits knits groups together. . . . They begin having pot-luck lunches; and they begin forming neighborhood crime watch things, and they begin looking after each other and checking in; and they begin to set up food bank coops. [It] seems to act as a catalyst for the creation of group cohesion in a society where that kind of catalyst is difficult to find.[18]

Update on the Pioneers

The pioneering private exchange models that we have looked at in this chapter continue to function and proliferate, but some, it appears, function at a reduced rate and with diminished vigor. The first wave has washed up on the beach and receded. The second wave is now breaking. It is bigger and more global in scope, but its impact has yet to be assessed.

There has been a shakeout in the commercial "barter" industry, which has left it better off. As in any new industry, a period of exuberant, often reckless, expansion is being followed by consolidation, as poorly managed and under-funded companies fail or are absorbed by stronger ones. Unscrupulous operators thus reap their proper reward. Also to the good is the reduction or elimination of the practice of trade exchanges buying and selling for their own account, a questionable practice that led to credit inflation (debasement) in some companies. As the industry has matured, it has grown stronger and more significant. The growth of both the volume of transactions and the number of participating businesses continues to be strong. According to one industry source, "The current outlook calls for consolidation of independent exchanges into larger, more sophisticated, electronic clearinghouses where professional barter brokers come together to help their clients increase sales, improve cash flow, and develop new profits."[19]

LETSystems continue to pop up here and there but not in the numbers previously experienced, and some have faltered and fallen by the wayside. Most have reached a leveling off place, serving a small, stable or slowly declining, active membership. Many of the hundreds of LETSystems around the world have experimented with design modifications. Some of these have improved performance, while some have not. The biggest shortcoming with LETS and related variants seems to be their inability to attract significant participation by established businesses. Still, LETS and the commercial barter industry have demonstrated the simplicity, effectiveness, and tremendous potential of credit clearing or mutual credit.

Ithaca has continued to attract the attention of journalists and social activists from around the world, and HOURS currencies modeled after Ithaca HOURS have been started in a number of communities, though none has yet equaled the success of the original.

Time Dollars have landed in Britain and, under the sponsorship of the New Economics Foundation, have begun to impact the social services delivery system there. The British variant allows volunteers to earn *Time Credits,* which are stored in *Time Banks* for later redemption or donation to those in need.

The next chapter will describe a few of the more recently established currencies and exchange systems, each one notable and unique in some way, and each one capable of providing additional insights into the problems, solutions, and design features of private exchange mechanisms.

Chapter 11

~

Recent Models and Developments

Money That Builds Community

—MOTTO OF TORONTO DOLLARS

THE COMMUNITY CURRENCY MOVEMENT continues to develop, with new systems being launched almost every week. Each presents a new opportunity to experiment and innovate. While most of these systems follow closely one of the two most popular models—LETS and Ithaca HOURS—some have unique features. This chapter describes a few of the more interesting cases, which, as they continue to develop, may be worth emulating.

Tucson Traders

After a series of meetings in 1997 that included the author and several other interested people, Tucson Traders was launched in early 1998. The core group wanted to establish a community exchange system that would be fiscally sound and easy and inexpensive both to set up and to operate. It was agreed that a mutual credit system using a set of ledger accounts best satisfied these criteria. It was thought that by keeping the financial and labor overhead low, the system could be allowed to grow at its own pace and without much risk of failure or core group burnout. While the group recognized some of the advantages of circulating paper notes, it was thought that they could be phased in later after the system had become well established.

The group even decided to pass up the usual computerized ledger systems commonly used by LETS and other mutual credit systems and, for the time being at least, to opt for a simple pen and paper accounting system. This took the form of a loose-leaf notebook that contained a page for each member. All members' trades were recorded on these pages. Periodic account statements could easily be provided to each member by simply mailing a photocopy of his or her page. A sample page of this type is shown below in figure 11.1.

The name "Tucson Token" was chosen for the value measure and unit of account, which would have a value equivalent to that of the United States dollar. It was decided that each member should have an initial line of credit of TT200 (200 Tucson Tokens), meaning that their account could not exceed a debit balance of two hundred tokens. A voice-mail telephone line was obtained for members to use in reporting their trades, for communication of news and events, and for prospective members to request information packets. Out of the core group of organizers, a decision-making body called the steering committee emerged. The steering committee is a nonhierarchical body that makes decisions using a consensus process, and participation is open to the entire membership.

Community Mutual Credit Exchange

Member Name: _____

Membership Number: _____

Date	Provider	Recipient	Description	Debit for Purchase	Credit for Sale	Balance

Figure 11.1. A pencil and paper accounting system.

As the word spread, the size of the membership grew rapidly, and, after less than a year, the steering committee decided that it was time to computerize the accounts. However, rather than adopting one of the available LETS accounting programs, the accounts were set up on a standard database program. It was early recognized that, given the geographic size of Tucson and the wide distances that separated many of the members from one another, some way would need to be found to make trading more convenient. Various approaches were tried as a way of bringing members together periodically. What seemed to work best was the Saturday trading "bazaars," which were held once every other month at a neighborhood center operated by the city. The bazaars gave members a chance to socialize, to sell their products, and to sell items they no longer needed.

As time went on, however, attendance at these events dropped off. Some members objected to selling their quality handcrafted items in a "flea market" atmosphere. Also, there seemed to be a number of problems with the venue. First was the "sterile" atmosphere at the center, which had fluorescent lights, white walls, and unaesthetic decor. Another was the location, which some people thought was inconvenient. Unloading and loading things that members brought to sell was also less than convenient. Besides that, the rules imposed by the neighborhood center would not permit any exchange of official cash to be part of the transactions. Venues that do not impose such limitations are being sought. A more ideal place would be one where vehicles can get close to the activity space and where traders have a choice of setting up their display tables either indoors or outdoors. There has also been some discussion about possibly shifting from trading bazaars, which have been limited to members only, to "community flea markets," which would be open to all. Some people believe that a more open event will increase the quantity and assortment of goods and services offered for sale, which will attract a greater number of people and provide an opportunity to recruit new members.

Toward the end of 1999, the steering committee began a serious review of the system structures and procedures. This arose from the fact that some problems were making administration of the system burdensome, and also from a desire to broaden the base of the membership. First of all, it was agreed that it was important to recruit more businesses to participate in the community exchange process, but most of the businesses that were approached were not interested in joining a ledger system because of the extra labor overhead that would entail. Second, it was felt that some members were misperceiving the role of the steering committee and making inappropriate demands on it. Specifically, some members who were less than satisfied with some of their trades thought it appropriate to bring their complaints to the system accountant or others in the volunteer core. The system administrators felt that their job was to record trades and update members' accounts and that mediating disputes between traders was a burden they could not bear.

Figure 11.2. TT Twenty Token note—front side.

Figure 11.3. TT Twenty Token note—reverse side.

Another problem was that two or three members had exceeded their allowable debit limit of two hundred tokens. In one case, in fact, the limit had been exceeded by about five hundred tokens. This situation was thought to be detrimental to the health of the system. Various ways of dealing with the problem were considered, but none was entirely satisfactory. As the computerized accounting system was improved and it became easier to check account balances, the system accountant started refusing to post transactions that would cause the debit limit to be exceeded. This, of course, caused some ill feeling on the part of those who had made such sales in good faith and expected their account to be credited.

It soon became clear that it was time to implement the use of paper currency. This would, at one stroke, solve a number of problems and offer a number of advantages for trading and system expansion. It would reduce the workload considerably by eliminating the need to record every trade and reducing the frequency of sending out account statements. Further, although it would not remedy the existing cases of excessive debit balances, it would prevent overspending in the future. By going to a "currency only" exchange system, Tucson Traders could easily enforce the debit limit. No more than two hundred tokens would be issued to any member, so that would be the maximum they could spend into circulation. Shortly after making the shift to paper currency, the system accountant reported that "the greater advantage so far seems to be a change in people's attitude about TT's administrative role— many folks came to us with their personal disputes about trades. Now that there's nobody to report their trades to, there's less temptation to report their complaints as well."

In March of the year 2000, at its second anniversary celebration, Tucson Traders made the shift to circulating paper currency notes. One-token, five-token, and twenty-token notes, each designed by a different artist, were printed by a local printer who also happened to be a member of the steering committee. Figures 11.2 and 11.3 show the two sides of the twenty-token note. The celebration was held at a popular café/restaurant that had just become a member and agreed to accept 25 percent payment in tokens. For this special event, the café offered selected menu items for either 50 percent or 100 percent tokens.

Any Tucson Token notes issued to a member would be debited to his or her account. Since almost every member already had an account balance, a way had to be found to make the transition to paper currency work smoothly and equitably. It was decided to retain the existing debit limit of TT200 and allow members to draw token notes up to that amount. For those who already had a debit balance, the amount of token notes that could be drawn was reduced by the amount of their current debit balance. Thus, a member who had an existing debit balance of 60 tokens would be allowed to draw notes amounting to only 140 tokens. Likewise, those members with a credit balance would be allowed to draw more than 200 tokens in notes. Thus, a member who had an existing credit balance of 100 tokens would be allowed to draw up to 300 tokens in notes. It was recommended, however, that members draw out only 50 tokens to start. It was decided that new members would automatically receive TT50 upon joining and be informed that they could request more, up to the 200 token limit.

Each member was asked to sign a new agreement acknowledging that any debit balance, which included Tucson Token notes issued to them, represented an effective "loan" extended to them by the members in general, and

---

Tucson Traders Membership Agreement

By signing this agreement, I state that I will, upon (or prior to) termination or expiration of my membership with Tucson Traders (TT), reimburse TT for the total amount of tokens that have been issued to me throughout the course of my membership, according to TT's recourds. If I am unable to obtain that amount in Tucson Tokens, I will present the equivalent amounti n federal money.

Printed Name:_____

Signature: _____ Date: _____

Figure 11.4. Tucson Traders membership agreement.

that this "loan" must be paid back if and when their membership was terminated. The exact agreement is shown in figure 11.4.

At the same time, the steering committee agreed that it would allow members to submit requests for loans of more than two hundred tokens. These loan requests must be submitted in writing and will be reviewed by the steering committee. While the formal criteria for approval are still being developed, consideration is being given to the applicant's past account history and the purpose for which the loan proceeds will be used.

Prior to making these changes, the membership was asked for its consent. Almost everyone seemed to agree that the changes would be beneficial and they were eagerly endorsed. Time will tell how successful these strategies will prove to be, but Tucson Traders will be an interesting case to watch.

The döMAK "Barter" Circle

In the eastern German town of Halle, a group has come up with an utterly simple approach to the recordkeeping problem. They have formed a trading system that they call "The Barter Circle." Its accounting unit is equivalent in value to one German mark.

Like most other mutual credit systems, the döMAK system provides for interest-free reciprocal exchange among its members, but unlike the typical mutual credit systems or LETS, there is no central recordkeeping of exchange information. Instead, each member of the döMAK system is issued a logbook in which only his or her transactions are recorded. When a trade is negotiated between two members, it is recorded in each of their logbooks. There is a space for each important item of information: a description of the goods or services traded, the amount of döMAKs debited or credited, the updated account balance, and the validation signature of the other party in the exchange. Recording transactions in this way provides the two parties to the trade with instant, up-to-date information about the status of each other's account—whether they have a debit balance or a credit balance, and whether its amount is within the agreed limits.

This solves one of the common concerns of mutual credit systems, which is to prevent members from overdrawing their accounts. If, instead, there is a central ledger, the only way a seller can check a prospective buyer's account balance is to contact the registrar. This is usually not possible except perhaps in a few very large systems that have regular paid staff, and even then only within limited business hours. Moreover, the central account information may be much out of date, depending on the timely reporting of trades by the members and the frequency and diligence of the registrar in posting transaction information to the ledger of accounts. This leaves overdrafts to be dealt with after the fact, which causes a great deal of trouble and ill will.

Another advantage of the döMAK system is that only those who need to know, the traders themselves, have access to their personal trading information. A possible downside, of course, is the chance that someone will falsify entries in a log book, causing it to show more credits than were actually earned. The system has a partial safeguard against this in that members must exchange their logbooks for new ones at the end of each year, at which time entries are checked by the management group. Still, this leaves plenty of room for fraud in the interim. For this reason, the döMAK approach will probably work best within a relatively small community of people who know and trust one another. Larger, more impersonal systems would seem to call for tighter, more secure procedures.

Toronto Dollars, "Money That Builds Community"

The St. Lawrence Market is a matrix of historic streets and buildings in the heart of old Toronto, and the focal point of the St. Lawrence neighborhood. The Toronto Dollar local currency was instigated by renowned Canadian author and neighborhood resident Joy Kogawa. Working together with her partner, John Flanders, and a small core group of supporters, including businessman David Walsh, the community currency project gradually took shape. A not-for-profit community group called Toronto Dollar Community Projects Inc. was formed specifically for the purpose of issuing the currency, which was launched in December 1998 when, according to Flanders, "amidst much hoopla and media coverage, Toronto's Mayor, Mel Lastman, kicked it off at the historic St. Lawrence Market by exchanging his Canadian federal dollars for Toronto Dollars and spending them with participating local businesses."

Toronto Dollars are a prime example of what I call a *fully funded* currency, in that it comes into circulation when someone buys it, dollar for dollar, with official currency. (This type of currency will be described more fully in chapter 14.) The Canadian dollars received from the sale of Toronto Dollars go into a Toronto Dollar Reserve Fund that provides the means for later redemption of Toronto Dollars back into Canadian dollars. Participating businesses agree to accept Toronto Dollars at par with the Canadian dollar.

ESSENTIAL FEATURES OF TORONTO DOLLARS

- Toronto Dollars are issued by Toronto Dollar Community Projects Inc., a not-for-profit organization.
- People exchange their Canadian dollars for Toronto Dollars at par, one Toronto Dollar for one Canadian dollar.
- They then use Toronto Dollars (as they would Canadian dollars) to pay for goods and services offered by participating businesses and organizations.
- For each Canadian dollar exchanged, ninety cents is put into a Toronto

Dollar Reserve Fund administered by Toronto's First Post Office to back the Toronto Dollar. The other ten cents goes into a Community Trust Fund, to be used for community improvement projects, or is retained by nonprofit groups that sell Toronto Dollars to the public.

- Businesses that accept Toronto Dollars can choose to use them at par by making purchases at other participating merchants, or they can redeem them, receiving 90 percent of the face value in Canadian dollars from the reserve fund. Only businesses are allowed to redeem Toronto Dollars.

- The ten cents on each dollar that is held back is given to community organizations chosen by the Toronto Dollar organizing group.

- The interest income earned on the reserve fund deposits is used to offset administrative expenses.

- Toronto Dollars are printed in denominations of one, five, ten, and twenty dollars using standard anticounterfeiting techniques.

- Toronto Dollar notes carry an expiration date. They have a two-year (or less) life.

Figures 11.5 and 11.6 show the two sides of the Toronto Dollar ten dollar note.

The Evolution of Toronto Dollars

Toronto Dollars is a volunteer community project of St. Lawrence Works, "a coalition of business and cultural groups interested in putting its collective

Figure 11.5. Toronto Dollar ten dollar note—front side.

Figure 11.6. Toronto Dollar ten dollar note— reverse side.

shoulder to the wheel to help community initiatives."[1] According to John Flanders, one of the founders, the Toronto Dollar project evolved in the following way. Toward the end of 1997, several people from LETS Toronto met with community leaders and business people in the St. Lawrence area of Toronto with the intention of setting up a local LETS as part of the dream of a multi-LETS project. They found it difficult, however, to interest the business community. There were various reasons for this, including the internal difficulties that LETS Toronto was then experiencing. In addition, the telephone reporting system used by LETS Toronto was seen by some as being too cumbersome for small retail stores.

The group saw that business participation was vital to the realization of a community currency system that would have broad-based support and wide distribution. LETS typically suffer from a lack of business involvement, which severely limits the usefulness of LETS credits. A primary goal of the Toronto group was to transcend this limitation.

The group then looked to the Ithaca HOUR as a possible model. Ithaca, New York, has managed for several years to sustain a paper currency that appeals to both businesspeople and individuals within the Ithaca area. It was estimated that, at the time, there were more than 3,500 participants in that system, including 350 businesses that offered a range of useful products and services.

For a while, the Toronto organizers considered blending the Ithaca HOUR model with the LETS model but decided, for the time being, to drop LETS altogether and develop a paper currency. But because of merchant concerns "about getting stuck with large amounts of Toronto Dollars," a substantial departure from the Ithaca model was made. Another of the founders, businessman David Walsh, insisted that Toronto Dollars should be issued based on the payment of Canadian dollars, and that they should expire at some point. It was recognized that tying the Toronto Dollar so closely to the Canadian dollar would limit its empowerment potential, but it would provide the level of safety needed to satisfy the business community and achieve the primary goal of broad-based acceptance of the local currency.

The existence of the Toronto Dollar Reserve Fund and the option of redeeming community currency for federal currency were seen as powerful selling points in gaining the participation of the business community. Indeed, the participating merchants generally view Toronto Dollars as safe, credible, and risk-free.

CURRENT STATUS

By the end of 1999, slightly more than 100,000 Toronto Dollars had been sold. The organizers estimate that the average amount in circulation at any one time has been between $30,000 and $35,000. There were about 105 participating businesses, including about 40 food vendors in the St. Lawrence

Market and 17 restaurants, all of which accept 100 percent payment in Toronto Dollars.[2] Partnerships with two community newspapers had been formed to carry advertisements from program participants. In mid-1999, the project got a big boost when CIBC (Canadian Imperial Bank of Commerce), one of North America's leading financial institutions, agreed to sell Toronto Dollars at two of its central Toronto branches.[3] During 1999, the Toronto Dollar project gave $10,200 in donations to eighteen community groups. A "Toronto Dollar Party" sponsored by the St. Lawrence Market, in which thirty community groups participated with display tables and a silent auction, was attended by more than three thousand people. This is planned to be an annual event.

The organizers' current ambitions include expanding the number of participants to include businesses in adjoining neighborhoods and communities and "closing the loop" of production and distribution to make the currency more useful to all players in the local economy: basic producers, manufacturers, wholesale distributors, retailers, workers, and consumers.

How Does it Work?

Since Toronto Dollars are presently accepted only by businesses within the St. Lawrence neighborhood, their circulation tends to be geographically limited to that area. Anyone, however, is free to accept them, and many people who live outside the area do accept them, knowing that they can always spend them when they visit the St. Lawrence neighborhood. Residents, local businesses, community organizations, and visitors exchange their Toronto Dollars with each other, as well.

Toronto Dollars are fully backed by official money but only participating merchants are allowed to redeem them, and then only at ninety cents on the dollar. These provisions are designed to encourage circulation and to discourage redemption. Using Toronto Dollars costs the consumers nothing since they receive the same amount of goods and services as if they were spending Canadian dollars. The 10 percent redemption fee is borne by the merchant who redeems the Toronto Dollars. The more times a Toronto Dollar changes hands before being redeemed, the more the local economy is stimulated and strengthened. The greater the amount of Toronto Dollars bought into circulation, the greater the boost to the local economy and the greater the amount of money that goes to support local charities.

Ten percent of the federal dollars exchanged go directly into the Community Trust Fund, while the remaining 90 percent is deposited in a Toronto Dollar Reserve Fund, which is held in liquid asset form for redemption of Toronto Dollars back into Canadian dollars. The main purpose of the Community Trust Fund is to finance community initiatives and groups that support those who are on low incomes, unemployed, or homeless. These funds can be immediately distributed. The first beneficiary of the fund was an important volunteer project to help the homeless, called "Out of the Cold." The earnings from the reserve fund could eventually offset all of the Toronto Dollar administrative expenses and provide additional funding for community projects.

Toronto's First Post Office, a contract agency of the Canadian postal service, has been engaged to serve as a central distribution center. It sells Toronto Dollars and also has been given responsibility for the management of the Toronto Dollar Reserve Trust Fund. There are plans to have additional exchange agents located conveniently throughout the St. Lawrence neighborhood and elsewhere as the trading area expands to other neighborhoods. Distinctive Toronto Dollar decals are displayed by businesses accepting Toronto Dollars.

The Toronto Dollar currency is printed by the Canadian Bank Note Company, which also prints Canadian federal currency. It utilizes standard security features to protect against counterfeiting, including special paper and ink that cannot be copied. Each note issued has a serial number that is recorded.

AN EXAMPLE

Future Bakery in the St. Lawrence Market is one business that will take Toronto Dollars. Let's say it has received sixty Toronto Dollars from Joan and forty from Lee for baked goods. The bakery now has a choice: it can spend the Toronto Dollars at Frida Crafts on Front Street or at other participating businesses within the community, or it can cash them in, receiving ninety Canadian dollars. The remaining ten dollars become, in effect, a donation for job creation and other community projects.

And how did Joan and Lee get Toronto Dollars in the first place? Joan and Lee each exchanged Canadian dollars and received Toronto Dollars at the Toronto Dollar booth in the St. Lawrence Market. Neither lost any money. They received the same amount of merchandise as if they had paid with Canadian dollars. Their actions *got* the ball rolling. They supported local businesses and generated ten dollars in donations to support community improvement projects. The Future Bakery took the hundred Toronto Dollars from Joan and Lee and used them to buy flour and other supplies from other participating merchants in the Market. It *kept* the ball rolling.

BUSINESS BENEFITS AND CONSIDERATIONS

Among the benefits that business participants realize from acceptance of Toronto Dollars are the following:

Businesses gain additional advertising exposure and the goodwill of the community. They attract new customers and additional cash business, improve their image as a concerned member of the community, increase their contact with other local businesses, build a loyal customer base, enrich their home community, and attract tourist dollars.

Merchants are not required to accept 100 percent payment for merchandise in Toronto Dollars. They can choose to accept whatever percentage they want. Businesses that have a high cost of goods sold (low profit margin) can choose to accept a small percentage of payment in Toronto Dollars and the rest in Canadian dollars, thus assuring that their cash costs are covered. Merchants with a high *value added* or excess capacity can afford to accept a higher percentage in local currency. A beauty parlor, for example, has very little in the way of cash costs, so it can afford to accept a high percentage of payment in local currency, while a boutique selling imported merchandise needs a considerable amount of cash to pay for its stock. A movie house may be able to sell seats that otherwise would remain empty. If it can fill some of those seats with customers who pay in local currency, it is better off.

The merchants' costs and their administrative burden are minimal. A merchant pays a small initial fee of only twenty-five dollars. There are no monthly fees, no transaction fees, and no surcharges. The only additional cash cost is the 10 percent redemption fee for early cash-out, which can be avoided if the merchant spends any Toronto Dollars received from customers instead of redeeming them. Redemption must be in hundred-dollar multiples.

Toronto Dollar notes have an expiration date that is two years after the date they are printed. This feature provides control over the inventory of Toronto Dollars in circulation and eliminates the uncertainty of supply usually associated with circulating currencies. When notes get lost or are otherwise taken out of circulation, the redemption fund can be reduced accordingly. It is estimated that about 10 percent of the notes sold will never be redeemed; therefore, when they expire, the corresponding amount of Canadian dollars from the reserve fund can be spent on charitable or community improvement projects. No one need lose out on account of the expiration feature, however, since Toronto Dollar notes that are nearing expiration may be exchanged at par for other Toronto Dollar notes that have a later expiration date.

Start-up costs of operating the Toronto Dollar project have been covered mainly by donations from supporters. In the first eighteen months, the project had received donations amounting to about $25,000, plus a grant of $10,000 from the City of Toronto. For the time being, the interest income received on the Toronto Dollar Reserve Fund is retained by Toronto's First Post Office as compensation for its administrative services.

Friendly Favors

Friendly Favors is the creation of a team of experts associated with Sergio Lub, a successful California artist, craftsman, and entrepreneur, who for several years has had a keen interest in community economics in general and community exchange in particular.

Friendly Favors is a voluntary World Wide Web–based association of people who acknowledge one another by awarding *THANKYOUS*. It resembles a mutual credit system in its essential features. Membership is free and open to all, but a new member must be sponsored by an existing sponsoring member, thus building a chain of trust. Each member services his or her own data page, which includes a photograph and a description of the member's skills, interests, products, and services. The idea is to offer members access to the resources made available by all other members at the maximum discount that can be sustained by the members offering them. Discounts vary from 10 percent to 100 percent (free). Prices and discounts are visible on the Web and can be modified by the member offering them. This service doubles for members as free Internet advertising for their products or services. Discounts among members are given freely as favors. Members are expected, but not obliged, to acknowledge the generous act they receive with THANKYOUS. The accounting of those THANKYOUS is hassle-free, is kept openly on the Web for each member to see, and represents the favors that members have acknowledged for each other. The idea is that recognition promotes further desirable behavior.

The Friendly Favors network uses THANKYOUS as a way of measuring generosity. Members give THANKYOUS to each other for the favors they receive. One THANKYOU is equivalent to one United States dollar saved because of the discount received. THANKYOUS can also be assigned to someone simply to express gratitude for the various contributions that person has made to the community. They are not redeemable, and according to professional accounting advice, they are not taxable. THANKYOUS do not measure wealth but goodwill. They can be transferred electronically or given as a written *Thankyou Note* to be entered later on the Web by a trained host member. Members issuing THANKYOUS are morally committed to reciprocate, in turn, with someone else who needs their gifts. This reciprocity allows for favors to spread as "ripples in a pond."

Account statements are maintained on the web. A 10 percent "tithing" of the total THANKYOUS received each month goes to the nonprofit *cause member* and to the volunteer *host member* of each member's choice. A 1 percent demurrage fee on monthly balances above 100 or below –100 goes to acknowledge Friendly Favors's services. Friendly Favors was launched on the Web in August 1999, having Victor Grey as its webmaster, a veteran Internet strategist and author of "Web without a Weaver." Friendly Favors has been praised for its ease of use and the willingness of its developers to consider suggestions for improvement submitted by the members who use it. The commercial development of a complex interactive software of this magnitude by a corporate developer was priced by *Wired* magazine to be in the neighborhood of $3 million. Most remarkably, all the development, service, equipment, office, and server spaces have been contributed by members as favors and have been acknowledged with THANKYOUS. Because of its unique structure, Friendly Favors has no bank account and therefore cannot accept monetary contributions. Friendly Favors freeware should be completed sometime in 2001 and will be made available for other developers to improve.

As of January 2001, two years since its inception, the Friendly Favors network had more than seven thousand participants, living in 120 different countries, offering a diverse array of professional services, including business, career, and health counseling, writing, editing, media production, a variety of practical and building skills, and hospitality. According to the founders, about one thousand members have already acknowledged almost 5,000 favors online totaling about 280,000 THANKYOUS.[4] But, aside from the gifts and discounts that members provide to one another, THANKYOUS are also given in recognition of good work that a person does that may not directly benefit the person giving the THANKYOUS.

The self-maintained personal profiles that members keep on the Friendly Favors Web site, with the support of a sophisticated search engine, help members to keep connected and allow people with similar interests to find one another. Anyone wishing to be included in this pioneer program can apply on line at www.Favors.org. See the Sources and Resources section for contact information. The motto of Friendly Favors is: "A friendly way to account for the favors we do for each other."

Equal Dollars (=$s)

Equal Dollars are the currency units used in a community exchange project of Resources for Human Development (RHD), a large Philadelphia-based nonprofit social service organization. Equal Dollars exist mainly as credits on the books in a mutual credit system, although members are also allowed to draw paper Equal Dollar notes against their lines of credit in the system. Launched in 1996, the Equal Dollar system had reached, by mid-1999, a membership of about eight hundred. The amount of credit outstanding was about sixty thousand Equal Dollars, including about six hundred in the form of circulating paper notes.

The Equal Dollar program is unique in its mission of supporting the economic improvement of its disadvantaged inner-city constituency. Here's what the RHD brochure says about it: "Although it is open to all, we are particularly interested in promoting the productive capacity of those individuals who are significantly underemployed or left out of the mainstream of the U.S. $ economic system. This is a nonprofit banking system without interest which provides credit to all members. It has stimulated over $300,000 in economic activity since its inception."[5]

As a supporting adjunct to the Equal Dollar program, RHD has established a small-scale micro-lending program. While assisting inner-city entrepreneurs by providing no-interest short-term micro-loans, RHD has given the Equal Dollar program a boost by requiring that each loan recipient have some link to the Equal Dollar program, either by accepting Equal Dollars as partial payment from customers or by employing workers and paying them partly in Equal Dollars. The maximum loan that can be obtained is five hundred dollars, and each loan must be repaid within a period of three to six months. This is a new program, and by the end of 1999, only six loans had been made, but all have performed satisfactorily. RHD is planning to gradually expand the program.

The Developing World Takes the Lead

During the 1980s, the first decade of the new wave, activity within the grassroots exchange movement was confined mainly to the English-speaking world, with a few systems eventually popping up elsewhere. From the early 1990s onward, however, activity in the rest of the world has burgeoned, with new organizations and networks showing up in a variety of cultural contexts, first on the European continent, then in Asia and Latin America. Much of this later activity was undoubtedly inspired by those earlier pioneers, but the development in South America has been unique and mainly homegrown.

THE GLOBAL TRADING NETWORK (RED GLOBAL DE TRUEQUE, OR RGT)[6]

The megalopolis of Buenos Aires stretches out along the Rio Plata; 120 miles long and 30 miles wide, it is home to about half of Argentina's forty million people. It is also the birthplace of a phenomenal modern manifestation of complementary exchange which has come to be known as Red Global de Trueque, or Global Trading Network. Beginning with the organization of a single "barter club" in an outlying sector of Buenos Aires in 1995, the *social money* movement, as it is called in Latin America, has exploded into a socioeconomic phenomenon involving hundreds of thousands of people in at least nine South American countries.

The emergence of social money in Latin America has occurred within the broader context of a movement toward community building and "social solidarity" that has arisen largely as a response to economic globalization. The Argentine government, like others in the region, over the past several years has been engaged in an aggressive program of privatization and has pursued policies favorable to the increasing dominance of multinational companies in Argentine markets. As part of its new economic strategy, the government has now rigidly linked the Argentine peso to the United States dollar.[7] Although these policies may have brought benefits to some, they have wreaked tremendous hardships on the poor and middle classes. Unemployment has reached high levels, at times officially estimated to be around 20 percent. The reality is much worse than that. In many of the barrios of Buenos Aires, and in some rural villages, up to 50 percent are without paid work. Even skilled professionals have had a hard time. The social "safety net" in Argentina is both flimsy and full of holes, making subsistence very difficult for people without employment. The people have responded to this challenge with tremendous energy, initiative, creativity, and courage, building networks of mutual assistance that are leading them toward greater self-reliance and social cohesiveness.

The Beginning   The first barter club in Argentina arose in 1995 when a group of neighbors initiated weekly meetings to enact direct barter trades of food and clothing. They quickly expanded their economic interactions into a kind of mutual credit trading (what they call "multireciprocal barter"[8]) involving a wider variety of goods and services. Since then, the organization of local clubs or "nodos" has proliferated among groups of poor and marginalized people throughout Latin America. The following is a slightly edited version of Heloisa Primavera's description of the birth and development of the RGT system.

> It was on the 1st of May 1995 that a group of ecologists, worried about the impact unemployment was having on the quality of life, created the first Barter Club comprised of twenty people, in Bernal, thirty kilometers from Buenos Aires in Argentina. Every Saturday, group members met to exchange their products (at the beginning, bread, various foodstuffs, fruit and vegetables, tarts, handcrafts, and afterwards, services—dental care, hairdressing, massage, therapy, etc.). Some months later the first club opened in Buenos Aires. . . . One year later, a television program gave a great impulse to further growth, which up to then had been rather slow and led by the early pioneers. The accounts, which from the outset had been recorded in a centralized notebook, were soon computerized because of the increase in the number of transactions. Sometime later, a system of cheques was set up—similar to the French SEL system.[9] However, people quickly began using these cheques as currency for other transactions, endorsing them and using them to pay for purchases. This was possible because the people knew each other and could trust the vouchers (cheques) coming from a friend or trusted acquaintance. This was how the first ticket trueque (an exchange voucher) came into being, which was transferable to anyone that was part of the system. Right from the start the units were called creditos because of their association with the trust that existed between partic-

ipants [each credito or credit is equivalent in value to one Argentine peso, which is equivalent to one U.S. dollar]. On becoming a member of the club, each participant would receive the same number of credits, thus encouraging and greatly multiplying the speed of transactions. Since everyone receives the same number of credits, the initial "equality" surprises new members, and at the same time stimulates the creation of new clubs. Since each member must produce and consume to be in the system, they are called "prosumers," a term suggested by Alvin Toffler's *Third Wave*.

Thus it was that two years later it was possible to find groups organized in different regions of Greater Buenos Aires as well as in the interior of the country. A form of administration linking the groups soon turned out to be necessary in view of the complexity of the exchanges that took place between members of different clubs, which is the richest aspect of the network. So the Barter Network came into being, with the clubs starting to call themselves nodos (knots). This central government enabled equality to be maintained between the groups and the members of those groups.

The founding group defined some ethical principles, but without doubt each autonomous group has freely interpreted them. Today there exist a great number of interconnected groups, but also many others that are completely independent of the founding group. Although the media was responsible for the initial spread of this initiative, it was the city government of Buenos Aires that provided the first government support, firstly, from the Department of Social Affairs, and afterwards from the Department of Industry, Trade and Commerce. This attitude encouraged other towns to do the same and five years later there are more than forty that have given their backing to similar initiatives, in one way or another.

Within three years of its creation, the Red Global de Trueque had grown to more than 100,000 members. Representatives were invited to Helsinki to show this experiment to other community activists who were working to ameliorate the negative effects of economic globalization. The members of the Network therefore started to see their success (speed of growth, numbers of active members, for example) in an entirely new light. Various training systems were set up and diffusion throughout other Latin American countries began on a systematic basis, all within the context of creating a critical mass, political visibility, variety in the experiments, and to join together with other forms of the Economy of Solidarity.

The Present   By the early part of 2001, "nodos" or trading clubs had been set up in fourteen Argentine provinces and eight other countries of South and Central American, including Bolivia, Brazil, Chile, Colombia, Ecuador, El Salvador, Peru, and Uruguay. Creditos now take the form of a great assortment of "papelitos"[10] or paper notes, which are printed by the larger clubs and issued to the new members of new or existing clubs. While firm statistics are not available, it is estimated that within Argentina alone there are between 500 and

1,000 trading clubs with a total combined membership of more than 300,000. Many of these are family memberships involving several people. Further, creditos notes are circulated among nonmembers as well, so that the number of active participants in this parallel economy is much greater, perhaps as high as half a million people. According to Primavera, the circulation of creditos notes "provides, on average, between one and four minimum wages (about 300 U.S. dollars per month) per family; public tax returns have multiplied as a result of private agreements held by governments with individual prosumers from which products or services are accepted, and a judge has even authorized the payment of a living allowance in social money!"

A large proportion of the trading using these community currencies takes place at local trading fairs that are held at regularly scheduled times, some once or twice a week, others much more frequently. I was told by one of the movement leaders that on any given day, approximately twenty trading fairs are going on in various clubs around the country. In April 2001 I went to Argentina, where I visited several trading clubs around greater Buenos Aires and had an opportunity to observe a few of their trading fairs. One of them, held in the "west zone," was particularly impressive. It was held on a Wednesday afternoon in a large community center and involved upwards of four hundred people buying and selling. The atmosphere of excitement and vitality was truly astonishing, and not a single peso or dollar was involved in any of the thousands of transactions that were made. Instead, one could see a variety of paper notes passing from hand to hand. These were the creditos notes issued by the clubs in this zone, as well as those issued in several other zones. Figure 11.7 shows a few of these notes. Within the trading fairs, no official money is exchanged. Pesos and dollars are not permitted because of the tax implications. Argentina has a value added tax (VAT), which is a kind of sales tax. As long as no official money is involved, trades are not taxed. What people do outside the fairs is, of course, a personal matter between the buyer and the seller.

Another club, located in a poor neighborhood, operates out of a former factory building. It is open for trading seven hours a day, six days a week. It was organized in the year 2000 by two men from the community and is presently administered by a team of three people who have complete responsibility and control. Member participation is insignificant. This nodo does not issue its own notes but utilizes the notes issued by other nodos.

The organizers have recently taken a five-year lease on the factory property for a monthly rental fee of 2,500 pesos (equivalent to U.S.$2,500). It is a large property that includes a huge main building, a more modest sized outbuilding, a parking lot, and a very large adjacent field. During our two-hour visit to one of their trading fairs we estimated there must have been about three hundred people buying and selling. We were told that on the previous day more than two thousand people had passed through.

Figure 11-7. Various currency notes used within Argentina's Red Global de Trueque network.

The costs of operation of the center are covered by admission fees, which are 20 centavos (20 cents) plus one half a credito. Assuming a modest figure of 500 paid admissions per day and 25 days of operation monthly, estimated total monthly revenues would amount to 2,500 pesos (dollars) and 6,250 creditos. This is enough to pay the rent, which must be paid in pesos, and to pay the organizers and their helpers in creditos to administer and maintain the operation. One would presume that utilities must also be paid in pesos and that this amount of activity would not provide sufficient peso income to meet that expense. The administrators told us, however, that their early fairs had been almost overwhelmed by throngs of people, which they numbered in the thousands. Based on that experience, they estimate that their membership will soon reach 10,000 and they expect to have no problems raising the peso income they need.

We were also told that when they do have surplus peso income they use it to buy goods in the formal market to be sold for creditos in the trading fairs. These goods consist mainly of basic foods and ingredients, such as meat, vegetables, fruit, oil, wheat, eggs, and sugar. This practice effectively links the resources available in the formal (peso) market with the income-earning possibilities of the trueque (creditos) market without suffering the negative effects that would result from a direct currency exchange.

The organizers told us of their plans for the various resources at their disposal on the site. They intend to continue using the main building for the daily trading fairs. They plan to convert half of the outbuilding into production spaces, such as woodworking shops, and to utilize the other half as classroom space for training people in basic skills. The adjacent field, which is covered with grass and has several large trees, will be made into a campground.

Organization and Operation   Each nodo or club is autonomous and is responsible for its own organization, administration, budget, and finances. The Network has no centralized administration, only regular monthly meetings within each zone and a monthly interzonal meeting. At present, clubs follow several models of organization and the issuance of the currency notes is not uniform. Administrative costs are covered in different ways by the different clubs. Some impose a monthly membership fee while others, such as the one described above, require buyers and sellers to pay a small admission fee to participate in the many trading fairs. Some nodos are organized with an emphasis on building social solidarity among their members, while others are organized mainly as an economic expedient to provide a way for cash-poor people to meet their material needs. The former are more participatory, while the latter tend to be more paternalistically administered by a core group of organizers.

The network provides marginalized people with opportunities they cannot find in the formal market economy. It is not seen as a substitute for the formal economy, but as a parallel and complementary economy. While helping people to satisfy their immediate needs, it also gives them an opportunity to develop confidence, skills, products, and services that can also enable them to function in the formal economy.

All kinds of goods and services are to be found within the barter clubs, including bakers, dentists, bricklayers, and other tradespeople and professionals who can't find a place in the labor market. Reliable statistics do not exist, but estimates of the total amount of creditos that have been issued by all the clubs in Argentina range from around 6 million on up. Currently, the volume of trading within this barter network amounts to a minimum of 800 million pesos (equal to 800 million U.S. dollars) annually.

The National Government Offers Support The national government of Argentina has officially recognized the value and usefulness of "barter" exchange as a weapon against unemployment and has lent its support to the promotion of "multireciprocal exchange of goods and services" throughout the country. In December 2000, the government of Argentina signed an agreement with Red Global de Trueque.[11] Among the specific items of support is a commitment by the government to assist the network to develop its organizational infrastructure to help it reach larger numbers of people across a wider area of the country. The government will help to promote interregional exchange by means of an Internet-based communications system that will link the various clubs in the network. They hope that this "partnership" can promote the formation of efficient enterprises that contribute to the creation of jobs and enable marginalized workers to develop skills and tools that may permit their entry into the "productive tissue" of the economy. The government has stated its clear intention to help, but not force, participants into the mainstream economy. It has committed to provide training and support that will assist "the gradual and orderly transition of the prosumers circuit ruled by social money (vouchers), toward the formal economy's area, building genuine ventures," but it will allow prosumers to continue their participation in the barter circuit, as they wish.

"We believe this network has had a great development but very low profile. Now we want to give it a better organization on the national level and use it as a good tool for development," said Secretary of Small and Middle-sized Enterprises Enrique Martinez. Martinez thinks that "barter has been built as an element that jobless people recognize as a transition step toward the formal economy, or a substitute. From barter, people feel encouraged again. We cannot be absent from such a rich project." The dual goal of the government is, on the one hand, to establish and expand the barter of goods and services as a substitute for the formal economic system, while, on the other hand, to make it easy for such people to go back into the labor market. Whether or not this government involvement will prove helpful remains to be seen.

Close observers point to a number of factors contributing to the success of RGT. Among these are:

- The regular membership meetings convened by each nodo
- The use of only social money in most transactions
- More reliance upon ethical behavior and peer pressure and less reliance upon formal rules
- A great deal of local group autonomy and the avoidance of centralized leadership and control
- Only a few shared rules that define a loose federation of nodos at both the regional and the national levels
- A decision-making process that seeks consensus.

Some of the more active participants in several nodos, believe that the success of the RGT could lead to the creation of more far-reaching networks of socioeconomic solidarity. For this reason the Latin American Socioeconomic Solidarity Network (Redlases) was created in 1999, and the Global Socioeconomic Solidarity Network (Red Global de Socioeconomía Solidaria—RGSES) in 2001. The latter came out of the first World Social Forum that took place in January 2001 in Porto Alegre, Brazil. The focus of these initiatives is to rebuild the social fabric and create an *Economy of Solidarity* based on social money systems and other complementary economic, cultural, and social strategies that address the whole economic process: *production, trading, and consumption*, and simultaneous financial strategies such as micro-loans using a combination of both formal and social money.

Principles   As the trading network has evolved, the participants have adopted a set of twelve principles that define the values, objectives, and operating characteristics of the associated clubs. These were proposed by the founders and include (among others) the following:

- We are not trying to promote articles or services, but to mutually help ourselves to obtain a higher meaning of life through the intermediary of work, mutual understanding, and equitable exchange.
- We maintain that it is possible to replace sterile competition, selfish gain, and speculation with mutual exchange between people.
- We believe that our actions, products, and services can respond to ethical and ecological norms, rather than the dictates of the market, consumerism, and the quest for short-term benefits.
- The only conditions to which members of the Red Global de Trueque are bound are: to take part in periodic group meetings, to be involved in training programs, to produce and consume goods, services, and knowledge

available within the Network, in the spirit of the recommendations of the various Circles of Quality and Mutual Aid.
- We believe that it is possible to combine group autonomy in the administration of its internal affairs with the fundamental ethical principles of the Network.

Over the past few years, the Latin American Socioeconomic Solidarity Network has debated adopting a thirteenth principle regarding whether, and how, the club organizers should be compensated. Discussions have led to consideration of the role of volunteer help overall. There seems to be a widespread belief that reliance upon uncompensated work "has encouraged 'corrupt' practices very similar to those in political life." Thus, the network is now advocating adoption of the following additional principle:

- In the Economy of Solidarity nothing is wasted, nothing is volunteered, everything is recycled, everything must be paid for, and everything is divided in equal conditions!

Problems and Prospects   It should come as no surprise that a complex organization that has grown so large and so fast should manifest some difficulties. The autonomy of the various clubs has resulted in a plethora of local currencies issued in a variety of ways, some of which may be questionable from the standpoint of strict reciprocity. Some of the larger issuers are unable to give a proper accounting of all the notes they have issued. While a strong desire exists among the various clubs in the network to accept each other's notes, concerns and uncertainties have led some nodos to refuse to accept the notes of others, causing some confusion and dismay among the people.

Adding to the confusion is the actuality of counterfeiting. This is the first real counterfeiting of a community currency that has come to my attention. Counterfeit versions of at least one of the larger note issues have been injected into the network. This does not seem to have done significant harm, since their number has been small and the counterfeit notes are not very difficult to distinguish from the genuine ones. What happens when someone discovers that they have accepted a counterfeit note? Practice varies. Sometimes the person will simply pass it along, but quite often the local club or the issuing club will destroy the note and absorb the loss rather than force the holder to take the loss.

Another developing problem is the emergence of political factionalism and a struggle for leadership within the movement. One faction is attempting to become the spokesman for the entire network and wants to replace the various local currencies with its own currency to be used throughout the country. This faction, led by the founders of the first Barter Club, is the one that signed the agreement with the Argentine government. Another faction is seriously concerned about preserving the autonomy of the local clubs and wants to negotiate a consensus about the critical issues facing the movement, but the first faction is not willing to participate.

It will be interesting to see how this conflict plays out over the coming year or two. If the network is to avoid disintegration, the various clubs will need to come to some clear agreement on standards of practice for the proper issuance and management of their currencies.

PART III

MONETARY TRANSFORMATION AND COMMUNITY EMPOWERMENT

In this part of the book we get into the particulars of money and the design elements of cooperative exchange systems and community currencies—the essential features, the forms and devices, the procedures and methodologies. Part 3 includes, in chapter 13, a primer on mutual credit, which is the foundation on which any private exchange system should be built. It addresses the major issues in currency design—such as basis of issue, backing, credit and debit limits, system revenues and costs, savings and investment—and tackles the thorny question of usury and interest.

Chapter 12

~

Currency Fundamentals

Every piece of money is essentially a credit instrument.

—Hugo Bilgram and L. E. Levy

Bilgram and Levy remind us that **"every piece of money is essentially a credit instrument, an acknowledgment of debt, accepted in the market as a medium of exchange, and . . . its value depends solely on the value of the credit on which it is based."**[1] This is the most important principle about money that needs to be understood, and it applies to community currencies and mutual credit systems just as much as to ordinary kinds of money. The exception, of course, would be full-valued commodity moneys such as gold and silver coins, but that kind of money is all but extinct and does not concern us here. The common types of paper currency and "checkbook" money we have become accustomed to using in this modern era are simply credit instruments. Likewise, the contemporary community exchange examples described in previous chapters and the democratic exchange media that I advocate and describe herein are also credit instruments.

Keeping that fact in mind, it becomes clear that the first requisite in evaluating any exchange system is to assess, as Bilgram and Levy put it, "the value of the credit on which it [the money] is based." Monetary theory speaks of several factors that contribute to a sound currency or credit system. The most essential of these factors can be highlighted in the following questions:

1. What should be the basis on which money is issued into circulation?
2. What factors should determine the amount of money to be issued?
3. Who should have the power to issue money?
4. How should the power to issue be allocated among those empowered to issue, and what should be the limits on the amount issued?

As we shall see, the answer to the second question follows naturally from the first, while the answer to the fourth question is implied by the criteria selected in answering the third.

Basis of Issue

The most important factor in the creation of an exchange medium is the *basis of issue*. Historically, money has been issued on the basis of various financial instruments such as bonds, promissory notes, mortgage deeds of trust, and other claims to real value. **Ideally, the creation and issuance into circulation of a unit of currency or credit should be coincident with the actual transfer of value (goods and services) from a seller to a buyer.** That transfer should also give rise to a "commitment" on the part of the original issuer (the buyer) to redeem the currency, in the market, by providing equivalent value in exchange for the currency, that is, the issuer should be obligated to accept his or her currency at par or face value from anyone wishing to buy his or her goods or services. The form of the redemption need not necessarily be limited to a particular commodity but may be in the form of any desired goods or services that the original issuer offers for sale. This is the way LETS and other mutual credit systems operate. The "credits" that the seller receives are, in effect, money, created by the buyer, who is "committed" to redeem those credits later by providing goods or services to someone in the system.

The use of the term *credit* may cause some confusion, since it has more than one meaning. It can be said that goods are delivered on "credit." In this case the seller is giving the buyer "economic credit," that is, trusting the buyer to pay equivalent value later. In a mutual exchange system, however, it is the seller's account that receives "accounting credit" on the books of the exchange, indicating that the seller has so much value "coming to her." Thus, the buyer receives economic credit (in the form of goods or services), while the seller receives the corresponding accounting credit, which represents her claim to value within the system.

Regulation of the Amount of Exchange Media Supplied

It is a fundamental principle of monetary theory that the quantity of the exchange medium being created and put into circulation should be *balanced* by the flow of goods and services coming into the market. In an ideal system, the quantity of money in circulation should be *self-adjusting*.

Much is made of the "quantity (or volume) theory of the value of money," and it is generally accepted as valid. But as shown in chapter 9, it is not the quantity of money per se that determines its value; so it is not the quantity that needs to be controlled.[2] If money is properly issued, there will never be any problem of undersupply or oversupply. The quantity of money will always be just the right amount to purchase the goods and services that it represents. Capital goods, land, purchases by consumers, and ever expanding government debt should therefore all be excluded as allowable bases of issue. It is only the politicization of money and the monopolization of its issuance and control that have caused the focus of attention to be shifted away from its true value foundation onto its mere volume. **The proper basis of issue is the transfer of value, as it is being exchanged, from a producer to another (potential) producer.**

In a mutual credit system, credits are created as needed to mediate an exchange, and there is no interest burden placed on the associated debits. The total amount of credits is always balanced with an equal amount of total debits; so there can never be an artificial shortage or surplus, as there is in the official monetary system.

Power to Issue

The third important factor is the *power to issue*. In conventional banking, it is the bankers who have the power to decide who should be allowed to create money by being granted a "loan." The bankers, thus, designate some people as being "creditworthy" and others not. Those who are granted "loans" are, of course, required to pay the bankers interest, even though the bankers have not loaned anything but merely allowed the borrower to monetize the value of his or her assets.

In a truly free society, power of all kinds, including economic and financial power, should be widely distributed. Our objectives in promoting community currencies and exchange systems are to make trading more facile and to democratize economics. Thus, the association of issuers (traders) should be open to anyone willing and able to abide by its agreements and rules, which should be minimal, and there should be no restriction on the formation of competing associations. Just as we have competing credit card companies and businesses, the issuance of exchange media should be open to competing associations of issuing groups. This will tend to ensure that proper procedures are followed and will contribute to the innovative development of the exchange process.

With that said, it follows that **everyone should be empowered to issue exchange media based on their demonstrated ability and willingness to contribute valuable goods and services to the community.** Everyone is considered creditworthy to some degree, so each participant should be allowed to issue some minimum amount of currency into circulation (by buying). The guiding principle that seems most appropriate here is that an issuer should, in the normal course of business, be able to redeem his or her issue within a reasonable period of time. A good rule of thumb, based on past monetary experience, is that **a participant is qualified to put into circulation an amount of**

"money" up to the amount of his or her sales over a two- to three-month period. For example, if my sales over time have been averaging three thousand dollars per month, it would be appropriate for me to issue into circulation no more than nine thousand dollars of community currency.

What Gives a Currency Credibility?

As we have seen, the soundness of a currency in circulation derives from the basis on which it is issued. The ultimate "backing" for it is the commitment of the issuers to redeem it by accepting it as payment when they sell their goods and services. Each of the following issues has a bearing on the credibility of a circulating currency.

AUTHORITY BASED ON AGREEMENT

There has been considerable debate about whether or not an issuing authority is needed for a community currency or mutual exchange system and, if so, what the power of that authority should be. As we have pointed out, the basis of any exchange system is the agreement, either formal or tacit, among the participants. **It is the agreement that constitutes the authority under which the system operates, not the administrator or board of directors,** which are empowered only to administer the agreement by making certain specified decisions and/or taking limited actions, which are spelled out in the agreement.

The agreement should define, clearly and precisely, the rights and responsibilities of each of the parties to the agreement. In the case of a mutual credit system, it is fundamental that each participant is given the right to issue credits, and that each participant has the obligation of redeeming the credits that she or he issues. In addition there are matters of governance and administration: someone has to sign up new participants, keep the membership list, record transactions, and keep track of account balances. These functions must all be included in the agreement.

It is important that each participant have a full understanding and a palpable sense of his or her commitment. This is more likely to occur in a system in which there is formal "membership" status and a *written* agreement. This agreement might require members to "settle" their accounts if and when they terminate their membership. Thus, in a mutual credit system, a member with a debit balance would be obligated to earn enough credits to bring his or her account balance back to zero or, perhaps, to pay an equivalent amount in official money. Similarly, if a community exchange system uses paper currency notes, a member to whom notes have been allocated would agree to return a like amount of notes or cash.

A periodic renewal of membership provides an opportunity for each member to reaffirm his or her commitment. If a person fails to renew membership, then the management could "call" his or her commitment, that is, ask that the member settle the account. The obvious question, though, is How shall the agreement be enforced? I believe that a community-based exchange system, in contrast to the dominant system with which we are all familiar, should not depend on legal enforcement of contracts. As with any voluntary association, apart from crime and malfeasance, there should be no legal penalties for failure to honor one's commitment. Sanctions should be internal, such as suspension of membership privileges or expulsion from the association. In a limited, local, more personal system, we can probably do without a formal enforcement mechanism of coercion and penalties, trusting instead the good faith of the members and the subtle social pressures that regulate behavior in any community. In less personal, wide-area community exchange systems, some more formal and conventional surety mechanisms might need to be employed.

Though neither the nominal LETSystem nor Ithaca HOURS strictly follow all the theoretical directions suggested above, they seem to be working fairly well. This is probably due to the intensive educational efforts mounted by their proponents and the strong community spirit in the areas where they have prospered. In the case of Ithaca HOURS, it is probably also due to the rapid growth in the number of participants, the close control over the amount of HOURS placed in circulation, and the fact that a large number of HOUR notes have been taken away as souvenirs without being spent. With only about five to six HOURS per participant issued, there should be little risk of HOURS being discounted in the market. As the system reaches maturity, however, the need for more formal protocols will likely become apparent.

THE UNIT OF ACCOUNT

In mutual credit and LETSystems, the unit of account is called a "green dollar" or whatever the local group wishes to call it (for instance, *cowries, credits, oaks, tokens, ecos,* and so on). People naturally equate the value of a "green dollar" to that of an official unit of money since they have no other practical referent. People tend to value things in terms they are accustomed to using: in the United States, it's the *dollar,* in the United Kingdom, the *pound,* in Germany the *mark,* in France the *franc,* and so on. This does not mean that the local currency is bound to the government and the banking system. On the contrary, even though we might use the same "measuring stick" to determine the value of things traded, we are *not* limited to using the currency provided by the banking system or the government. **The great advantage of community currencies is that the participants empower themselves to create their own currency, interest-free, as needed to transact trades.**

Given the use of official currency units to measure values, the value of *green dollars* will undoubtedly depreciate along with the official dollar as inflation proceeds. This is not a great concern, since the primary purpose of a community currency is to facilitate trading within the community. A community currency should not be used as a savings medium. The diminishing value of the currency unit over time may actually be advantageous in providing traders with an incentive to circulate the currency rapidly, thus providing a further stimulus to trading.

Nevertheless, as communities eventually begin to address the need for savings and investment mechanisms, it will be desirable to define a different, more objective unit of account. I would prefer something more precise than labor time, such as the unit of account based on a composite commodity standard, as I proposed in my book *Money and Debt: A Solution to the Global Crisis.*[3] Such a standard, based on a "market basket" of commodities, would tend to be both stable and nonpolitical.

Alternatively, some single commodity that has special importance for the local economy could be used as a standard of value for a local currency. This could be a cord of wood, a bushel of corn, a bale of cotton, or some other commodity that is widely traded in local commerce. However, a unit of account based on a single commodity has drawbacks. Its value is more influenced by transitory conditions like weather, and the market for a single commodity can be more easily manipulated by governments and large-volume traders.

The community currency being used in Ithaca, New York, which was described in chapter 10, is denominated in HOURS. The founders hoped that by using a unit of time their currency would have a market value somewhat independent of the ever declining value of Federal Reserve currency. Also, they hoped that focusing on labor time would promote a tendency for people to value all labor equally. Although an "Ithaca HOUR" is not precisely defined, people tend to think of it as having a value more or less equal to the local average hourly wage. This is what the Ithaca founders encourage, and this is what seems to be happening in practice. Ithaca HOURS, from their initial launch in 1991, were said to have a nominal value of about ten dollars. After several years in circulation, traders still seem to accept that assessment of an HOUR having a value of ten dollars, despite significant inflation of the official dollar during that period. As the dollar continued to be debased, one would have expected the hourly wage to have risen and the value of the HOUR currency, in terms of dollars, to have risen also, but that has not happened. It remains an open question as to whether the HOUR concept can become independent of the dollar concept for measuring values of goods and services exchanged.

WHAT ABOUT BACKING AND REDEEMABILITY?

Many present-day monetary reformers lament the passing of the redemption feature of paper currency and bank credit. They yearn for a return to the "gold standard," by which they mean not only the definition of the dollar in terms of a particular weight of gold but also the redeemability of paper currency into gold. In the past, paper money was redeemable, at the option of the holder, for silver or gold coins. This option of exchanging one kind of money for another did indeed play a major role in keeping political paper money honest by limiting the amount of paper that could be issued. The reinstitution of redeemability would certainly be one way of restoring discipline on the issuing authorities, but it would also have negative side effects and is far from the ideal approach. The main problem is that when gold is used to back redeemable paper notes, the supply of money cannot grow larger than the supply of gold unless the system uses "fractional reserves," which creates still more problems.

The desire for redeemability in a currency is an anachronistic bit of psychology left over from the days of commodity money. As was described in chapter 4, paper bills and bank credit began as "claim checks" for *real* money (called "specie"), which was gold and silver. Thus, there were actually two kinds of money, paper and specie (gold or silver). The "real" money was, of course, the metal, and the paper was only a symbolic representation of it.

Under such a system, redeemability was absolutely necessary to prevent the banks and/or other issuing authorities from issuing too much paper. With expanding economic activity, however, there was a chronic shortage of metallic money. This led to the expedient of what is known as "fractional reserve banking," in which banks were allowed to issue paper money in amounts that were several times the value of their gold holdings. The paper was still redeemable for gold, but there was not enough gold to redeem all the paper. The potential problem with such a system is obvious, and indeed bank runs and panics were recurrent and common. The issuance of paper was often unsound (and therefore excessive), and whenever the public got a sense of this they exercised their option to redeem paper for gold, depleting bank reserves of gold.

Unfortunately, rather than ending the abuses and developing a sound system, monetary authorities addressed the problem of bank runs by centralizing control of the banking system and putting an end to redeemability. Thus they eliminated the only effective means of imposing discipline on the issuers and opened the way for abuse on a grand scale. Discipline is certainly necessary in a monetary system, especially when the issuer has a monopoly and competing currencies may be excluded from the marketplace. In a free environment, however, there are better ways to impose discipline. The ultimate test of a currency is its acceptability in the marketplace and its "redeemability" for goods and services there. When traders have the freedom to refuse to accept a currency, or to accept it at a discount from its face value, then they can protect themselves from the effects of improper and excessive issuance of a currency. In the words of Friedrich von Hayek:

There could be no more effective check against the abuse of money by government *(or any other issuer)* than if people were free to refuse any money they distrusted and to prefer money in which they had confidence."[4]

This, of course, means having a choice, which community currencies provide. In any event, computers and communications technologies have long since obviated the need for "claim check" kinds of money. Rather than revert to this anachronistic form of discipline, it is now necessary to move away from monopolized, political, and coercive monetary systems toward free, non-governmental, democratic exchange media based on the honor and productive capacity of associated producers.

What, then, will provide the "backing" for a democratic, privately issued, credit-type of money that we are considering? This question was answered very well by E. C. Riegel:

> "Reserves" and metal hoards are but window dressing. Only that which is purchasable is back of money.
> . . . like any money unit, until something has been exchanged for it, nothing is back of it. When it has been exchanged for something, that something is back of it. Money's material backing is that which the seller surrenders in exchange for it; its moral backing is the buyer's promise to back it with an equivalent value when in turn he becomes the seller."[5]

SURETY

Although we have put to rest the question of convertibility, the matter of surety or collateral remains open. As discussed above, it makes little sense to back one kind of money with another kind of money. Yet we may want to consider means of securing the promises made by the issuing members of a community exchange system.

Historically, financial commitments have often been "secured" by valuable property. Thus, a mortgage loan on your house is secured by the value of the house and land on which it stands. If you fail to abide by the agreement spelled out in the mortgage contract, the lender can use the legal system to take ownership and possession of the house. Likewise, the contract for an auto loan gives the lender the legal right to *repossess* your car if you should fail to make the payments. While most contemporary community exchange systems are based on the unsecured promises of their members, it might be appropriate in some cases to consider the possibility of requiring that lines of credit be secured. The WIR circle, described in chapter 8, requires its members to provide security for their lines of credit, and perhaps its success over more than sixty years has derived, in part, from this kind of operational rigor.

Forms and Devices

Whether it involves a mutual credit system, a circulating paper currency, or both, any complementary exchange system, in order to be easily implemented and readily accepted, should, as much as possible, use familiar devices and procedures. People are accustomed to using paper notes (bills), checks, bank accounts, debit and credit cards, and more recently smart cards and electronic wallets. These inventions have demonstrated their efficiency and effectiveness in handling the payment problem, the process of transferring funds from one trader to another. They are the mechanical aspects of money and banking, and there is no reason why the new, democratic community exchange systems should not use similar devices.

New ideas and approaches do, however, require different terminology. In order to minimize confusion and any suggestion of antagonism with existing monetary and financial structures, it might be wise for community exchange systems to avoid completely the use of words like *money* and *dollar*. Community exchange media are complementary to official money and can be referred to as *credits, coupons, notes,* or *scrip*. They have been developing in parallel with official monetary systems and, over time, can be expected to assume a larger and larger portion of the burden of mediating exchange. As people gain experience with the new systems, they will come to understand the simple essence of exchange media and sense the economic empowerment that community-based solutions provide.

Chapter 13

⌁

Mutual Credit: The Foundation for Community Currencies

The composite credit of private competitive traders, based as it is, upon actual exchange of goods and services, forms the only substance of money.

—E. C. RIEGEL

THE PURPOSE OF EVERY community currency or exchange system is to provide a payment medium that is separate from, and supplemental to, official money, and that originates not in banks or government but in the community of members. What do the members have to offer one another in exchange for their goods and services? Only their own goods and services. Ultimately, we each have only one currency with which to pay, and that is our own production. What is needed is some device, a "placeholder," if you will, that allows both time and opportunity for accounts to be balanced. All that this requires is a willingness to wait and a willingness to trust. In a word, the members of the trading community must be willing to give each other "credit."

What Is Mutual Credit?

Mutual credit is the essential agreement that underlies any complementary exchange system or community currency. Any community currency that is not based on a clear agreement among those who are empowered to issue it will be difficult to manage and prone to failure. Just as your dollars can be held in the form of either Federal Reserve notes or account balances in a bank or credit union, so too can community currencies take the form of either paper notes or account balances. A community exchange system may utilize any of the various financial instruments and protocols with which we are already familiar. It may utilize physical objects that circulate from hand to hand, such as paper notes, coins, or tokens; it may be comprised of accounts and ledgers on which debits and credits are recorded; or it may involve some combination of these. Whatever form the exchange media may take, whether paper notes or account balances, the same basic principles apply. Therefore, when we speak of "currency," it should be understood that the term also includes credits in a ledger (bookkeeping) system. Further, it should be pointed out that while accounts may be kept on a computer, a ledger system can be as simple as a pen and a notebook.

Mutual credit is the generic term that we use to describe an association of traders who have agreed to create and utilize their own exchange medium. Anyone familiar with LETS, described in chapter 10, already has a basic understanding of what mutual credit looks like. LETS is a particular type or "brand" of mutual credit. It has its own particular procedures and protocols. A mutual credit system might, like LETS, use a ledger or system of accounts for recording the trades and tracking the account balances of its members, but it might also utilize circulating notes. These notes can be issued to members against their credit lines, in effect providing a physical representation of that credit. Just as a cash withdrawal is debited against (subtracted from) a bank account, the amount of any notes thus issued would be debited against the members' mutual credit account. Indeed, the use of circulating notes may be employed to eliminate completely the need to record members' transactions. The passing of notes from hand to hand is just an alternative way of keeping score in the economic game of give and take. This is the path that Tucson Traders has elected to take, as described in chapter 11.

A mutual credit system is designed to surmount the limitations of barter. Like money, it provides an intermediary device that allows two parties to trade even though one of them may have nothing the other wants. For example, suppose Martha knits sweaters and John wants to buy one but has nothing that Martha presently needs. Using mutual credit, John can still get the sweater by giving Martha "credits" for the agreed price. Where does John get the credits to give to Martha? He creates them. Just as banks create dollars to give to someone who requests a loan, John creates the credits to pay Martha for the sweater. Martha can then spend those credits when she buys something from anyone else in the system. When John creates credits to pay Martha, he obligates himself to accept credits from someone in the system at some future time in payment for his own goods or services. In this way, by making a sale, he "redeems" the credits that he originally issued. This is shown pictorially in figure 13.1. It can be seen that the process is essentially identical to that of the ideal money circuit described in chapter 4 and to the LETS trading circuit described in chapter 10.

In a mutual credit system, the members empower themselves to do the same thing that banks have done for years, essentially creating their own money in the form of credit but saving the cost of interest, while distributing the money themselves according to their own needs. In such a system, holding credits is evidence that so much value has been delivered to the community, while a debit balance indicates that a member has received that much more from the community than she or he has delivered. A debit balance thus represents a person's commitment to deliver that much value to the community sometime in the near future.

How a Mutual Credit System Works

Mutual credit can be viewed as an extension of the long-established practice of the trade credit that businesses offer to one another in the normal course of business. Businesses often sell to their customers on what is called "open account," which means that they deliver the merchandise and bill their customers for the amount due. A certain amount of time is allowed for payment to be made. It may be fifteen, thirty, sixty days or more, depending on the customs and needs of that particular line of business. Often, a discount may be given for prompt payment. In the terminology of business, an example of typical trade terms might be "2%/10; net 30 days," which means that payment is due within thirty days of the billing date, but a 2 percent discount may be taken if payment is made within ten days.

The basic idea of a mutual credit system is to extend the practice of trade credit to a wider group of participants, each of whom has the power to buy without cash and, at the same time, to lengthen the duration within which balances may be outstanding. The ideal, at least with respect to empowerment of the participants and local control of the local economy, is to eliminate completely the requirement of payment in official currency. In actual practice, the exchange of goods and services within a mutual credit system involves the payment of some combination of community credits and official cash. Since a seller must usually incur some cash costs in providing goods or services to the buyer, she or he must be able to earn enough cash to cover those costs.

Over the long run, individual mutual credit account balances will move up and down, some months ending with a credit balance and some months ending with a debit balance, but averaging out around a balance of zero. As long as debit balances do not become chronic or extreme, the system can handle these situations readily. Indeed, since the total of credits in the system must be balanced by an equal amount of total debits, outstanding debit balances are a necessary feature of the system and will have no adverse effect on its opera-

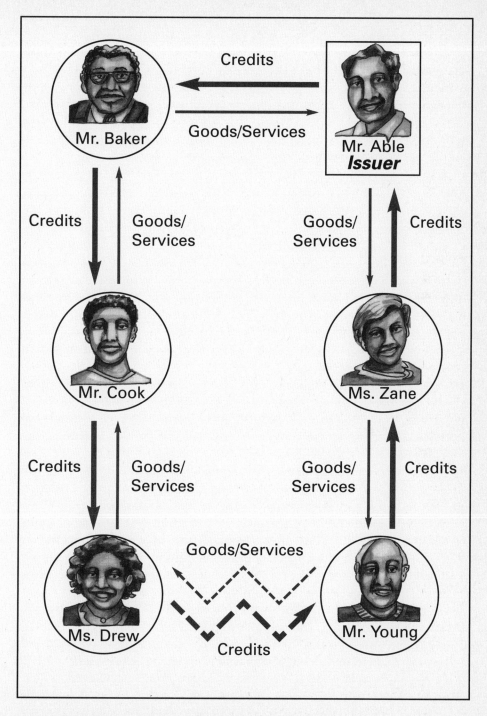

Figure 13.1. The mutual credit trading circuit.

tion. If a particular participant develops a chronic debit balance, steps can be taken by the group to help him or her to increase sales and/or reduce purchases. This may involve retraining or the kind of friendly assistance that is typical within mutual support networks.

Basic Steps in Organizing a Mutual Credit System

Here, in brief, are the essential steps involved in starting a mutual credit trading system (these will be elaborated upon in chapter 18):

1. Organize a core group of people and organizations to begin trading among themselves using trade credit units as the exchange medium. It is best if the founding group is composed of people who already know and trust one another or who have some affinity or common interest. The group can be expanded, as appropriate, by inviting other friends, family, acquaintances, and business associates to join. New members might be provisional for some specified period of time, after which they would have the same status as founding members. Provisional members might have a debit limit that is lower than the limit for full members. Over time the membership can be made more inclusive, but there needs to be a balance between system integrity and inclusivity.
2. Choose some unique name for the system credits to distinguish them from official currency. They might be called "sand dollars," "green dollars," "acorns," "credits," "tokens," "hours," and so forth. However, to avoid confusion, I suggest that the use of the word *dollar* be avoided in naming the local unit.
3. Place a limit on debit balances in members' accounts. Initially, every full member account should have the same maximum debit (negative) balance. The amount is arguable, but an equivalent of about two hundred or three hundred dollars might be reasonable. As trading develops, debit limits might be raised for those who demonstrate the capacity to carry a higher amount by selling more within the system. A good rule of thumb for setting debit limits is that a person's debit limit should be no more than two or three times his or her average monthly community credit sales.
4. Designate someone to assume the role of "registrar" for the system, to maintain the account ledger and membership list. The accounts can be kept as pages in a notebook, on file cards, or on a computer. The registrar will record transactions (debits and credits), update members' account balances, and periodically issue account statements. Members can report their transactions using a standard form similar to a check, or transactions can be reported to a telephone answering machine. The simplest accounting system is a loose-leaf notebook that contains a page for each member. The

```
┌─────────────────────────────────────────────────────────────┐
│  Thomas A. Trader              Member Number 1066             │
│  P.O. Box 42663, Tucson, AZ 85733                             │
│  Date: _____                                          │
│  Credit the                                                   │
│  Account of: _____ TT _____           │
│                                                               │
│  _____ Tucson Tokens             │
│                                                               │
│  For _____ Signed _____          │
│                                                               │
│  Tucson Traders • P.O. Box 1842 • Tucson, Arizona, 85722      │
└─────────────────────────────────────────────────────────────┘
```

Figure 13.2. A mutual credit system check.

page should contain spaces for transactions to be recorded, columns for debits and credits, and a column for the running balance. Periodic account statements could consist simply of a photocopy of each member's page. Such an account page as used by Tucson Traders was shown in chapter 11 (figure 11.1). Figure 13.2 shows a typical mutual credit system check.

5. Produce and distribute at regular intervals a system status report showing each member's balance and trading volume. This will help to establish a completely open information system and allow every member to know the health of the system and be aware of any developing problems with chronic or excessive balances. It might also highlight the identity of the most active and productive participants.

6. Designate someone to produce a newsletter containing classified ads listing both offers of, and requests for, goods and services. This could be part of the registrar's duties, or it could be done by someone else.

7. Since the mutual credit system has operating expenses, it must generate some revenue. This can be accomplished by charging fees for some or all of the services provided. Fixed fees may be applied for such services as recording transactions, advertising offers and requests, and generating and mailing account statements and reports. Some of these fees can be in system credits, but some are needed in official currency to cover costs such as postage, printing, or supplies that cannot be obtained within the system. These cash expenses might also be covered by an annual membership fee.

8. Schedule regular gatherings of the membership. These are useful not only to take care of system business but to get to know one another, to trade, and to have some fun. Try potluck suppers, fairs, trading bazaars, celebrations, picnics, auctions, and rummage sales.

9. Consider the possibility of charging a small percentage, in system credits, at the end of each quarter or year on all balances, both credit and debit. The percentage charged should be the same for both types of balance. This will have several positive effects. It is intended mainly to stimulate the circulation of credits and avoid stagnation of balances. In addition, it will provide a supplementary source of system credits with which to pay for system operation and development. This will assure more adequate compensation for the registrar, newsletter editor, and others who provide services to the system. Any surpluses that develop might be used to fund community projects or for other purposes that the members determine by consensus. (This item is among the more controversial issues in mutual credit and will be discussed further in chapters 15 and 18.)

As the mutual credit system develops, members will likely find that they are supporting one another in a variety of ways—as friends, confidants, counselors, and more. Some direct barter and informal trading will occur. This should be encouraged rather than discouraged. Even though private and informal transactions bypass the system and avoid paying fees into it, they also reduce the workload. The primary objective, after all, is to foster the development of mutually supportive relationships. If the system works for people, they will help to maintain it through donations and volunteer labor. **Sometimes it's better not to keep score.**

Continuing Issues in Mutual Credit Systems

This chapter is intended to provide a quick overview of mutual credit. The steps and suggestions outlined above are by no means the final word on the matter and will be looked at in later chapters. Each group will have to work out for itself many of the answers to the recurrent problems of exchange, but full advantage should be taken of the experience of others. The questions and issues that need to be addressed in establishing and operating a mutual credit system are essentially the same as those which exist in any system of money and banking, and if not properly handled can lead to disastrous consequences. Various groups have dealt with them in different ways, but some approaches are superior to others. Here are some of the major issues that need to be highlighted:

Debit Limits

How are limits on individual accounts to be set? What amounts are reasonable in allowing members maximum purchasing power without becoming a drag on the system? What provisions should be made for monitoring accounts, preventing overdrafts, and correcting imbalances?

Account settlement agreements

How long should account balances be allowed to remain stagnant? What should be done when a member drops out? What provisions, if any, should be made for periodic clearing or settlement of accounts?

Savings and Investment Provisions

What if people want to save some of their credits over extended periods of time? Can that be accommodated without diminishing the effectiveness of mutual credit as a medium of exchange? If not, what mechanisms should be used to limit the use of mutual credit as a savings and investment medium?

Interest/Demurrage on Account Balances

Should interest and/or demurrage charges be levied on debit and/or credit balances?

Coresponsibility Groups

Should membership be completely open or should it be required that new members be sponsored by existing members? Should participation be based on individual membership or should everyone be part of an affinity group in which the group members take some responsibility for each others' balances?

Group/Organizational/Family Memberships

Should the system provide fee discounts to people who join as part of an organization, group, or family, and if so how much? How is "family" defined? What limitations should be placed on family or group memberships, if any?

Taxability/Reportability

There is a considerable amount of confusion and controversy about whether cashless trading is taxable, either constitutionally or under IRS regulations, and whether or not members need to report their trading on their tax returns. If trades are reported, should the seller report the credits she or he received, or should the buyer report the value of the goods and services received? Which party has received income? Is the system administrator responsible for reporting members' business transactions to the IRS or other tax authorities?

Advertising and Transaction Fees

How much should be charged for publishing notices/ads and recording transactions? What portion of the charges should be charged in official currency and what portion in system credits? How can meeting the general cash needs for operating the system be assured?

Strategies for Enhancing Mutual Credit
Systems and Gaining Acceptance

Many community exchange systems begin with a flurry of enthusiasm and then gradually grind to a halt. Here are some suggestions for improving the likelihood of sustained success.

1. Utilize familiar financial devices such as notes or tokens, checks, and credit/debit cards to facilitate exchange transactions and provide more reliable accounting. Most mutual credit systems, like LETS, rely mainly on telephone reporting as the basis for updating member accounts. While that may be perfectly adequate for small systems, larger systems may require a more foolproof recording process and a paper trail for verification.
2. Involve as many established businesses as possible, especially locally owned retail establishments that potential members are accustomed to patronizing. The participation of established businesses provides a mutual credit system with instant credibility and makes the system more useful to potential members. Effort should be made to help retail businesses find ways to spend their community currency income.
3. Hold frequent trading fairs or bazaars to bring members together for the purpose of trading, socializing, and celebrating. Schools, community centers, church halls, and parks can often be obtained at no cost or low cost for such activities. These events must be well organized and well publicized to be effective. Low attendance can be demoralizing and inhibit attendance at subsequent events.
4. Establish some form of community store that enables members to buy and sell their goods and services for local currency. The store should operate in a familiar organized retail setting with more or less regular business hours. Such a "cooperative" gives members with low sales volume an outlet for their goods without having to incur prohibitive overhead expenses. It also encourages more habitual trading.
5. Make a special effort to involve marginalized and underutilized groups, for instance retirees and youth, who have lots of time and/or less than adequate money income. These groups have a greater need for exchange alternatives and are able to devote more time and effort to making trades and helping to run the system.
6. Enlist the support and encouragement of government officials, especially at the local level, and of the private nonprofit sector, especially social service providers, but be sure to maintain control in the hands of a volunteer core. Be careful when dealing with bureaucracies: they can take up a lot of your time and energy in futile activity.

Chapter 14

◆

Basic Currency Types: A Classification Scheme

The most powerful type of community currency is not *issued on the basis of a national currency or any other existing currency, but is issued into circulation as a credit obligation of some group or organization other than the government or the banking establishment.*

—GRECO

T HE FOREGOING CHAPTERS have described numerous historic and contemporary currencies and exchange systems. In this chapter, we will examine the similarities and differences among them and offer a taxonomy or classification scheme based on their essential characteristics.

Different Breeds of Cat: Community Currencies Are Not All Created Equal

Currencies can be classified into various categories based on how they are issued, circulated, and redeemed; the functions they are intended to serve; and the type of "backing" they have. It is important to distinguish between the *essential nature* of an exchange medium (currency), on the one hand, and its physical form, mechanical details, protocols, and procedures, on the other. Its essential nature is determined by the answers to such questions as: Who is the issuer? How is it created? How is it put into circulation? How is it redeemed? What is its backing?

Most of the remaining questions have to do with mere accounting details: Does the currency exist in the form of paper notes, tokens, ledger entries, account balances, or smart card balances? Does the payment process and transfer of the currency take the form of passing paper notes and tokens from hand to hand, or is this managed by writing checks or by phoning in orders to the account registrar or community currency "bank," or does a card reader move credits from one person's card or account to another person's card or account?

Good Paper vs. Bad Paper

The first thing to understand about community currencies is that, like contemporary national currencies, they are all "credit instruments," or IOUs. Regardless of whether we are considering a paper note, like a Federal Reserve note, or the numbers in your checking account at the bank, that fact applies, and we need to ask the question "Who owes what to whom? What "stands behind" or "backs" a currency—the thing that makes it valuable—is the promise of the issuer to accept the currency as payment for real goods and/or services, or the ability to "redeem" it for something of real value. So, ultimately, the value of any currency is determined by the belief that people have in the issuer's promise. If people perceive that the issuer is *ready, willing,* and *able* to fulfill the promise stated or implied by the currency, people will accept it as a medium of exchange. To the extent that any of these is in doubt, people will either refuse the currency completely (if they have a choice) or "discount" it (accept it at less than face value).

Community currencies can take many forms. Some are more credible and secure than others; some are more generally accepted than others; some are more empowering for the participants than others. As we proceed, we will look at the various design elements of community currency and how they impinge on these factors of credibility, acceptance, and empowerment.

Before we get to the details, the reader should review the way in which banks bring money into circulation, which was described in chapter 4. This will provide a benchmark for comparison and a point of departure for assessing the degree of improvement that a particular type of community currency might offer.

Types of Currencies

Most of the contemporary community currencies are, technically, not currencies at all but merely limited-use substitutes for official money. It is extremely important to differentiate among these currency types, because their characteristics and capabilities differ considerably. The differences can be as extreme as those between a bicycle and a freight train. While the bicycle has the advantages of light weight, environmental friendliness, and efficiency, the freight train is capable of carrying much greater loads.

In my view, to qualify as an actual community currency, an issue should change hands many times before being returned to the issuer for redemption, and it should not be issued on the basis of some other (presumably, national) currency. **The most powerful type of community currency is *not* issued on the basis of a national currency or any other existing currency, but is issued into circulation as a credit obligation of some group or organization other than the government or the banking establishment.** Nevertheless, for the sake of convenience in our discussion, we will accept the popular usage of the term "currency" to include money substitutes as well as true community currencies.

The classic example of a limited-use money substitute is the chips used in gambling casinos. Anyone who has been to Las Vegas, Atlantic City, or any of the many other gaming centers is familiar with these. There are a number of reasons for using chips rather than cash at the gaming tables. First, they are easier to handle than paper notes; second, their denominations can be determined at a glance; and third, they enable a psychological denial that is advantageous for the casino. It is easier for most people to toss off a five-dollar chip than to part with a five-dollar bill, much less a ten or a twenty. People seem to "forget" that the chips represent real money, causing them to be a bit more reckless in wagering and spending them.

A community currency, on the other hand, is intended to empower the members of the community. It achieves this primarily by enabling them to issue currency on the basis of their own labor and resources. Those resources might include official money, but a currency that requires official money for its existence will always be dependent on, and limited by, the policies and actions of the monetary authorities. While such a currency can be useful for the purpose of funding community improvement projects and promoting "buy local" initiatives, the level of empowerment and independence that it provides is minimal in comparison with community currencies created by the people themselves and "backed" by their own labor and resources.

The following classification scheme is useful in describing the various possibilities. These possible types of currency will be described along with their distinguishing features, uses, and limitations, and the familiar examples will be fit into this overall classification scheme.

First of all, two fundamental classes of currency can be described. They are distinguished from each other according to how they are issued into circulation. Namely, a currency can be either *cash-based,* that is, issued by some entity or authority that transfers the currency to a buyer who pays for it with official money; or it can be *wealth-based,* that is, issued by some individual or group or authority that transfers the currency as payment to a seller of commodities, merchandise, or services. The former uses an existing currency to pay for another currency, while the latter uses the transfer of real wealth as the occasion to create a completely new currency. Each of these fundamental classes can be subdivided as shown in figure 14.1, which also fits various real currencies into the classifying scheme.

CASH-BASED CURRENCIES

Within the fundamental class of cash-based currencies, there are at least two subcategories that are distinguished from one another on the basis of how, and with what, they may be redeemed. These two subcategories emulate the familiar models of (1) gift certificates and (2) traveler's checks.

The Gift Certificate Type of Currency   Most people have had some experience in using gift certificates. These are certificates that can be bought from a business and then used later to pay for goods or services received from that business. They have been quite popular among such businesses as department stores, clothing stores, and restaurants. The appeal of a gift certificate is that it allows someone to give a gift, while allowing the recipient to choose the specific item or service. It is, in effect, a receipt acknowledging prepayment.

Many so-called local currencies have the same basic characteristics of a gift certificate. Those currencies are purchased for cash and are then redeemable for particular types of merchandise or services at designated businesses. The Farm Preserve Notes and Deli Dollars, described in chapter 10 are examples of this type of local currency. In each case, a potential customer buys the notes for cash from the issuing business. The business then redeems the notes for merchandise during some specified time period.

Often, the cash amount paid is something less than the face value of the certificate or note. In the case of Farm Preserve Notes, a ten-dollar note could be bought for nine dollars in cash, then redeemed at harvesttime for ten dollars worth of produce. Likewise, the Deli Dollars were purchased for cash, then used at some later time to purchase meals at the Deli.

Various issues of this type have become popular in recent years as fundraisers. They are often referred to as "scrip," and scrip has become big business. Major retailers, such as the Safeway supermarket chain, have been selling scrip that is good for the purchase of groceries and other merchandise. The scrip is typically sold through nonprofit and community organizations such as the Boy Scouts. For example, the retailer might offer books of coupons (scrip) good for twenty dollars worth of groceries. These might be sold to the Boy Scouts for nineteen dollars (a 5 percent discount). The Boy Scouts then sell the coupon books to supporters and the general public for cash at full face value, keeping the difference. The retailer, thus, may be able to presell a considerable amount of merchandise while gaining goodwill and benefiting charitable groups. The discount cost plus the incidental costs of running the program may well be made up by extra sales.

Types of Cash Substitutes			True Community Currencies	
Gift Certificate	Traveler's Check	Special Purpose	Unfunded	Funded
Deli Dollars	Traveler's check	Casino Chips	Mutual Credit	Warehouse Receipt Scrip
Farm Preserve Notes	Toronto Notes	Toronto Dollars	LETS Dollars	
Supermarket Scrip	Harvey Bucks	Harvey Bucks	Ithaca HOURS	
			Provincial "Bonds"	
			Larkin Merchandise "Bonds"	
			Railway Notes	

Figure 14.1. Basic classification of community currency types, with examples.

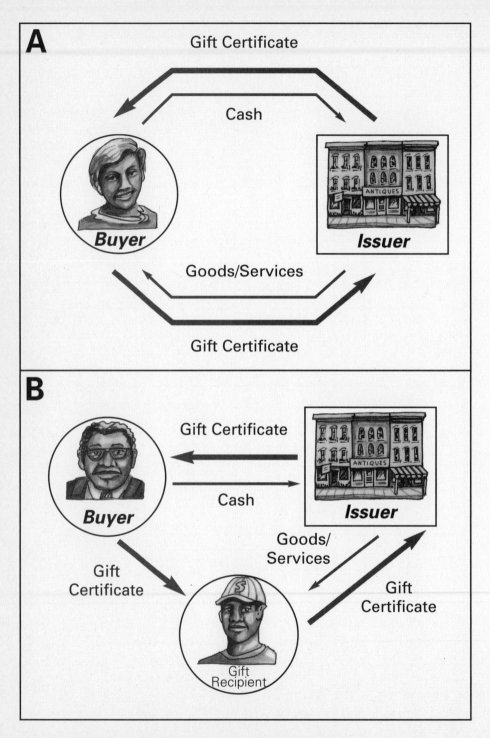

Figure 14.2. Gift certificate issuance, transfer, and redemption.

Gift certificates do not generally circulate as currency. They have limited life, and their circulation is extremely limited. They go from the issuer to a buyer to the gift recipient and then back to the issuer, or, in the case of the "scrip" described above, they go from issuer to agent (like a nonprofit group) to buyer to issuer. These cases are depicted in figures 14.2 and 14.3, respectively. Gift certificates do not normally function as a medium of exchange. This has been a major concern for the organization that issues and promotes Toronto Dollars (see chapter 11). It would like to see the community currency change hands many times before being presented for redemption. That is why it is making a great effort to extend the reach of the currency to include the entire Metro Toronto region and to recruit a wider variety of business types. As the businesses themselves find that they too can get what they need by spending Toronto Dollars, they will be less inclined to cash them in.

The Traveler's Check Type of Currency   A traveler's check differs from a gift certificate in two main respects. First, traveler's checks are more widely accepted and are not limited to one company or group of merchants. Second, while gift certificates are normally redeemable only for goods or services, traveler's checks are (ultimately) redeemed for cash. The original issuer who sells the traveler's checks for cash is committed to accept them back from anyone and to redeem them for cash. This makes them acceptable to a wide range of third parties, particularly merchants, who can cash them or deposit them at most any bank. Another major factor in their general acceptance is the prestige and name recognition of issuers such as American Express and Thomas Cooke.

The primary appeal of traditional traveler's checks is the safety they provide over cash. For a small percentage fee, usually about 1 percent or 2 percent, a buyer can receive protection against loss in the event the checks are lost or stolen. The issuing company provides this protection by guaranteeing to replace the checks. These checks must be signed in order to be negotiable. The buyer of the traveler's checks signs them once when purchased and again when she or he cashes them or uses them to buy something. Technically, the two signatures must match in order for the checks to be honored for redemption by the issuing company.

Why is the issuing company willing to provide this protection for such a seemingly low cost to the "traveler"? Actually, the traveler's check business is quite lucrative for the issuer. Companies that issue them, such as American Express and Thomas Cooke, make considerable profit. First, the money they receive for their traveler's checks can be invested to earn an income that accrues the whole time the traveler's check remains outstanding. Even the most conservative investments, such as government notes, will yield an annual rate of 5 percent to 6 percent. Furthermore, it is estimated that about

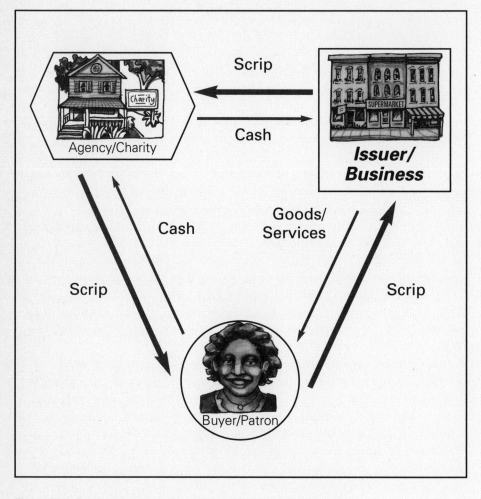

Figure 14.3. Fundraising scrip issuance, transfer, and redemption.

8 percent of all traveler's checks issued are *never* redeemed. This represents a windfall profit for the issuing company.

Traveler's checks can be purchased from various agents, including most banks and credit unions, and are often issued free to members by such organizations as the American Automobile Association (AAA). As in the case of gift certificates, traveler's checks do not usually circulate as currency. Their usual life span is a matter of weeks or months, and their circulation is generally limited, going from issuer to agent to buyer to merchant to a bank, and back to the issuer (through the check-clearing mechanisms of the banking system), as depicted in figure 14.4.

Special Purpose Cash-Substitute Scrip   *Toronto Dollars Revisited.* Toronto Dollars are a special case, which we will use to describe this class of special purpose *cash-substitute scrip.* Toronto Dollars have the basic characteristics of a gift certificate but also bear some resemblance to a traveler's check. They are sold for official money, in this case Canadian dollars. A ten-dollar Toronto Dollar note is purchased for ten Canadian dollars. Toronto Dollars can be spent at any of a fairly large number of businesses, and the number of merchants willing to accept them is continually growing. The characteristics that make Toronto Dollars resemble traveler's checks are that (1) many businesses accept them and (2) each business has the option of redeeming them for cash.

Toronto Dollars also serve as a fund-raising device since each one hundred Toronto Dollars redeemed return only ninety Canadian dollars. The 10 percent redemption fee is used to fund community projects and charities. Like most gift certificates, Toronto Dollars have an expiration date.

One additional feature that distinguishes Toronto Dollars is the fact that, unlike a typical gift certificate or traveler's check, *they are intended to continue circulating as currency.* The main question that still remains to be fully answered is, How can they be made to do so? One way is by advertising them as a currency and describing the benefits of circulating them. Another way is to broaden the scope of their usefulness. The greater the variety of goods and services that can be bought with a scrip, the more it will tend to be used as a currency. Further, cash redemption can be discouraged by placing carefully tailored limitations on redemption. Specifically, the redemption value can be discounted from the face value, and/or the scrip can have a redemption date that is months or years after the issuance date.

Some of the stamp scrip issued during the Great Depression had characteristics of this kind. In the case of the most elegant stamp scrip model, the official money was not tendered in advance but was accumulated over the life of the scrip through the purchase of the stamps. If the stamps were affixed each week as required, enough cash would have been accumulated within a year to allow for cash redemption of the scrip.

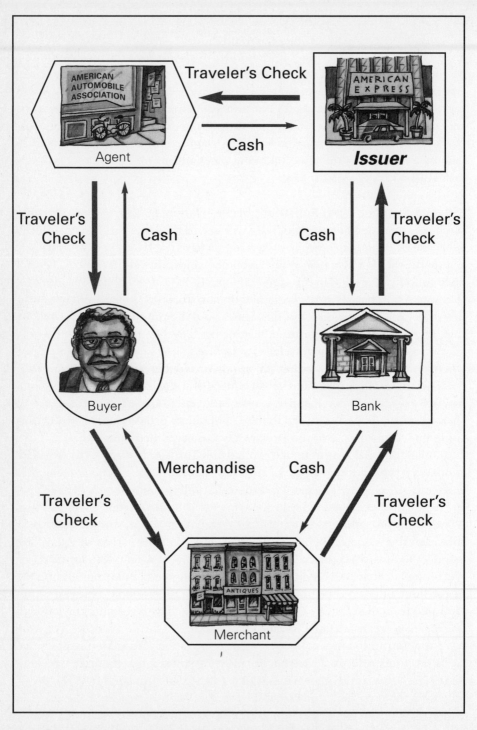

Figure 14.4. Traveler's check issuance, transfer, and redemption.

I have designed a scrip that is intended to assist some specific target groups, such as unemployed youth, the details of which are described in chapter 22. Given the widespread desire of people to be helpful, such currencies could, I think, find ready acceptance in the mainstream local economy. Scrip could be sold for cash with the guarantee that it will be redeemed for cash at some later date. The guarantee can be made almost ironclad by depositing the cash in an escrow account and designating a trust company as the redemption agent. Among the provisions that might be applied to encourage circulation and retard or discourage redemption are:

1. to specify that only particular entities are allowed to redeem the scrip for cash, for example, nonprofit organizations and/or sponsoring merchants;
2. to apply some discount from face value when the scrip is presented for redemption; and
3. to allow redemption only after the passage of some period of time.

In the meantime, the scrip can be exchanged for goods and services and will change hands repeatedly if people understand the benefits that accrue to the target group, the local economy, and the general community by using it in that way. The Toronto Dollars mentioned above aspire to become more than a gift certificate or traveler's check, and some of their redemption provisions are intended to accomplish that. These include the first two items mentioned above. First of all, only sponsoring businesses are allowed to redeem Toronto Dollars for cash, and only in multiples of one hundred dollars. Second, each Toronto Dollar redeemed receives only ninety cents in Canadian cash. The remaining ten cents is donated to nonprofit and community action groups.

There is no waiting period on the redemption of Toronto Dollars, however. A participating merchant who receives them in trade can cash them in immediately if she or he wishes. If a waiting period of, say, six months or a year were to be imposed before Toronto Dollars could be redeemed, they would, no doubt, change hands more times prior to redemption. This increased circulation would allow each Toronto Dollar issued to mediate more trades.

What would be the trade-off in implementing such a waiting period? It might be more difficult to recruit businesses to participate in the Toronto Dollar program if such a restriction were imposed. At this stage of development of the community currency movement, gaining the trust and participation of the business community is a primary requirement. This has been the Toronto Dollar project's major success. At some point, however, it may become possible to add such time restrictions on redemption without losing support.

Figure 14.5 depicts the issuance, circulation, and redemption of Toronto Dollars. The dashed lines in the lower portion of the diagram are intended to represent an indeterminate number of exchanges taking place before the Toronto Dollar notes are presented for redemption.

Shortcomings and Advantages   As mentioned above, all forms of scrip that are sold for official money are not true supplemental currencies. They do not ordinarily circulate as a payment medium, and they do not supplement the total supply of money in the local economy; they merely substitute a limited or local form of payment for official currency that is already in circulation. This may, arguably, not be true in the case of Harvey Bucks (see the sidebar), since they are issued by a bank. By making a loan, the bank does indeed increase the overall money supply. Initially, this increase is in the form of the local scrip, Christmas Cash. But when the merchant redeems the local scrip, it is converted (95 percent of it) to official money. The outstanding balance on the aggregate of all Christmas Cash loans represents money in circulation issued by the bank.

In order for the total supply of money to be increased, a nonofficial currency must be issued into circulation on the basis of some form of value other than the official currency. Only through bypassing the conventional banking channels and monetization mechanisms can a community currency add to the total money supply and be called a true supplemental currency.

Nonetheless, the cash-based money substitutes just described do have some significant advantages.

1. They can provide a means of temporary financing for local businesses.
2. They can serve a fund-raising function for local charities and community service groups that buy them at a discount.
3. Perhaps most important, they ensure that the amount of money converted will be spent within the community, bolstering the entire local economy.

If a cash-based scrip has appropriate design features and is promoted as a spendable currency, it can change hands many times. Thus it would be spent not just once but over and over again, stimulating local business instead of going elsewhere to buy imports. Further, cash substitutes can be a significant first step in introducing the idea, and gaining acceptance of, nongovernment community currencies and private exchange alternatives.

Uses of Cash Paid In   The natural question to be asked in all these cash-substitute cases is, What happens to the official money paid in to purchase the scrip? Actually, there are a number of possibilities. Consider first the gift certificate type. The cash will normally go into the general fund of the issuer to

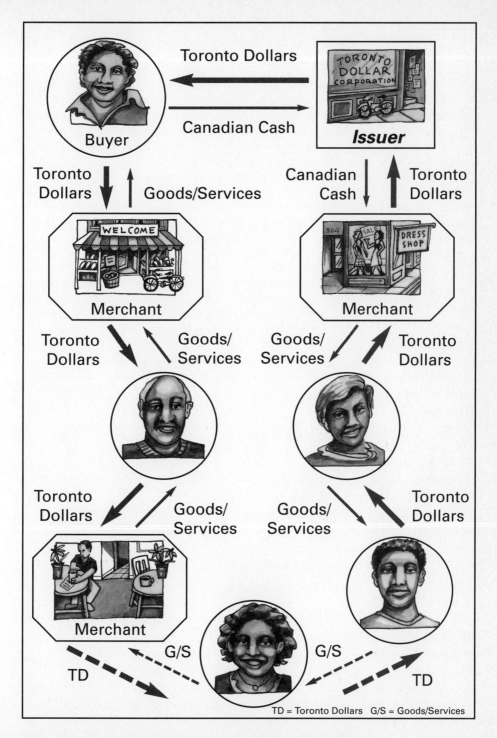

Toronto Dollars

Canadian Cash

Buyer

Issuer

Toronto Dollars

Goods/Services

Canadian Cash

Toronto Dollars

Merchant

Merchant

Toronto Dollars

Goods/ Services

Goods/ Services

Toronto Dollars

Toronto Dollars

Goods/ Services

Goods/ Services

Toronto Dollars

Merchant

G/S

G/S

TD

TD

TD = Toronto Dollars   G/S = Goods/Services

Figure 14.5. Toronto Dollars issuance, circulation, and redemption.

Harvey Bucks

―

Harvey Bucks are unique in my experience, and difficult to classify. The First State Bank of Harvey (North Dakota) has a novel no-interest Christmas loan program that involves the issuance of Harvey Christmas Cash, or Harvey Bucks. Like Toronto Dollars, these too have some characteristics of both a gift certificate and a traveler's check, but there is an added "twist." Here's the way it works.

Prior to the Christmas holidays, the bank takes applications for Christmas loans on which it charges no interest. If the application is approved, the borrower receives the loan proceeds in Harvey Christmas Cash, which can be used to purchase merchandise from participating retail stores in the Harvey area. These 0 percent interest loans are repaid in cash over a nine-month period. Merchants who accept Christmas Cash from customers redeem it for official money at the bank and pay a 5 percent redemption fee. Thus, when a merchant brings one hundred dollars worth of Christmas Cash to the bank, he or she receives ninety-five dollars in official money. In effect, the merchant pays the bank a fee of 5 percent in return for becoming a preferred supplier of goods to a particular group of shoppers (the loan recipients).

The primary benefit of a program of this type is that it keeps people's spending power in the local community. By substituting for official money that can be spent anywhere a type of money that can only be spent locally, local merchants gain an advantage in attracting the shopping dollars of the borrowers.

The following lists summarize the benefits of such a program to the various participants.

The bank gets:

- a $5 processing fee for each loan application,
- a 5% redemption fee on the total amount loaned (which is the total amount of Christmas Cash issued),
- new loan customers,
- merchant traffic into the bank,
- indirect benefits of helping its local business customers prosper, and
- the goodwill of the community.

The merchant gets:

- increased customer traffic and
- increased sales (at the cost of an effective 5% discount).

The customer/borrower gets:

- an interest-free loan.

The bank reports that the program, which has been operating since 1991, "has been a pretty good program to help keep money in our town."[1]

The Harvey example is quite unique in that the bank is the issuer, not the merchant, and the cash payment by the recipient for the currency comes after the fact rather than prior to the issuance. Again, the Christmas Cash does not generally circulate but moves rather quickly from bank to borrower to merchant and back to the bank.

be used as working capital, or it may be allocated to a special purpose. In the case of Deli Dollars, it was used to pay the expense of moving the Deli. In any event, it should be used in a way that enhances the ability of the business to deliver the goods or services promised by the note.

In the case of actual traveler's checks, the cash is invested in income-producing assets, probably government and corporate securities and perhaps commercial real estate. This provides the main source of profit for the companies that issue traveler's checks. Local issuers can do the same but will more likely deposit the money in an escrow account at a local bank, where it might be invested in such things as CDs (certificates of deposit). In any case, the money will earn an income return. This cash income can then be used to support the project by paying its development and/or overhead expenses. Any surplus earnings might be allocated to charitable or community improvement projects.

The question is often asked, Why not invest that money locally in productive enterprises that will enhance the local economy instead of giving it over to governments, banks, or megacorporations to use elsewhere? This is a very good question, and answering it requires a discussion of investment theory and practice that is beyond the scope of this present work. Suffice it to say that the primary objectives in investing such a redemption fund are (1) preservation of capital and (2) liquidity. The cash paid into a redemption fund should be invested in such a way as to assure that the value of the fund does not decline and that the investments can be liquidated as needed to meet redemption demands. To the extent that these objectives can be met, it would be most beneficial to invest the cash funds in local enterprises.

COMMODITY-, MERCHANDISE-, OR SERVICE-BASED CURRENCIES — TRUE SUPPLEMENTARY CURRENCIES

Banks issue currency (bank credit) on the basis of promissory notes signed by their customers (borrowers). These notes may be secured or unsecured. A secured loan has specific assets named as collateral, such as a car or a house. An unsecured note has no specific collateral assets pledged to assure repayment of the loan. In the former case, if the borrower fails to make the payments as specified in the loan agreement, the bank can seize the collateral. Thus, cars are sometimes "repossessed," and houses are "foreclosed." So the bank, in actuality, *monetizes* your promise to repay. Or, to put it another way, the bank monetizes the value of your assets in the case of a secured loan, or the value of your labor and skills if your note is unsecured.

A true supplementary currency is one that is issued on the basis of the transfer of real value, that is, goods and services. Typically, it is issued by the buyer of goods or services at the time of purchase, and backed by his or her promise to redeem it by accepting it back as payment for goods or services she or he sells.

This kind of exchange is usually accomplished in conjunction with an agent acting on behalf of a group of traders who have agreed to cooperate with one another in the process. The currency involved can be thought of as an IOU issued in recognition of the delivery of some valuable good or service; however, it is not a personal IOU but a community IOU supported by the members collectively. Mutual credit systems, LETS, and commercial trade exchanges all provide supplementary exchange media or currency. They are not dependent on the payment of official money. Thus, they add to the total supply of exchange media in circulation, supplementing the supply of official money. They actually allow the members of the association to collectively *monetize the value contained in the labor or goods exchanged.* They do not require the involvement of any government, bank, or ordinary financial institution.

If you give me a ten-dollar Federal Reserve note and I write an IOU and give it to you in return, we have not increased the total supply of money. But if you give me ten dollars worth of fresh vegetables and I give you my IOU in return, we have potentially increased the supply of money by ten dollars—not official money, but our own money, my IOU. If you allow me to redeem my IOU by delivering goods and services instead of official money, we need never be dependent on the supply of official money, the policies of the Federal Reserve system, or the lending practices of the banks.

Funded vs. Nonfunded Currencies and Exchange Systems   Most of the community currency and credit systems discussed thus far have been nonfunded. Nonfunded currencies are characterized as follows:

1. A nonfunded currency is one that is issued on the basis of some exchange transaction or agreement. No assets are held as "cover" by the issuing agency, and the currency is therefore not redeemable, except, of course, in the market, for goods and services.
2. The currency may be issued on the basis of the transfer of value between two parties, one of which (the buyer) is authorized to issue such currency under an agreement with others willing to accept it as payment.[1]
3. The "backing" for a nonfunded currency is simply the formal or implied commitment of the buyer to deliver equal value to someone at some future time in return for the currency that the buyer has created and issued. Thus, she or he "redeems" it by making a sale.
4. As already pointed out, there must be a limit to the amount of currency that each individual party to the agreement can issue. This limit should be determined by the person's ability to produce, and his or her willingness to deliver valuable goods and services to the community. Experience indicates that the limit should not exceed a value equivalent to his or her normal sales volume within a two- or three-month period.

In contrast, the essential features of a funded currency or credit system are as follows:

1. A funded currency is one that is issued on the basis of the transfer to the issuing agency of some valuable assets held as "cover" or "reserves."
2. These assets are held by the issuing agency against future redemption of the currency. The currency may be redeemable on demand of the holder, or its redemption may be restricted in some way. For example, it may be redeemable only at certain times, or under certain specified conditions, and/or only by certain specified classes of individuals or groups.
3. The assets that are accepted can be in most any form; however, some assets serve the purpose better than others. Historically, gold and silver have often served this purpose, along with government bonds and other securities, or even other currencies. Some "third world" countries use United States dollars as reserves for their national currencies.
4. It is best to use assets that represent value on the way to market or assets that can be easily liquidated in fractional amounts. Thus, the use of real estate or capital equipment is not recommended, unless the rate of redemption is restricted to conform to the productivity or rate of liquidation of such assets in the normal course of business.
5. One of the usual errors that banks and governments have made is to issue more currency notes than the value of the assets held. This is known as "fractional reserve banking," which should be avoided.
6. If a currency is made redeemable, it should be backed 100 percent by the assets in which it is to be redeemed. In other words, to be "fully funded," the amount of currency issued must not exceed the value of the assets held for redemption.
7. If the value of the assets held should decline in terms of some other currency or value measure, the value of the currency itself would decline in relation to that same measure.
8. If some official currency, such as the United States dollar or securities denominated in dollars, is used as backing (reserves) for a funded local currency, then the buying power of the local currency will fluctuate in accordance with the buying power of the official currency.

Using Official Money as Reserves. One of the simplest and most straightforward approaches to issuing a community currency is simply to sell it for official currency. This would be a cash-based currency, such as the gift certificate type or the traveler's check type discussed above. Again, while such a currency can be useful for the purpose of funding community improvement projects and promoting "buy local" initiatives, the level of empowerment and independence that it provides is minimal in comparison with community currencies that are "backed" by people's own labor, resources, and material goods.

The main advantage of a cash-based community currency is that it is easier to establish credibility for it and gain its acceptance by the general community. The primary disadvantage is that such a currency, which requires official money for its existence, will always be dependent on, and limited by, the policies and actions of the monetary authorities that determine its supply and cost.

Using Inventories as Reserves. A better way of issuing a funded currency would be to use the value of inventories as the basis of issue. This approach provides the security of real-value backing while allowing issuance on the basis of local production, cutting the dependence on the availability of official money. Since inventories must be maintained anyway as part of the process of doing business, why not use the value of those inventories to provide a sound medium of exchange? The purpose could be served by most any kind of inventories, including consumer goods in retail shops, manufactured goods in warehouses, even crops in the field, but some types of inventories are more advantageous than others. Basic commodities in inventory would, perhaps, provide the best basis of issue, since they provide the foundational inputs for subsequent stages of production, and they provide as well an early indicator of the value of manufactured goods on the way to market. They would provide a medium of exchange grounded in reality and subject to all the natural limitations of the physical commodities that the chosen exchange medium represents. The supply of money thus created could become more or less self-regulating, expanding and contracting in step with changes in the supplies of goods available for purchase.

One might envision such a currency being issued through a network of local merchant banks or business associations. The system would be decentralized, locally controlled, open, and subject to audit by a public service, nongovernmental agency. "Grain banks" have often been used in lesser developed countries. An example of a funded currency based on deposits of grain will be presented in chapter 20.

Historical Examples of True Community Currencies and Their Basis of Issue   We have examined in this and in previous chapters many truly supplementary currencies. The table in figure 14.6 provides a summary list of several historical examples of private and community currencies, together with their bases of issue and means of issuance into circulation.

Type	Issuer	Basis of Issue	How Issued
Merchandise notes or bonds	Retail merchants	Merchandise inventory	Paid to suppliers, contractors, employees
Tax anticipation warrants	Municipal governments	Anticipated tax revenues	Paid to suppliers, contractors, employees
Transportation coupons/notes	Transportation companies	Capacity for providing transportation	Paid to suppliers, contractors, employees services
Utility notes	Utility companies	Capacity for providing utility services	Paid to suppliers, contractors, employees
Manufacturer's notes	Manufacturing companies	Inventory of manufactured goods	Paid to suppliers, contractors, employees
Farm produce certificates	Farmers, in association or individually	Farm produce either in the field or in a warehouse	Paid to suppliers, contractors, employees
Clearinghouse certificates	Clearing houses	Members; credit, secured by financial assets	Paid to other members to settle clearing imbalances

Figure 14.6. Historical examples of true community currencies and their basis of issue.

Chapter 15

⌐

A Note on Interest

There was probably no other person in the whole country who had medi-
tated so much on the question of interest. Maragaya's mind was full of it.
Night and day he sat and brooded over it. The more he thought of it the
more it seemed to him the greatest wonder of creation. It combined in it the
mystery of birth and multiplication. Otherwise how could you account for
the fact that a hundred rupees in a savings bank became one hundred
and twenty in course of time? It was something like the ripening corn.
Every rupee, Maragaya felt, contained in it the seed of another rupee,
and that seed in it another seed and so on and on to infinity. It was some-
thing like the firmament, endless stars and within each star an endless
firmament and within each a further endless. . . . It bordered on mystic
perception. It gave him the feeling of being part of an infinite existence.

—R. K. NARAYAN, *THE FINANCIAL EXPERT*

THE PRESENT OFFICIAL MONETARY REGIME is founded on the charging of interest, which, as previous chapters have shown, creates an instability in the system and leads to economic inequities. Most of what today is called "interest" is actually usury. Three of the world's great religious traditions, Judaism, Christianity, and Islam, all have prohibitions against the practice of usury. Of these, only Islam today makes much of an issue of it, though the current opposition seems generally ineffective and appears not to be taken very seriously except in the more fundamentalist circles.

My arguments against usury and interest are not religious or ideological, but economic and practical. Religious prohibitions do not provide a rational basis for evaluating the pros and cons of a particular practice. I have shown in earlier chapters that the foundation of our monetary system on interest-bearing debt creates a cancerous growth in debt. That, in turn, leads to a "growth imperative" for the entire economy, which causes both ecological devastation and social decay.[1] I believe that it would be generally beneficial if we would work toward economic and financial arrangements in which interest is minimized. But most important, it is essential that we establish an exchange (monetary) system that avoids the imposition of interest on the medium of exchange at its creation. I believe, however, that this might be done without resorting to legal prohibitions. The objective of economic equity can be achieved by means of better monetary and financial arrangements that are voluntarily applied.

Interest or Usury?

The word *usury* has become taboo in our culture, particularly in academic and financial circles It is almost never mentioned in the media anymore. But if we are to remedy the obvious inequities in the economy and discover a sustainable way of life, it is vital that we reexamine this concept and understand its economic and social impact. We need to know how it affects people in their daily lives—their ability to meet basic needs, to provide for their families, to enjoy lives that fulfill their creative potential. Those who call themselves economists have, for the most part, been derelict in their duty to provide such analysis. The few who have ventured onto this path have been ignored, repressed, and even vilified.

Still, there is plenty of useful material available if one is willing to look for it. There seems to be no disagreement that the effects of usury are, indeed, profound. The argument, rather, centers on the precise nature of those effects and whether they are, in total, good or evil. My study of the matter has convinced me that the evolution of money during the 20th century, including the incorporation of usury into its creation in the form of bank credit money, has placed an engine of destruction in our midst. Now, money must be borrowed into circulation. That, by itself, is not necessarily a problem. What *is* a problem is that banks charge interest on these debts. The interest (usury) feature of bank credit money causes debt to grow exponentially. This, in turn, puts pressure on the economy to grow exponentially as well, which of course is impossible in the long run. Among the consequences of this cancerous growth of debt are the voracious consumption of natural resources, the production of superfluous goods, destructive competition for markets and scarce money, and the maldistribution of wealth.[2]

But what is usury, and how does it differ from interest? Is there really a difference, or is the word *interest* simply a euphemism? Is one benign and the other malevolent? How can we distinguish between them?

Sidney Homer provides some clues in his book *A History of Interest Rates*. He points out that both words, *usury* and *interest,* are derived from Latin:

> The Latin word *usura* means the "use" of anything, in this case, the use of borrowed capital; hence usury was the price paid for the use of money. The Latin verb *intereo* means "to be lost." A substantive form, *interisse,* developed into the modern term "interest." Interest was not profit but loss. Compensation for loans was not licit if it was a gain to the lender, but became licit if the compensation was not a net gain but reimbursement for loss or expense.[3]

It is undeniable that there *are* costs associated with the act of lending. In historic times, these might have included the cost of transporting and safeguarding the gold or silver money, the cost of drafting and legally registering the loan contract, and the cost of insuring against default. In modern times, there are similar "loan placement" expenses. It is entirely reasonable and equitable that the borrower should be asked to bear these costs. Thus, interest became an allowable exception under Canon law, since it was seen, not as profit, but as compensation for loss or expense.

It is not surprising that self-serving lenders would seek to justify *all* their charges as interest to avoid being labeled usurers and incurring sanctions under law. This accounts for the gradual confusion between the two terms, confusion that we can assume was not only welcomed but fostered by money lenders and bankers. Over time, people came to understand usury not as "interest" itself but only an *excessive* rate of interest, making the distinction appear to be quantitative rather than qualitative.

Throughout the 20th century, the influence of established religion has steadily declined. At the same time, the rise of modernism opened the way for formerly forbidden practices to be sold to the public as scientific and rational. Usury, for example, could be rationalized. Although there has never been an adequate scientific case made to support the practice of usury, it has become generally accepted. Indeed, in the orthodox body of economic thought it is now considered to be a necessary element in the allocation of material resources among competing uses in the economy and an important lever in the management of the monetary system.

The principle of the "time value of money" is now an unquestioned axiom of business and economics, and almost everyone supports the pretense that any rational "economic man" would prefer a sum of money now to the same sum of money later. But this applies only in situations where money can command an interest return, and an interest return is possible only when there is no free market for money. The matter becomes more clear if we look at real values rather than monetary values. For example, a person can eat only so much at one time. Once your hunger is satisfied, would you prefer more food now or more food later? The answer is obvious. Your concern is not just to satisfy your present need for food but also to satisfy your future need. Why should money be any different? You would like to save money that is surplus to your present needs in order to be able to satisfy your future needs. The additional incentive of interest is obviously unnecessary. Does that mean that we must forego any possibility of capital growth when we save? Not at all. A thorough treatment of investment philosophy is beyond the scope of this book, but we can say that the answer lies in the general direction of equity investment or ownership shares.[4] Silvio Gesell's Robinson Crusoe vignette, adapted in the accompanying sidebar, provides, I think, a convincing argument against the imposition of interest on loans.

Toward Better Forms of Exchange

We can take a giant step toward economic equity and general prosperity by designing complementary currency systems that avoid the imposition of interest. It is one thing for holders of already created money which they have earned, to ask for interest on that part of their earnings they wish to "save." It is quite another thing to charge interest on newly created money, such as debit balances in a mutual credit system. If we can avoid the latter, the former will gradually wither away as well.

Given our cultural conditioning and the prevailing practice within the conventional systems of money and finance, there may be a tendency to want to impose a levy or charge on debit balances, these balances being thought of as loans to the "debitor" and the levy representing an interest charge. Considering what has been said above, it is reasonable for us to reconsider those attitudes and practices.

What about Charges on Credit Balances?

In accordance with the rationale put forth by Silvio Gesell, some have argued that, in order to keep an exchange system vital, a periodic levy should be made on credit (positive) balances. This kind of charge, sometimes called "negative interest," is known as "demurrage."[5] The argument is that demurrage would encourage the spending, and discourage the holding or saving, of currency or credit balances, thus ensuring the lively flow of "money" (credits) through the system. That is not to say that saving is "bad" but rather that it should be accomplished using some other medium than the exchange medium.[6]

The imposition of levies on either debit or credit balances, or both, will undoubtedly promote their use as an exchange medium, deter their use as a savings/investment medium, and prevent stagnation. However, such levies may have a negative effect on the other primary objectives of reciprocity and equity.

The idea of reciprocity is that the value received by a trader should be equivalent to the value that he or she delivered. The discriminatory imposition of a levy on only one or the other type of balance, debit or credit, upsets this ideal. The case for imposing levies on balances may be a strong one. However, since everyone benefits from the operation of the system, if a levy is imposed on balances, both debit balances and credit balances should be charged at equal rates.

A Story of Robinson Crusoe: An Introduction to the Theory of Interest

by Silvio Gesell[1]

Robinson Crusoe, as is well known, built his house, from motives of health, on the south side of the mountain, whereas his crops grew on the damp but fruitful northern slopes. He was therefore obliged to carry his harvests over the mountain. To eliminate this labor he decided to construct a canal around the mountain. The time required for this enterprise, which, to avoid silting, would have to be carried out without interruption, he estimated at three years.

He slaughtered some pigs, and cured their flesh with salt; he filled a deep trench with wheat, covering it carefully with earth. He tanned a dozen buckskins for suits and nailed them up in a chest, enclosing also the stink glands of a skunk as a precaution against moths. In short, he provided amply, and as he thought, wisely, for the coming three years.

As he sat calculating for the last time whether his "capital" was sufficient for the projected undertaking, he was startled by the approach of a stranger, obviously the survivor of a shipwreck.

"Hallo, Crusoe!" shouted the stranger as he approached, "my ship has gone down, but I like your island and intend to settle here. Will you help me with some provisions until I have brought a field into cultivation and harvested my first crops?"

At these words, Crusoe's thoughts flew from his provisions to the possibility of interest and the attractions of life as a gentleman of independent means. He hastened to answer "yes."

"That's splendid!" replied the stranger, "but I must say at once that I shall pay no interest. I would prefer to keep myself alive by hunting and fishing, for my religion forbids me to pay, or to receive, interest."

ROBINSON CRUSOE: An admirable religion! But from what motive do you expect me to advance you provisions from my stores if you pay me no interest?

STRANGER: From pure egoism, my dear fellow, from your self-interest rightly understood. Because you gain, and gain enormously.

RC: That, stranger, you have yet to prove. I confess that I can see no advantage in lending you my provisions free of interest.

S: I shall prove it in black and white, and if you can follow my proof, you will agree to loan without interest, and thank me into the bargain. I need, first of all, clothes, for, as you see, I am naked. Have you a supply of clothes?

RC: That chest is packed with buckskin suits.

S: My dear Crusoe! I had more respect for your intelligence. Just fancy nailing up clothes for three years in a chest—buckskins, the favorite diet of moths! And buckskins must be kept aired and rubbed with grease, otherwise they become hard and brittle.

RC: That is true, but I have no choice in the matter. They would be no safer in my clothes cupboard—less safe, indeed, for it is infested by rats and mice as well as by moths.

S: The mice will get them in any case. Look how they have already started to gnaw their way in!

RC: Confound the brutes! I am helpless against them.

S: What! A human being helpless against mice! I will show you how to protect yourself against rats and mice and moths, against thieves and brittleness, dust and mildew. Lend me those clothes for one, two or three years, and I will agree to make you new clothes as soon as you require them. You will receive as many suits as you have lent me, and the new suits will be far superior to those you would have taken from this chest. Nor will you regret the absence of the particular perfume you have employed! Do you agree?

RC: Yes, stranger, I agree to lend you the chest of clothes; I see that in this case, the loan, even without interest, is to my advantage.

S: Now show me your wheat; I need some for bread and seed.

RC: It is buried in this mound.

S: Wheat buried for three years! What about mildew and beetles?

RC: I have thought about them and considered every other possibility, but this is the best I can do.

S: Just bend down a moment. Observe the beetle crawling on the surface of the mound. Note the garbage and the spreading patch of mildew. It is high time to take out and air the wheat.

RC: This capital will be my ruin! If I only could find some method of protecting myself against the thousand destructive forces of nature!

S: Let me tell you, Crusoe, how we manage at home. We build a dry and airy shed and shake out the wheat on a boarded floor. Every three weeks the whole mass is turned over with wooden shovels. We also keep a number of cats; we set mouse traps and insure against fire. In this way we keep the annual depreciation down to ten percent.

RC: But the labor and expense!

S: Exactly! You shrink from the labor and expense. In that case you have another course. Lend me your wheat and I shall replace it pound for pound, sack for sack, with fresh wheat from my harvest. You thus save the labor of building a shed and turning over the wheat; you need feed no cats, you avoid the loss of weight, and instead of mouldy rubbish, you will have fresh nutritious wheat.

RC: With all my heart, I accept your proposal.

S: That is you will lend me your wheat free of interest?

RC: Certainly; without interest and with my best thanks.

S: But I can only use part of the wheat, I do not need it all.

RC: Suppose I give you the whole store with the understanding that for every ten sacks lent you give me back nine sacks?

S: I must decline your offer, for it would mean interest—not indeed positive, but negative interest. The receiver, not the giver of the loan would be a capitalist, and my religion does not permit usury; even negative interest is forbidden. I propose therefore the following agreement. Entrust me with the supervision of your wheat, the construction of the shed, and whatever else is necessary. In return, you can pay me, annually, from every ten sacks two sacks as wages.

RC: It makes no difference to me whether your service comes under the heading of usury or labor. The agreement is, then, that I give you ten sacks and you give me back eight sacks?

S: But I need other articles, a plough, a cart and tools. Do you consent to lend them, also, without interest? I promise to return everything in perfect order, a new spade for a new spade, a new, un-rusted, chain for a new chain, and so forth.

RC: Of course I consent. All I have at present from my stores is work. Lately the river overflowed and flooded the shed, covering everything with mud. Then a storm blew off the roof and everything was damaged by rain. Now we have drought, and the wind is blowing in sand and dust. Rust, decay, breakage, drought, light, darkness, dry-rot, ants, keep up a never-ending attack. We can congratulate ourselves here upon having, at least, no thieves and incendiaries. I am delighted that, by means of a loan, I can now store my belongings without expense, labor, loss or vexation, until I need them later.

S: That is, you now see the advantage you gain by lending me your provisions free of interest?

RC: Of course I do. But the question now occurs to me, why do similar stores of provisions at home bring their possessors interest?

S: The explanation lies in money which is there the medium of such transactions.

RC: What? The cause of interest lies in money? That is impossible. . . .

S: . . . From their nature and destination your goods are the purest form of what is usually called capital. I challenge you to take up the position of a capitalist towards me. I need your stuff. No worker ever appeared before a capitalist as naked as I stand before you. Never has there been so clear an illustration of the relation between the owner of capital and the individual in need of capital. And now make the attempt to exact interest! Shall we begin our bargaining again from the beginning?

RC: I surrender! Rats, moths and rust have broken my power as a capitalist. But tell me, what is your explanation of interest?

S: The explanation is simple enough. If there were a monetary system on this island and I, as a shipwrecked traveler, needed a loan, I would have to apply to a money-lender for money to buy the things which you have just lent me without interest. But a money-lender has not to worry about rats, moths, rust and roof-repairing, so I could not have taken up the position towards him that I have taken up towards you. The loss inseparable from the ownership of goods (there is a dog running off with one of your—or rather my—buckskins!) is borne, not by money-lenders, but by those who have to store the goods. The money-lender is free from such cares and is unmoved by the ingenious arguments which found the joints in your armor. You did not nail up your chest of buckskins when I refused to pay interest; the nature of your capital made you willing to continue the negotiations. Not so the money capitalist; he would bang the door of his strong-room before my face if I announced that I would pay no interest. Yet, I do not need the money itself, I only need money to buy buckskins. The buckskins you give me without interest; but upon the money to buy buckskins I must pay interest!

RC: Then the cause of interest is to be sought in money? And Marx is wrong?

S: Of course Marx is wrong. He underestimated the importance of money, the nervous system of economic life, so it is not surprising that he went wrong on other things of fundamental importance. Like all his disciples he made the mistake of excluding money from the scope of his inquiry. He was fascinated by the shining metal disks, otherwise he could never have used the following words: "Gold and silver are not by nature money, but money is by nature gold and silver, witness the coincidence of their natural properties with its functions."

RC: Practice certainly does not agree with Marx's theory—that has been clearly proved by our negotiations. Money is for Marx only a medium of exchange; but money does more, it seems, than "merely pay the price of the goods it purchases." When the borrower refuses to pay interest, the banker can bang the door of his safe without experiencing any of the cares which beset the owner of goods (capital)—that is the root of the matter.

S: Rats, moths and rust are powerful logicians! A single hour of economic practice has taught you more than years of study of the text-books.

Chapter 16

~

Medium of Exchange or Savings Medium?

If the purpose of money is exchange, it should be spent; if the purpose is saving, it should be held.

—WALTER ZANDER

As PREVIOUSLY DISCUSSED, the primary problem to be overcome in facilitating trade is the "barter limitation": the fact that the buyer may not have anything the seller wants. By creating an intermediary "medium of exchange," for example, money or trade credits, a "space" is created within which the seller may go ahead and supply the buyer's need anyway and then proceed to find a supplier for his or her own needs, using money or trade credits to pay for whatever is eventually bought. This is a "space" in time, but, more important, it is interpersonal, a matter of finding someone in the market who is able to supply one's particular needs or wants. In other words, a medium of exchange provides some slack within which people can find one another so that all can have their needs satisfied.

Conflicting Roles of Money

A community currency is intended to provide a medium of exchange that is complementary to official government and central bank currencies. Its primary function is to enable the exchange of goods and services, that is, buying and selling. Another important function of "old-fashioned money" was to provide a way for people to save their current surplus value for use later on. But if the purpose of money is exchange, it should be spent; if the purpose is saving, it should be held. These are mutually contradictory objectives that we must find a way to separate.

Saving and Investment

When economists speak of money being a "store of value," they are speaking metaphorically. Since value is an abstract concept and not a physical quantity, it cannot really be stored. Cabbages can be stored, wheat can be stored, building materials can be stored, metals can be stored, but each, of course, is subject to some degree of spoilage or deterioration over time. The primary problem to be solved by storage is the asynchrony of needs and supplies. The very idea of storage is based on the desire to match present supplies with future needs. We save the extra food from today's meal to satisfy tomorrow's hunger. We put aside the extra food from the garden in summer to satisfy our hunger next winter when the garden will not be producing. Similarly, we save during our productive years so that we can have a livelihood during our retirement years. But unlike our storage of food from the garden, which we do directly, our saving for retirement we do socially. Saving, in financial terms, must involve other people. The way we save value is by letting other people use it, with the expectation that they will return value to us later.

Ultimately, at any point in time, nonproducers, such as young children and retirees, depend on current producers for the satisfaction of their material needs and desires. The mechanisms by which nonproducer needs are met are varied and often complex, based on factors such as cultural values, ethics, social norms, legal statutes, and financial agreements. In our retirement years, for example, we depend mainly on two basic arrangements: (1) legislated, involuntary redistribution of wealth by governments in the form of such programs as FICA taxes and Social Security benefits and welfare, and (2) contractual agreements of a form usually called "investments," which consist of such financial instruments as pensions, annuities, insurance, stocks, bonds, mutual fund shares, bank deposits, and so on.

Both legislated programs and investments provide the recipient with a "claim" against the collective current and/or future production. The question as to which claims may or may not be "legitimate" is, of course, always open to debate and disagreement, and the question of which claims may or may not be honored is always a matter of concern. The satisfaction of any claim always depends on the ability and willingness of those who are asked to bear its burden.

How Do We Save?

Most people have experience with bank accounts of some sort. It is all but impossible to function today without having at least a checking account, and most people have a savings account as well. What is the difference between a checking account and a savings account? While the distinctions have become quite blurred in recent times, it is useful to describe them according to their original purposes and functions. The first thing that one must understand is that when you deposit money in a bank, the bank does not simply lock it up in a vault and leave it there waiting for you to come and claim it; *the bank lends that money out.* Thus, your savings are "invested" by the bank, perhaps as a loan to a local business that needs additional capital to expand or perhaps as a mortgage on a house that your neighbor has bought.

In banking terms, funds deposited in a checking account are known as "demand deposits": they are subject to immediate withdrawal or transfer at your request (which you may do by writing a check). As such, the bank, in its role as depository, has only limited opportunity to lend out your funds. It must keep them "liquid" just in case you need them. The bank may hold a large portion of total demand deposits as cash or in short-term loans. Funds deposited in savings accounts, on the other hand, are expected to remain on deposit for a longer period of time, making them available for longer-term investments. While you may be allowed to withdraw funds from your savings account anytime you wish, there is the expectation that few depositors will want to do so. Further, the bank may have the option of delaying payment if too many people ask for their money all at once. The now popular CDs (certificates of deposit) provide a clear example of how banks try to match the term of savings deposits more closely to the terms of the loans they make. With a CD, you agree to leave your money on deposit for a specific period of time, which may be six months, a year, three years, or longer.

"Capital formation" is the process of creating the means of production, including the creation of new businesses or the expansion and improvement of existing ones. It includes construction of buildings, improvement of land, production of tools and equipment, and other expenditures that take a long period of time to recover (through the sale of consumer products or services). The financing of capital formation is accomplished through the use of people's savings. So we see that, as stated above, saving is a social process. Your current surplus (savings) is, ideally, allocated to others who will use it productively (for capital formation) so that the products you need will be there when you need them.

Preventing Stagnation in Mutual Credit Systems

To repeat, the primary purpose of a mutual credit or currency system is to provide a medium of exchange. One problem that may arise in any system of exchange, and that is worthy of special attention, is the stagnation of circulation. In a mutual credit system, stagnation takes the form of idle balances, either debit or credit. Those holding *debit* balances have bought more than they have sold. If such an account is idle, that member, in effect, is not honoring her or his commitment to the members of the system. Having received value, she or he is "committed" to deliver like value. Although there may be no specified time limit for honoring such a commitment, there is the expectation that a continuing effort will be made to move the account balance back toward zero. Some activity in earning credits shows "good faith" and indicates that a member is willing and able to provide something that the community needs or wants. If a member does develop a chronic debit balance, however, some action needs to be taken.

In keeping with the basic principles of a local, limited, personal, and convivial system, chronic debit balances should not be dealt with in a punitive fashion. A mutual credit system is designed to be friendly and helpful rather than dominating and exploitative. A chronic debit balance may indicate that a member is having some kind of personal trouble, in which case fellow members would probably want to help in some way. Perhaps that member has a spending addiction or limited abilities. Maybe she needs to improve the quality of the products or services she provides, or perhaps she needs to acquire some new skill to provide something the community needs. In a personal, local system, these matters can be handled in a helpful way by those closest to the problem, rather than impersonally and coercively by distant and unresponsive bureaucracies.

Those holding *credit* balances in a mutual credit system, on the other hand, have sold more than they have bought. If an account with a credit balance is idle, that member, in effect, is not demanding from the system value that is due him or her. Having delivered value, such a member is entitled to receive like value. Although there may be no specified time limit within which credits must be spent, the expectation is that credits will be spent, not saved. Saving credits has the effect of preventing, to some extent, those with debit balances from selling enough to get their account balances back to zero.

Current Account vs. Capital Account

With that understanding of the exchange versus saving functions, we can now consider a possible approach to dealing with the problem of idle balances in a mutual credit system. Each person might have two accounts, one a "demand" or "current" account and the other a "capital" or "savings/loan" account. The current account would be the normal "medium of exchange" account, while the capital account would provide a way for members to save surplus credits. The membership agreement would limit not only the amount of a member's debit balance but also the amount of a credit balance that could be maintained in the current or demand account. At the end of an accounting period, any amount in excess of the limit would be transferred to the capital account.

Mutual Credit Loans: An Example

As an example suppose that, at the end of the quarter, Betty has a credit balance of 900, but the maximum that may be carried over to the next period is 500. She must then find someone who needs the remaining 400 credits and make a private deal with that member, or she might "deposit" her excess credits in her capital account and the loan committee would invest them for her.

Suppose, too, that Gary wants to acquire enough credits to hire George to help him build a house. They agree on a price of 2,000 credits. But since the debit limit on all current accounts is, say, 500, Gary must "borrow" the remaining 1,500. He could make a deal with Betty, and maybe two or three other members, to use their excess credits for some specified period of time. During that time, of course, Betty would not be able to use those credits herself. Alternatively, Gary could go to the loan committee and request a loan of 1,500 credits. The loan committee would pool the savings of enough of its members to make the loan.

Anyone who desires to "save" surplus credits would have to find some suitable investment medium for accomplishing the storage of his or her value. She or he could do so independently or allow the excess credits to be automatically transferred to his or her capital account, to be invested by a loan committee.

On the other side of the equation, a member who wants long-term financing for any purpose would have to find someone willing to assign his or her surplus credits for a specified period of time. Alternatively, she or he could apply to the loan committee for a loan, which would be made from the collective savings of the membership. An outstanding loan would be represented on the books by a negative balance in that member's capital account. So what I am proposing here is the creation of a capital market alongside the mutual credit exchange, the exchange function being served by the mutual credit system and the saving/capital formation function being served by a kind of credit union that takes deposits and makes loans in local credits or currency.

Interest Revisited

This ability to save and lend surplus credits again raises questions about that old bugaboo, interest. Is preservation of capital in itself sufficient reward for saving? Given what we have seen regarding the destructive effects of usury, I would suggest that both savings deposits and loans be made interest-free. It can be expected, however, that in the aggregate some losses from defaulted loans will be inevitable. These can easily be handled by imposing a small insurance fee on all loans.

It may be argued that, if the local currency unit is equivalent to the official unit, for instance the dollar, savers would incur a loss as the official currency unit depreciates, unless they receive interest on their savings. This is a valid argument, but the problem might be handled by periodically adjusting for inflation both savings account balances and loan balances. This would solve the equity problem while still keeping the system in balance.

There have been a number of historical attempts to establish an interest-free system of saving and lending. The most notable and successful current example is a Swedish system called JAK. JAK stands for the Swedish words *Jord, Arbete, Kapital*—land, labor, capital in English. Founded as a cooperative savings and loan association in 1965, JAK was officially recognized as a bank by the Swedish government in 1997. Official bank status provides JAK members with the same deposit guarantees as with any other bank, and the additional security of regulatory oversight. The current members number some twenty thousand. They are serviced by eighty local representatives and twenty-five local offices scattered throughout Sweden. JAK's bank deposits in July 1999 totaled about SEK 440 million ($55 million), and outstanding loans were about SEK 397 million ($50 million).

The procedures of this interest-free banking are based on the expectation that members will be both savers and borrowers, with those two needs differing over time. In brief, members accumulate "savings points" based on the amount and duration of their savings. The amount of savings points accumulated, in turn, determines the amount that may be borrowed and the duration of the loan. There are, of course administrative expenses associated with the operation of this bank, just as any other. These costs are covered by the imposition of various fees on the borrowers. There is a "loan fee calculated at 3.5 percent of the loan amount and 1 percent of the loan amount for each repayment year." According to the Swedish Consumer Services Authority (Konsumentverket), these fees would compare to an effective rate of interest on conventional bank loans of 3 percent for a ten-year loan of SEK 100,000 (about $12,500). That rate is considerably less than normal bank rates.[1]

Basis of Issue Revisited

The creation of exchange media should be based on the exchange of current supplies of goods and services. It is a well-established principle of sound banking that "loans" for long-term assets should not be used as the basis for creating new money; funds for creating those assets should come out of "savings," which means money *that has already been created* but not spent on current consumption. Having both a "current" account and a "capital" account is a way of separating the "medium of exchange" from the "store of value." It is as easy as transferring deposits from your checking account to your savings account, or writing a check to buy shares of stock or a mutual fund. Indeed, along with empowering people by allowing them to create their own exchange medium, it is also important to provide some method for saving credits. In doing all this it is still important to follow sound banking practices. Since these practices have been largely forgotten and abandoned by the established monetary and financial institutions, new systems must be built from the ground up. These systems should be based on the principles of equity (justice), conviviality (they should be open to all), reciprocity (give as much as you get), and cooperation, and on a clear understanding of the effects of various financial practices.

In either case, whether in a current account or a capital account, a credit balance represents a "claim," and the activity that gives rise to the claim should determine whether it is "current" or "capital." In the current account, a credit is a short-term claim on the market, which is intended only to facilitate trade. In ordinary banking practice, it is a "demand" deposit that the market should be able to satisfy now. So it represents goods and services already there in the market. In the capital account, a credit is a claim against long-lived assets that are not liquid but will produce benefits in the future and bring value into the market gradually over a longer period of time. For example, if the claim has resulted from activity that has produced a building or machine, it will take time for the cost of these to be recovered. This recovery takes place in the normal course of their use in the production and sale of consumable goods.

One of the errors of the present banking establishment is that it has blurred this distinction between savings deposits (time deposits) and demand deposits (checking account deposits) and has issued money on the basis of, not only goods on the way to market, but also goods being taken from the market.[2] Properly, demand deposits represent goods (and services) presently in the market and available for purchase, and savings deposits represent investments in capital goods and durables. Formerly, banks paid no interest on demand deposits, because such deposits had to be kept available for payment of checks drawn on the account. Thus, they could not be invested in longer-term, interest-earning assets. Now, banks are paying interest on demand deposits and giving some savings deposits much the same liquidity as demand deposits. This is a practice that could become troublesome.

PART IV

CURRENCY DESIGN, IMPROVEMENT, AND INNOVATION

In addressing the megacrisis that confronts the world today, it should be clear that decisive changes will need to made in the methods we humans use to distribute political/economic power and allocate material resources. As pointed out earlier, the present dominant structures of money and finance, by their very nature, promote the concentration of power into fewer and fewer hands, increase disparities in the distribution of wealth, channel a huge portion of the earth's resources into wasteful production, and force both social and ecological degradation. The pinnacle of power today is the power to issue money. If that power can be democratized and focused in a direction that gives social and ecological concerns top priority, there may yet be hope for saving the world.

This section is a how-to-do-it guide. It contains a number of innovative proposals for achieving nothing less than world-saving reforms. All these proposals involve the use of community currencies to facilitate trade within local communities, and many of them also contain features for the empowerment of community improvement groups working to serve the common good. These proposals are described mainly in terms of circulating notes or certificates, but, as already stressed, exchange media could also take the form of accounting credits on a ledger. In fact any of the various devices such as notes, checks, smart cards, and debit cards may be used to transfer credits. The proposals described here could also be applied to empowering groups whose members are widely dispersed geographically, using the Internet and our highly developed information and communications infrastructure.

The basis of issuing money has, in times past, been more neutral than at present. Now, with the issuance of money controlled by the central bank/central government nexus, it has become a mechanism by which these centralized powers control the application of human and capital resources, allocating them to projects that are usually self-serving, wasteful of resources, and often downright destructive. Our objective should be to create exchange media issued on the basis of human service and Earth service rather than acquisitiveness and domination.

The exchange media described in this section put control of the exchange process into the hands of the people, giving them more choice over how they apply their energies and resources. The willingness of others in the community to accept the new exchange media in payment for goods and services, especially the necessities of life, does two things: it encourages the application of people's energies and resources to life-sustaining activities, and it provides the community with a medium of exchange that by its very nature is abundant, democratic, and locally controlled.

Any community, at any time, could implement the following model currency systems, with beneficial effects. The descriptions given here are "bare-bones" outlines. The precise details can be tailored to the needs and circumstances of the particular community.

Chapter 17

⌒

Improving Local Currencies, or How to Make a Good Thing Better

An effective community is a process, an ongoing collection of interactions and continuing relationships.

—MICHAEL LINTON

THE LOCAL CURRENCY AND EXCHANGE movement may be the most important development in human liberation since the Magna Carta. It evidences a move toward *economic* freedom that is every bit as important as political and religious freedom. The proliferation of mutual credit systems such as LETS, and local currencies such as Ithaca HOURS, and the "creditos" of South America, demonstrates the intensifying need that people feel for community, satisfaction of basic human needs, and greater control over their own destinies. It provides a hopeful sign that we are not powerless in the face of increasing concentration of money and power and the rapid globalization of capital and markets.

Those pioneers who have dedicated themselves to developing and implementing new prototypes for community currency deserve our deepest gratitude and respect. Nevertheless, there is still much to be done. Just as the early airplanes showed that manned flight was possible, these early exchange systems are demonstrating that the specialization of labor and the equitable exchange of value in the marketplace do not depend on centralized banks and national currencies. Indeed, they are providing a means by which communities can thrive economically and maintain high quality-of-life standards in the face of global competition and capital mobility. As the Wright brothers' early powered airplanes were not the last word in aircraft, so too our current community exchange prototypes are far from optimal. We should expect, and indeed require, refinement and improvement of our local currencies and systems of exchange. This chapter takes a closer look at the most popular models with an eye toward improving their design and implementation.

Gift Exchange vs. Reciprocal Exchange

The market has become the dominant institution in economic exchange, but, as pointed out earlier, market mechanisms are certainly not the only means of exchanging goods and services. An enormous amount of work is being done for which no money is paid, nor is it counted in the economic statistics; and many exchanges do not involve markets or money either. Indeed, the imposition of money into the exchange process can be destructive to the close interpersonal relationships that are necessary to healthy social units such as the family. Besides all the economic activity that goes on within households, a huge amount of goods and services change hands as gifts. I would contend that, in general, the more exchanges we can manage without the use of money and markets, the better. Nonetheless, I am a firm believer in the efficacy of markets in particular situations, provided that the markets are free and competitive and not dominated by any particular trader, company, or group. Markets are excellent mechanisms for allocating scarce resources, since they provide a means of reaching consensus.

Reciprocal exchange is the ideal to be sought within a market realm. We can think of the economy as a game of "put-and-take." Reciprocity demands that each person puts in as much as she or he takes out. In other words, in reciprocal exchange one is expected to give as much as she or he gets. This is an important point to keep in mind when designing community exchange systems.

Although altruism and charitable giving might be built into a local exchange system *as an adjunct,* the essential characteristic of such systems should be *reciprocity.* No one should be made, by virtue of a system's design or defect, an unwitting or unwilling donor to someone else's benefit. **An exchange system that has both equity and integrity must insist on strict reciprocity.** Charity and gift giving should better be left to individual choice.

Money Is an IOU

Although we may not refer to community currencies as money, they perform the same essential function as money and bear the same basic characteristics as money. This goes for credits in a ledger system as well as for circulating paper notes. Previous chapters have emphasized repeatedly *that every piece of money is a credit instrument.* That means it is an IOU. The natural question, then, is, Who owes what to whom? Who or what stands behind the IOU? The answer may not always be obvious. When a community of traders agrees to accept a particular currency, they are making a commitment to stand behind it, that is, to give real value in exchange for it. When others who are not a party to the agreement accept the currency, they are expressing their confidence that the issuers of the IOU will pay what is owed, although the time frame for payment may or may not be precisely specified.

Basis of Issue

Earlier chapters have also stressed the importance of the basis of issue of a currency. We need to know how it first comes into circulation. It is proper that a currency comes into circulation when someone first spends it, that is, when she or he gets real goods or services and the seller accepts the currency as payment. Reciprocity demands that the issuer be willing and able, at some point, to redeem that currency by accepting it as payment for the goods or services that she or he sells.

Mutual Credit and Paper Notes

As shown in chapter 10, there are presently two predominant forms of complementary exchange. These are mutual credit systems such as LETS, which use a ledger of accounts to keep track of exchanges, credits, and obligations; and local currency systems such as Ithaca HOURS, which use circulating paper notes to give people a way of tracking their exchanges. There are many variations on both themes. Some ledger systems that call themselves LETS may, in fact, depart significantly from the original and official LETS procedures and protocols. Likewise, there are many HOUR currencies springing up that correspond generally to the Ithaca model but may differ in procedural details. Further, there is no reason why a mutual credit system cannot use paper notes as well as ledger accounts, and there is no reason why an Ithaca HOUR–type currency system cannot also utilize ledger accounts, checks, and debit cards.

Essential Differences between LETS and HOURS

The essential difference between LETS and HOURS is *not* that LETS uses ledger accounts and HOURS uses paper notes. These are accounting details. The essential difference lies in how the currency is issued and what stands behind it, that is, in *the nature of the agreement*. A LETS is a membership association in which each member has an account. All accounts begin with a balance of zero. When a member sells something to another member, his or her account receives a credit (plus); when a member buys something, his or her account receives a debit (minus). A credit causes an account balance to increase, while a debit causes an account balance to decrease. Accounts are allowed to have negative as well as positive balances. In fact, there can be no positive balances unless some members have negative balances. In such a system of mutual credit, the total of all the credit balances must always equal the total of all the debit balances. What this means is that the amount of value owed by those who have debit balances is always equal to the amount that those with credit balances have delivered and expect to receive in return. This is a system of strict reciprocity. Of course, as in any system, there will always be some who will default on their obligations: they will fail to provide the amount of goods and services they committed themselves to when they incurred debits (by buying). These defaults should be recognized at some point and "written off." In doing so, the amount of debits being written off and an equal amount of credits must be taken off the ledger. What this suggests is the need for the system to have a capital fund or reserve fund, providing a supply of credits that can be used to offset "bad debts." How this fund might be provided will be discussed shortly.

In a mutual credit system, we may think of the "money supply" as being the total amount of debits or credits. Since these are two sides of the same coin, and since debits and credits are always equal, we should count only one side, not both. One of the elegant aspects of a mutual credit system is that the "money supply," within reasonable bounds, adjusts itself automatically in relation to the amount of trading that members wish, or need, to do. There need be no central authority that decides whether the supply of credits should be increased or decreased in order to maintain the market value of the credits. The only thing to be decided is the maximum amount of debit balance that should be allowed on each particular account to minimize the risk of default and the amount of potential loss. In usual practice, account balances remain well below that maximum amount.

The primary role in a mutual credit system is that of the *registrar* or *accountant,* which is strictly nonpolitical. The duties of the registrar are to record the transactions as reported by the members, and to update the members' account balances.

How HOURS Work

Ithaca HOURS, and the many similar HOUR currency systems modeled after it, are paper currency notes that circulate within a local economy. Unlike LETS, Ithaca HOURS is *not* a membership organization. The HOUR notes are put into circulation by the operator of a newspaper called *HOUR Town* (formerly *Ithaca Money*). The notes are delivered to advertisers when they buy an ad in the newspaper. As I understand it, those who advertise in *HOUR Town* informally agree to accept HOURS for at least partial payment but have no obligation to do so.

As mentioned before, it is important to ask, What is the basis of issue, and who or what stands behind the HOUR currency? There is generally a great deal of confusion about currency issuance and the obligations associated with it. It is crucial that we understand how and where the currency originates, how it is placed into circulation, how it will be redeemed, and who will be obliged to redeem it. In the case of Ithaca HOURS, the answers to these questions are not entirely clear. I think that the ambiguity can easily be resolved once we understand a few basic points.

Fish or Fowl?

A local currency must originate somewhere. Somehow the notes must be printed and distributed and their use in exchanging valuable goods and services must be initiated. Now here's the first point: the originator may be either a principal or an agent. What's the difference?

A *principal* is one who initially receives valuable goods and/or services and uses the notes to pay for them. It is the principal who actually *issues* the currency into circulation by buying goods and services with it. The currency notes are a generalized IOU that must be redeemed at some time. Redemption occurs when the notes are accepted by the principal in payment for the goods and services she or he sells. A currency that makes no adequate provision for redemption is bound for trouble. The collapse of innumerable government and bank-issued currencies throughout history testifies to this.

An agent performs a different role. An *agent* does not spend the currency notes into circulation. She or he does not issue the notes but merely *distributes* them to the principals who will issue them (spend them into circulation). The agent, therefore, is not responsible for redeeming the notes. That is the obligation of the principals, the ones who spend them into circulation. The agent also serves as registrar, recording the amount of notes distributed to, and received back from, each principal. As an example, Tucson Traders acts as agent when it prints and distributes Tucson Token notes to its members, who then spend them into circulation.

What we need to know about the *HOUR Town* newspaper is whether it acts as principal (issuer) or agent. If it acts as principal, *HOUR Town* must be willing and able to redeem its entire issue of HOURS by providing an equivalent amount of goods and/or services to those who hold the notes. In this case the HOUR notes represent its IOUs. Is that how *HOUR Town* regards the HOURS it distributes?

HOUR Town does accept HOURS in payment for advertising, but is it prepared (willing and able) to redeem the entire issue in this way? If *HOUR Town* is not so prepared, then there could, and likely will, develop an eventual prob-lem of currency debasement. In other words, of "too much currency chasing too few goods and services," which will show up as HOUR price inflation. In the worst-case scenario, the currency could collapse, which is to say lose the confidence of the community and cease to be widely accepted.

On the other hand, if *HOUR Town* acts only as agent, then the responsibil-ity for redemption of the notes rests on the advertisers who first received them from *HOUR Town*. They are the ones who first issue the notes into circulation by using them to pay for goods and services. Do the advertisers who receive the notes realize that they bear this responsibility? Is there a written agreement? Do they know what they must do in order to fulfill their responsibility? Is there adequate assurance that they will do so?

How might such assurance be obtained? I think that it is not at all neces-sary to be legalistic about obtaining it, but the nature of the agreement should be clear and explicit. One way to achieve this would be to have each advertiser to whom HOURS are distributed sign a simple agreement similar to the one used by Tucson Traders, which was described in chapter 11. This agreement might state:

HOUR Town is acting as agent for its advertisers, and anyone who accepts HOURS from the agent is obligated to return an equal number of HOURS to the agent if and when they choose to discontinue their participation in the program.

The next problem is to know when an advertiser has chosen to discontinue its participation. The actions or inactions that constitute discontinuation must be defined. It could be defined as being no longer willing to accept HOURS in payment for goods and/or services. This might not be enough, however, since there would probably be no formal declaration of that fact to the agent. The agreement could be greatly strengthened if discontinuation was defined as nonrenewal of an ad in *HOUR Town*. Even without any intention of following through with legal enforcement, having such an agreement would provide greater assurance that an advertiser will not spend HOURS and then fail to earn them back, that is, will not take value from the community without giv-ing back an equal amount (failure to reciprocate).

The requirement of returning HOURS to the agent would provide the needed proof that the IOUs issued by the advertiser have been honored (redeemed), the loop has been closed, and reciprocity achieved. Figures 17.1 and 17.2 show pictorially how currency notes are issued, circulated, and redeemed if *HOUR Town* acts as issuer or agent, respectively.

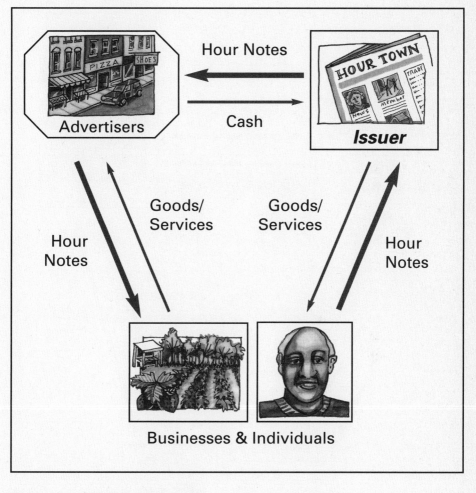

Figure 17.1. *HOUR Town* as issuer.

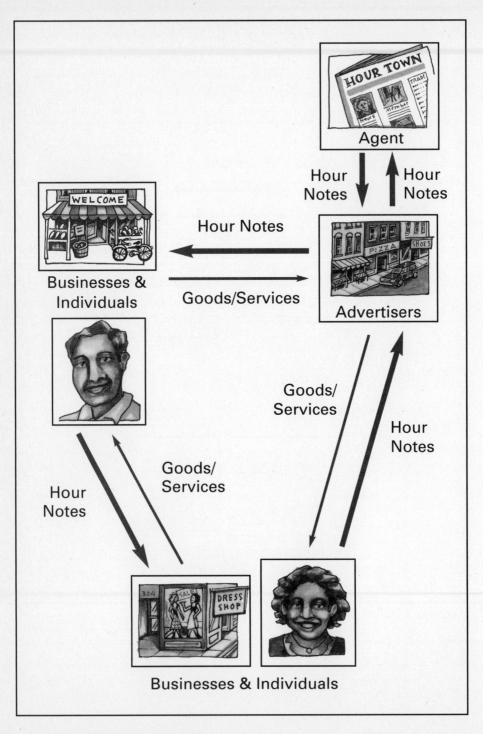

Figure 17.2. *HOUR Town* as agent.

How Are Ithaca HOURS Issued?

From the inception of Ithaca HOURS in 1991 until the present, the issuance of its notes has been slowly evolving. What was originally an unbacked currency has become a partially backed currency. In the beginning, *Ithaca MONEY,* the predecessor of *HOUR Town* newspaper, would give four HOURS to anyone who bought advertising in the newspaper. There was an understanding that advertisers would accept HOURS as at least partial payment for whatever they were selling, but the agreement was informal and implied, and there was no requirement that the HOURS be repaid. Later on, the amount issued to each advertiser was reduced from four to two HOURS. Still later, the administration began to make HOUR loans, in which case there is an agreement to repay. In addition to these HOUR gifts and loans, the administration issues some HOURS by making HOUR "grants" to local community improvement groups and nonprofit organizations. While the intention in doing this is laudable, it is not sound currency management practice. Grant recipients have no obligation to reciprocate; thus, HOURS issued in this way tend to debase the value of the HOURS already in circulation. Such grants, if they are given, should be specifically underwritten by individuals or businesses.

Let us recall from chapter 10 the various means in which Ithaca HOURS are now issued:

1. as payment to those who agree to be listed in *HOUR Town* (one or two HOURS per person/business),
2. as a bonus every eight months to participants "for reaffirming their participation,"
3. as a bonus to those who sign up or renew at a barter potluck,
4. as grants to community organizations (14% of HOURS),
5. as loans (10% of HOURS otherwise issued),
6. as payments made to the system itself for printing *HOUR Town,* HOUR notes, bumper stickers, office supplies, and so forth (5% of HOURS).

As pointed out before, the issuance of currency into circulation should be accompanied by the flow of goods and services into the economy, and the person or entity receiving those goods and services must be committed to redeeming that currency by accepting it in payment for whatever she or he sells. I have serious concerns, therefore, about many of the ways in which Ithaca HOURS are placed into circulation. It is evident that *HOUR Town* acts mainly as agent rather than issuer. Of the six means of issuance listed above, the first four appear to be gifts. Only the first of these implies any expectation that the recipient will reciprocate or redeem the notes she or he spends, but, in the absence of a formal agreement, I must have serious doubts about the recipients' strength of commitment. Only the fifth item, loans, carries a clear expectation of reciprocity. With the sixth item, payment to the system itself to cover its costs, *HOUR Town* may qualify as issuer rather than agent, since it is willing to accept HOURS as payment for the advertising services it offers. But it is unclear if the newspaper is willing and able to redeem the *entire* amount of the HOURS it issues in that way.

Like everyone involved in the community currency movement, I admire the sentiment behind the gifts and grants of Ithaca HOURS. But, as the saying goes, "there ain't no free lunch." Someone must ultimately pay. Simply giving out HOURS on a nonreciprocal basis produces an imbalance between HOURS in circulation and goods and services available to be purchased. This will gradually debase the currency. Everyone who uses the currency will end up paying for it, HOURS will be devalued in the market, and confidence in the currency will be diminished.

Why have these ill effects not been felt up to now? Conversations with the organizers have pointed to an answer. It seems that a large proportion of the HOURS issued have been permanently taken out of circulation by the large numbers of journalists and curiosity seekers who have collected them as souvenirs. This effect has helped to balance the supply of circulating currency with the supply of goods and services offered for HOURS. Such inadvertent subsidy, however, should not be expected to continue.

These defects in Ithaca HOURS need not be fatal. With a few relatively minor adjustments, the program should be able to consolidate its past success and assure its continued growth and viability. Here is what I recommend:

1. When *HOUR Town,* acting as agent, places HOURS into the hands of "participants," they should be asked to sign a formal agreement something like the one used by Tucson Traders (see chapter 11), in which they agree to accept HOURS in payment for the goods and services they sell and further agree to return the same amount in HOURS or cash if and when they stop their participation.
2. The system should increase the proportion of HOURS issued as loans made to support micro-enterprise. This will provide a sound basis of issue while helping to build the productive capacity of the local economy. Only loans that produce a fairly immediate increase in the flow of goods and services into the HOUR economy should be made.
3. When the system issues HOURS for its own account, it should issue no more than it is able to redeem. In other words, when the system issues HOURS to itself to pay some of its expenses, it should be willing and able to redeem all of them by providing goods and services. It must earn sufficient HOUR revenue to cover its HOUR expenditures.

4. HOURS issued by the system as grants or gifts should be underwritten by some individual or business that makes a prior commitment to donate back to the system the same amount of HOURS initially granted or given. Someone must be committed to deliver the value that the newly issued currency represents. How this can be done is described below.

Adding a Capital Cushion

When a conventional bank is established, the founders must put in some capital of their own. This capital fund (called "owners' equity") is necessary not only to cover start-up costs but also to provide added security for depositors in case some of the bank's assets, which back the deposits, should lose some or all of their value. The capital fund, then, provides the resources that can be used, if necessary, to cover the cost of bad debts or reduced asset value.

A community exchange system, too, is a sort of business. Although it may not be operated for profit, it still incurs costs of operation. While most contemporary systems have been started with grants and volunteer labor, that may not be an adequate basis for operation in the long run. In order for the system to be independently sustainable, it must eventually generate sufficient revenues to cover its costs. Some of these costs may be unavoidable cash costs, while others might be adequately covered with local currency. A capital fund will provide credits or backed currency against which bad debts can be charged. How might the system acquire a capital fund, and how might it generate sufficient revenues to sustain its operations?

Let us consider the latter question first. Operating revenues must generally come from fees that the system charges its clients and patrons for services such as advertising and/or accounting. But there is also another way to obtain revenues, which will be described in a moment. The capital fund can come from grants or loans, but it too might be obtained in another way. What is this other way?

Using Excess Business Capacity to Support Local Currency

Every community has an "economic base," which is comprised of its natural resources, built-up infrastructure, productive capacity, the skills of its people, and so forth. While each community has its own distinct array and assortment of these, there is almost always "excess capacity," which means that the businesses in the community are able to produce and sell more goods and services than they actually do. Further, the cost of that additional production is usually very low in comparison with the average cost per unit of output. Economists call this cost of the last unit produced the *marginal cost*. They argue that, since the marginal cost is lower than the average cost, a business can afford to sell additional units of output at a lower price.

Everyone is familiar with discount coupons. They are typically used by restaurants and retailers to attract more cash business and repeat customers, that is, to utilize some of their excess capacity. Since their marginal cost is low, they can afford to grant the discount and still add to their overall profit.

This phenomenon of excess capacity can be harnessed to accomplish at least three important community objectives. It can be a funding source for nonprofit and community improvement groups, including a local currency system, and at the same time it can provide a way of introducing and promoting the use of a local currency. Further, some of that excess business capacity can be donated to provide the local currency system with a capital fund, giving added security against loss of value of the currency.

Whether a system uses ledger credits (Community Way), transaction cards (Community Hero Card), or circulating paper notes like my Community Service Coupons, the process is conceptually the same.

The essential process for doing this has been variously described by at least three local currency/exchange advocates. In chapter 15 of *New Money for Healthy Communities,* I described a Community Service Credit System that uses this basic approach. Variations on that theme, which I have been trying to promote in recent years in the United States, are Community Service Coupons and Youth Employment Scrip. These will be described in chapters 21 and 22, respectively. Joel Hodroff has been promoting a plan in the Minneapolis/St. Paul area for several years. His efforts have come to fruition in a pilot project called the Community Hero Card, which was launched there in the spring of 1997. It involves a number of local businesses that use their excess capacity to underwrite the issuance of local exchange credits. Michael Linton and Ernie Yacub have been advocating an approach they call Community Way. Their article on Community Way provided a particularly elegant description of this basic approach. It was published in the summer of 1996 in a Canadian magazine, *Making Waves.*

There has been some movement toward implementation of Community Way in Vancouver, British Columbia; Santa Cruz, California; and the San Francisco Bay area. I believe that programs such as the Community Service Credit System, Community Way, and the Community Hero Card have the potential to shift tremendous amounts of resources into the "third sector" (nonprofits) and at the same time, give the community currency movement a big boost into the mainstream. Once the first prototype is up and running smoothly, I think that other systems based on this concept will proliferate rapidly.

How Does It Work?

Whether a system uses ledger credits (Community Way), transaction cards (Community Hero Card), or circulating paper notes like my Community Service Coupons, the process is conceptually the same. The bare-bones process for my coupon (note) version is this:

1. A business agrees to accept the local currency as partial payment for whatever it sells (just as it would its own discount coupon). It also agrees to donate back to the system a portion of its local currency revenue. This may be a fixed numerical amount paid over a specified period of time or a percentage of its periodic local currency income.
2. This commitment provides the system with a capital fund, collectible in local currency, which allows the system to issue (spend) notes or credits knowing that the business will redeem them, which completes the reciprocity circuit.
3. The system then allocates the notes or credits to nonprofit organizations or community service groups. These groups can use them to pay their volunteer workers, purchase supplies, or pay for services. The system can use some of these donated notes or credits to pay the people who do the work of running the system *and to build its capital fund cushion.*
4. The volunteer workers can then spend the notes at the businesses that have agreed to accept them, or they can sell them for cash to cash-rich supporters who spend them at the businesses that have agreed to accept them. Others in the community may also be willing to accept the notes as a payment medium, knowing that they can be redeemed at any participating business.
5. When the business donates back to the system the amount of notes it agreed to, the circuit is complete, the obligation has been discharged, and the notes are retired until that business or another business makes a donor commitment. Then the notes may be reissued.

Of course, the notes may change hands many times before they reach the donor business, and it is hoped that they will, allowing the notes to serve not only as a fund-raiser for charity and community improvement activities but also as a supplemental medium of exchange that benefits the entire local economy. What if a business takes in more notes than it agreed to donate back to the system? In this case, the business can spend the excess notes at other participating businesses, which will be eager to have them in order to fulfill their own donor obligation to the system.

There are a number of other details associated with such plans, but they need not be discussed here. Figure 17.3 shows pictorially how the notes are issued, circulated, and retired so that reciprocity is achieved.

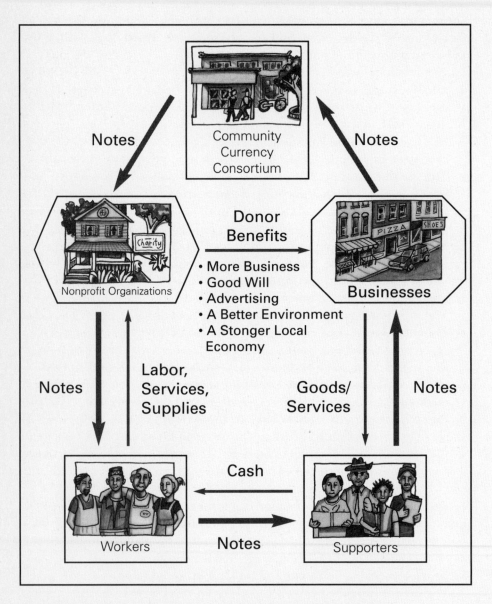

Figure 17.3. Using excess business capacity to support local currency.

Once the notes return to the system, they are retired. They may be reissued if and when another business commits to donate them back. The diagram shows who gets what when the notes change hands. The nonprofits, including the system, get labor, services, and supplies; the workers get cash or discounts at participating merchants; the cash-rich supporters get discounts at participating merchants; the participating merchants get the benefits associated with being a donor, which are (1) more business, (2) goodwill in the community, (3) advertising, (4) a better community environment in which to conduct business, and (5) a stronger local economy.

Now, the system may hold back on issuing some of the notes for which it has obtained a commitment. This would be the amount of the capital fund against which losses might be written off.

Here's an example. Let's consider an imaginary town called Cordial. The people of Cordial have heard about the Community Service Credit System and have decided to give it a try. They form a committee to organize and operate it. The committee in charge of printing and issuing the currency (coupons) decides that it will call the coupon value unit a "SERV," and coupons will be issued in one-, five-, ten-, and twenty-SERV denominations. A SERV will have a value equivalent to a dollar.

The subcommittee in charge of business recruitment has managed to get one hundred local businesses to agree to accept SERVs in partial payment for the goods and services they offer. Of those businesses, forty have also agreed to donate back to the system varying amounts of SERVs, which total 20,000 SERVs (equivalent to $20,000 worth of "discounts"). The committee then decides that it will issue only 15,000 SERVs and hold the remaining 5,000 as a reserve or capital fund. It will issue the 15,000 SERVs as follows: 5,000 will be used by the system itself to pay for printing the coupons, to buy office supplies and equipment, and for accounting and other services; 10,000 will be distributed to local nonprofit groups, which will use them to buy things they need or to reward their volunteers.

Now, if some merchants prove to be less than faithful in honoring their commitments, there should be no problem—the supply of coupons in circulation will still be less than the value of "discounts" pledged.

Combined Bases of Issue

In the example above, involving the fictitious town of Cordial, the currency is fully backed (and then some) by the donations that the local business community has already agreed to provide. This might be a good way to begin, but to rely entirely on donations, even in-kind donations, as a basis of issue would be much too limiting. Recall, however, that the standard mutual credit system allows its members to monetize their own credit, that is, to issue credits or notes on the basis of *their* commitment to provide goods and services equal in value to those they have received. It is these commitments that are more likely to become problematic. Adding the capital cushion provided by donation commitments described above improves the system in at least two ways:

1. It provides a fund against which "bad debts" can be written off.
2. It increases the total available supply of notes circulating, making it easier for those members choosing to leave the system to earn back and repay the notes or credits they owe.

A detailed outline of how to design and implement such a community exchange system is presented in the next chapter.

Chapter 18

‒

How to Design and Implement a Community Exchange System

Any sizeable group anywhere, any day, could start a nonpolitical monetary unit and system. There is no law against it, and no legislation need be invoked.

—E. C. RIEGEL

M Y LONG CONTINUING RESEARCH into monetary history and theory has been complemented over the past decade by my involvement in the design, development, and operation of various cashless community trading systems and currencies. These have included LETSonora, Tucson Traders, Equal Dollars, Tianguis Tlalocs and others, either as organizer, administrator, or consultant. These involvements have provided an opportunity for observation and experimentation with various exchange approaches, currency features, and system improvements. I have also maintained regular correspondence with others around the world who are active in the movement, and I have continued to monitor developments in LETS, HOURS, and the various other exchange and currency models currently in operation.

Although the current community exchange models may not be quite ideal, the fundamental soundness of some has been established, and the effectiveness of many of their features has been proven in practice. If we keep in mind the basic principles of social justice, economic equity, personal freedom, and inclusiveness, and equip ourselves with sound theoretical knowledge, we can continue our approach toward more ideal exchange systems. This chapter contains my prescription for a sound and effective community exchange system. It is a composite system that incorporates many of the ideas discussed in previous chapters. In brief, it is a mutual credit association that utilizes a variety of exchange devices, including circulating currency notes, but its essential feature is that it is a membership organization, and it is the explicit commitment of the members that gives credibility and value to the community currency as a medium of exchange.

Summary Prescription

Although some deviation might be appropriate in particular circumstances or to achieve particular objectives, I would recommend that complementary exchange systems be established according to the following guidelines:

1. *Organizational form.* Organize the system as a nonprofit cooperative association. It need not be legally incorporated, but as a system grows and develops it generally becomes advantageous to operate under a corporate umbrella with a formal management and control structure. In jurisdictions where the cooperative association is well defined as a legal structure, the cooperative form might be utilized.
2. *Type of exchange system.* Organize the system as a mutual credit system with a formal membership agreement that makes explicit the rights and responsibilities of membership. In particular, each member should acknowledge that any debit balance incurred represents a "loan" received from the community, which the member is obligated to repay.
3. *Membership.* Membership should be as open and inclusive as possible. The only basis for exclusion should be someone's failure to adhere to the agreements and rules of the system. Special efforts should be made to attract the participation of the local business community and of nonprofit organizations as well as individuals.
4. *Governance.* Power should ultimately be in the hands of the members. They should have the power to elect and recall the members of a board of governors or overseers who have the responsibility for establishing and managing the system. The powers of the governing body should be limited and clearly defined at the outset.
5. *Credit creation power.* Every member should be allowed to have some minimum line of credit, that is, debit balance limit. Higher debit balance limits should be established according to a definite formula involving the member's trading record and average level of sales over time.
6. *Exchange mechanisms.* A variety of devices to transfer credits from one member's account to another member's account may be employed. The use of credit checks or receipts may be less prone to error than the typical telephone reporting method (used by LETSystems) and provides a paper trail, which facilitates the detection and correction of any errors that may occur.

The use of circulating notes drawn against members' lines of credit provides a number of important advantages and should be considered.

7. *Membership fees and assessments.* The system should charge its members for the services rendered. Service charges should be fixed amounts based on the cost of the services provided. Charges may be levied for such items as directory listings, newsletter advertising, account statements, recording transactions, updating accounts, and so on. Charging interest on debit balances should be avoided. If system charges *are* levied against account balances, they should be assessed on both debit and credit balances equally, and in proportion to the balance.

8. *System trading account.* The system trading account needs to be managed properly. Make sure that the system generates sufficient credit earnings to cover its costs of operation. Avoid the common pitfall of running up a big debit balance in the system trading account. This can lead to "credit inflation" and loss of confidence in the system.

9. *Currency convertibility.* Do *not* provide the option of redeeming community currencies or credits for official currencies (dollars) unless the system has an adequate source of official currency income. Even then, redemption should be restricted to specific occasions and limited in amount.

Detailed Guidelines

Many details of how to achieve each of these objectives have been discussed throughout the previous chapters. The following is a recapitulation but also an elaboration on some of the more important points.

ORGANIZATIONAL FORM

The point was made earlier that banking should be conducted as a profession, not run as a corporate, for-profit business (see also appendix A for more background on this point). To avoid conflicts of interest in the operation of a community exchange system, it should be established as a cooperative or mutual association, "owned" by its members and run entirely for the benefit of the community. Legal incorporation provides liability safeguards for the people who take responsibility for management of the system. Still, it is the responsibility of the membership to hold administrators accountable. Open membership and democratic governing structures help to assure the safeguarding of the public interest.

MEMBERSHIP, RIGHTS, AND RESPONSIBILITIES

The spirit of community and inclusiveness should be paramount in a community currency system; thus, membership should be open to all. On the other hand, safeguards need to be built into the system to protect it from those who would exploit it. The use of a written membership agreement helps to clarify the rights and responsibilities of membership and leaves less room for argument and misinterpretation. A basic objective of a community currency system is to empower everyone to some extent to monetize the value of their own labor and resources. It must be understood, however, that any credits or currency that a member spends into circulation must be offset by his or her eventual earnings of credits. In a mutual credit system, a member who spends before earning will show a debit balance on his or her account. That debit balance should be considered to be a loan of real value from the community, which must eventually be repaid. In the normal course of events the repayment will be in the form of goods and services, not money. By selling goods and services, a member earns credits to offset previous debits. The membership agreement should clearly state that a member who chooses to withdraw from the system must first repay any remaining debit balance.

In a paper currency system, the same agreement should apply. When paper currency notes are originally allocated to the members, those notes should be debited to their account, and each member should understand that she or he is obligated to repay the same amount on withdrawal from the system.

The Governing Board

A community exchange system, whether it be simply a ledger system, a paper currency issue, or some combination of the two, requires some administrative group or authority. It is very important that the administrative board be constrained in its power. No matter how well intentioned the people might be, "power corrupts," as we have so often seen. That is the basic problem with the existing monetary and governmental structures. The powers of the board should be defined and limited. Its function should be to establish the basic rules at the outset, monitor the members' adherence to their agreements, and take the appropriate prescribed action in the event that they do not.

The board's role is mainly to create the initial structure, including the terms of membership, to set policy regarding membership and service fees and the establishment of debit and credit limits, and to oversee the administrative processes and staff. Any subsequent changes to these essential constitutional elements should be made by the members as a whole.

Credit Limits for Members

One of the fundamental questions in a mutual credit exchange system is that of how much credit to authorize to each individual or business member. This credit limit determines how large a debit balance each member should be allowed to carry, or, in monetary terms, how much currency each person should be allowed to issue. For ease of discussion, let us refer to any unit of local trade credit as a "val." This is the unit name used by E. C. Riegel, one of the most lucid thinkers on the question of money. The number of local currency units or local trade units that a business or individual is expected to redeem in the course of trade each month should be the only basis for deciding the amount of credit to be authorized, and it should be based on a formula relationship. The formula is based on the following rationale:

1. The member business itself decides what percentage of each sale to accept in vals. There is no apparent reason for the board to have any say about what this percentage should be. There is, however, a useful basis for making this decision. It is called "value added," a concept in managerial finance that refers to the value added by a particular stage of production or distribution. For example, a sawmill buys a load of logs from a logging company for $200, then cuts it into finished lumber that it sells for $350. The value added by that company would be the difference between its raw material cost and the revenue received from sale of its final products, in this case $350 − $200 = $150. The value added, then, can be a rough measure of how much value is added locally, and thus the amount of the business's costs and profits that could conceivably be paid for using local currency. As a matter of interest, many European countries impose a value-added tax (VAT) on businesses at every stage of production and distribution. Thus, a business with a 60 percent cost of goods sold (gross margin of 40 percent) and a net profit margin of 20 percent of sales, could choose to accept a percentage of vals anywhere between 20 and 40 percent, depending on how much of the administrative costs it expects to be able to pay with vals. One might expect a member business to start with the lower figure to be safe, then increase it as experience merits.

2. Adherents to the "German school" have pointed out that a viable currency should have at least a 1 percent daily reflux. At that rate, the whole volume of currency that an issuer puts into circulation flows back to the issuer within about a 100-day period. It might be prudent to agree, at least initially, to be conservative and seek a total reflux within a 60-day period. Each member business could then be authorized to issue an amount of vals up to the amount it would be expected to redeem in trade during an average 60-day period (two months). That's a simple formula calculation:

   Authorized Credit, vals = (2 x monthly sales) x (val payment percentage/100)

   For example, if a business has monthly sales of $80,000 and agrees to accept 20 percent payment in vals, it would be authorized to issue a total of 32,000 vals:

   32,000 vals = (2 x $80,000) x (20/100)

3. A member business should be allowed to adjust the percentage of vals it accepts upward or downward as it sees fit, up to the limit of its value added percentage.[1] If the adjustment is upward, it would be authorized to issue

more vals in accordance with the formula. If a business ever wanted to decrease its percentage, or drop out completely, all it would need to do would be to repay the difference in the amount of vals it was authorized to issue. If it did not have enough vals to do that, it would have to earn them in trade, or it could be allowed to pay the remainder in any mutually agreed on medium of exchange, presumably official currency.

Employee Participation

Employees of member businesses should be encouraged to become associate members. They would agree to accept a particular percentage of their wages in vals. In return, they themselves might be allowed to issue (spend into circulation) an amount of vals computed in the same way as the business authorization is determined.

Here's an example. If an employee earning $1,000 a month agrees to accept 30 percent of her salary in vals, she could be allowed to issue (spend into circulation) up to a total of 600 vals, which would be two months' val earnings. (She would also be getting 300 vals a month in her pay envelope, but these are vals she earns, not issues.)

Employees will, no doubt, want to jump onto the bandwagon when they see the system working. As unemployment becomes more of a problem, and official money becomes less available, people will probably be willing to accept wages in any kind of currency that they deem to be trustworthy. As we have seen in previous chapters, when there is not enough official currency circulating in the local economy, a complementary currency can put people to work and provide a means by which they can meet their needs.

Ledger Accounts, Credit Checks, or Circulating Paper Notes?

Conceptually, it doesn't matter whether the community exchange credits (vals) take the form of paper notes, tokens, or ledger balances (bookkeeping entries). These are all symbolic representations of the same thing—the values being exchanged—and each form of credit is "backed" by the same commitment of the issuers to redeem it. Just as cash is used as an adjunct to bank account balances in the official monetary system, so too can circulating paper notes be used as an adjunct to ledger accounts in a mutual credit system. Furthermore, the transfer of credits from one trader to another can be accomplished using any combination of notes, checks, debit cards, and electronic transfers, just as in the conventional money and banking system.

I strongly favor the use of circulating paper notes within a community exchange system, provided that they are properly issued. (See the section on Tucson Traders in chapter 11 for a description of one mutual credit system that has opted to use circulating paper notes.) Paper notes offer numerous advantages, including the following:

1. *Acceptability and familiarity.* Paper notes provide a physical representation of the exchange credits that the association members have created for themselves. People are accustomed to using paper currency. They are familiar with the way it works, and there is nothing new to learn; so it is easy to make the shift from using official currency to using community currency.

2. *Convenience and efficiency.* Cash is convenient. It requires no technology to use it, and a quick glance is all that's needed to recognize what it is. Issued in various small denominations, it efficiently performs the task of recording transfers of value between traders. This makes it easier for local businesses to participate in a community exchange system. From the standpoint of administrative efficiency, paper is better because it eliminates the need to record members' transactions and reduces the necessary frequency of account statements. This is particularly important within the context of lesser developed countries, where computers and telephones (and the skills to use them) may be lacking.

3. *Advertising, publicity, outreach, and recruitment.* Each community currency note is an advertisement for the system. Every time it is shown, offered, or transferred, it speaks for the credibility, effectiveness, and importance of the community exchange system, particularly if the notes are inscribed with a capsule agreement or pertinent slogan. Further, unlike recorded account credits, notes can be offered to nonmembers as payment, expanding the range of influence and usefulness of the community currency. They may be accepted and spent by anyone. Some businesses especially like the fact that there is nothing to join; they can accept or refuse the currency any time they wish.

4. *Limitation of issuance to the approved line of credit.* From a control standpoint, this assurance can be very important. In a ledger system in which each member account has a maximum approved debit balance, the problem is to assure that a member does not exceed that level. If a member has made a purchase that would cause his or her balance to exceed the approved limit, what can the system management do? The obvious answer is to refuse to record the transaction, but that creates ill will on the part of everyone, especially the person who earned the credits. The overall result is like that of a bounced check at a bank. Many mutual credit systems have found this to be a problem. *Using only circulating notes as the exchange mechanism within a mutual credit membership system completely avoids the problem of overdrafts.* You can't spend what you don't have. Moreover, by issuing notes to each member up to the amount of his or her allowable debit balance, we not only eliminate any possibility of overdrafts; we also avoid the work of recording each transaction.

5. *Enhancement of community spirit and culture.* The currency notes can be designed with features that promote a culture of civic pride, cooperation, and self-reliance. The design process itself can promote a spirit of commu-

nity by involving local artists, graphic designers, and various constituencies such as youths and senior citizens.

Proper Management of the System Trading Account

In the administration of mutual credit and community currency systems, a great deal of confusion derives from the failure to recognize one basic point: *The system administration involves two separate and distinct functions, (1) an administrative or "clearing" function and (2) a trading function.*

On the one hand, the system administration acts as agent for its members, providing credit clearing for their exchange transactions (using checks, cards, or some other accounting device) or distributing local currency notes to its members who then spend them into circulation. Note that it is the members who issue the notes into circulation, not the system administration. The administration, acting in its agent capacity, simply has the notes printed and distributes them to its members. These notes, like a line of credit, represent potential money, not actual money. They become actual money only when they are spent, that is when someone receives real value for them (goods and/or services). This is the point at which the notes are "issued" into circulation.

However, the system administration may also have its own trading account. In its role of trader, it acts like any other member of the association, buying and selling. In this capacity it *does* have the power to issue currency into circulation. Like any other member, it issues local currency into circulation when it receives valuable goods and services and pays for them using credits debited against its trading account or notes that have been allocated to it. When the administration does this, it is with the understanding that the system will be able to earn back an equal amount of credits or currency by selling services, such as credit clearing and advertising to the other members.

As emphasized repeatedly, every unit of local currency that is issued should give rise to a commitment by the issuer (the one who initially received value for it). This person (account) has agreed to take back the currency (credits) she or he issued as payment for goods and services she or he sells. With regard to each and every unit of local currency, we need to ask the following question: *Who initially received value for it?* That person (or entity) is the actual issuer. That person is the one who is expected to redeem the credits or currency by selling goods and services sometime in the future. It is that person's commitment on which the value of the credits or currency stands.

If the system account receives an amount of goods or services, or even official money, and gives local currency in exchange for it, then the system account is the issuer of that local currency. The system account is expected to redeem that currency by selling goods and services sometime in the near future. It is the commitment of the system account on which the value of those currency units stands; therefore the system must sell its services or have another source of local currency revenue.

The weight of experience shows mismanagement of the system trading account to be more the rule than the exception. In light of this, one might question whether the system should be allowed to have a trading account at all. It might be safer to restrict the system to providing the clearing function for its members and allocating paper currency notes as physical representations of their lines of credit. That part is pretty simple and straightforward. However, when a system begins trading on its own account, there is the temptation to overspend, that is, to incur debits far in excess of its ability to earn credits. Many LETS and local currency systems have fallen into this pit.

Given the costs of launching a system, some way must be found to capitalize the business and to recover that capital investment over a reasonable period of time. Systems have been launched with virtually no capital, but that option takes lots of volunteer labor. A system can make a quicker start if it has some start-up capital. To attempt to launch a system with no capital, and to finance the start-up by spending credits into circulation, is to court disaster.

Alas, a local exchange system is a business, and it must be run like a business. That means that adequate financing must be secured to start it, and proper accounts must be kept. In business, it is usually necessary to have some investment capital, not only to acquire equipment and supplies, but also to cover the shortfall of revenues relative to expenses while the business is building up its customer base and developing adequate revenues to keep it going. The start-up expenses are usually "capitalized," meaning that they are written off against future revenues rather than being charged against current revenues at the beginning. This is in keeping with the fundamental accounting principle of *matching revenues against expenses.*

Similarly, a fundamental principle of banking is that, in issuing any currency (or credits), **credits or notes issued should be matched against the means of their redemption, that is, goods and services available for purchase in the market.** For example, if it takes $50,000 to get a business started, that money must be obtained from somewhere, either as loans or as ownership shares, and it may take several years for that investment to be recovered (as profits) in the normal course of business. In the case of a mutual credit or local currency system, the services provided by the system to its members must ultimately be paid for by its members. Despite the fact that much volunteer labor is usually provided in the early stages, this cannot be expected to continue indefinitely. The system must become self-supporting. If it does not have sufficient revenues, it will not be sustainable. It may flourish for a while, but, like any business that has persistent losses, it must ultimately fail.

Those who do the work deserve to be paid. It makes perfect sense for a local trading or currency system to cover as much of its expenses as possible by using its own currency. To do so, of course, the system must have its own trading account. The question then resolves to laying out strict rules for managing the system trading account in order to avoid trouble because of overspending.

The system trading account should be viewed just the same as any other member's account. The debit limit on the system trading account should be established in the same way as the debit limit for any other member of the system. Whenever the system issues local currency on the basis of value it receives, it is committed to redeem that currency by selling goods and services. Normally, what the system has to sell is "clearing" (accounting services) and advertising. The administrative costs of operating the system, and recovery of the initial investment to start it, must be covered by fees and assessments charged to its members. If, for example, the system issues local currency in exchange for cash, or to pay its employees, it must recapture those local currency units within a reasonably short period of time by charging for the services it provides. Start-up and initial operating costs may, in addition, be covered not only by volunteer labor but also by grants, donations, or loans, but eventually the system will have to pay for itself. Another start-up option is to pay system staff in system credits on a *deferred basis*. Their salaries could be paid into a separate account that would recognize the value of the work done, but those credits could not be spent until some later time when the system's earnings have caught up with its expenses.

CONVERSION OF OFFICIAL CURRENCY TO COMMUNITY CURRENCY

An important question has been raised by a supporter of a community currency system being operated by a nonprofit organization in the eastern United States. This person wanted to inject some official cash into his local system to help it get better established. The question was whether it would be appropriate for the system to give him local currency in exchange for a cash contribution. Offhand, it would seem perfectly reasonable to do so, but the problem is to do it in a way that does not lead to local currency inflation. As explained above, a fundamental principle of accounting is to match revenues against the expenses incurred in producing those revenues. A fundamental principle of banking is to match the issuance of money against the flow of goods and services into the market, since they provide the value on which that money is based. So the problem boils down to one of both timing and the use to which the cash is put.

Suppose, for example, that this supporter provides the system with $500 in official money. Should he be given 500 vals (local units) to spend as he wishes? The answer is "it depends." What the success of this procedure depends on is how the official money is used by the system, and the ability of the system administration to convert that $500 contribution into immediately available goods and services. The important point is to match the local currency issued to the flow of goods and services into the local currency economy. Let's look at some possibilities.

If the system administration spent the $500 of official money on fresh produce from the farmers' market and offered that produce for sale for local currency, then it would be perfectly reasonable to make an immediate issue to the donor of 500 vals. The donor could spend the 500 vals into circulation, and he or others could use them to buy the produce; the circuit would be complete. Those local units would then be retired. Of course, the more likely scenario, and the one to be desired, is that the notes would change hands a few times before coming back to the issuer, which, in this case, is the system trading account.

Suppose, however, that the administration used the $500 in official money to buy food to give to poor families. Admirable as that is, it does nothing to put

The debit limit on the system trading account should be established in the same way as the debit limit for any other member of the system.

goods and services into the local currency economy. If the official money donor were to be issued local currency units, there would, in this case, be nothing for him to spend them on. This would cause local currency debasement (price inflation). This charitable procedure is like depositing money in one bank account and then writing checks against a different account.

Now this same nonprofit corporation operates a number of businesses that are designed to support its disadvantaged inner-city constituency. Among these is a tool library and a low-income housing business. The corporation wants to promote the use of the local currency within these businesses. These businesses should have their own trading accounts, separate from the system trading account.

Suppose a cash input is made to the tool library, for example, to buy the tools that will be rented out for local currency. That cash input should be considered as a loan. The lender can be repaid in local currency over a period of time as local currency rental income is acquired. Also, some of the expenses of operating the tool library can be paid for using local currency. However, some portion of the rental fees must be collected in cash so that the tools can be replaced when they eventually wear out.

Now consider what might be done when $500 in official money is contributed to the low-income housing project. That $500 might be spent to fix up a house that the project intends to rent out for official money. If the donor of the $500 were to be given 500 vals in return, that would cause local currency debasement (inflation), because this action adds nothing to the supply of goods and services available for purchase in the local currency economy.

On the other hand, if the low-income housing project would accept local currency for the rent, there would now be some value in the local currency economy that could absorb the newly issued currency units. However, attention needs to be paid to the timing within which that value becomes available. If the local units are issued at the time of the official money contribution and it takes six months for the house to be made ready for rental, there is an obvious mismatch between the flow of new currency into the local currency economy and the flow of real value into it. This, too, would cause inflation in the near term. In this case, it would be better to treat the official money contribution as a loan, since the money is used as a capital expenditure. That loan could be repaid in local currency, not in a lump sum at the beginning, but over a period of time that more closely matches the rental availability of the house. The local currency payments on the loan should start only after the renovations are completed and the house is ready to be rented. These payments should be spread out over the several-year life of the renovations that the cash contribution paid for.

Again, let me emphasize the fundamental principle that must be adhered to in order for the local currency to remain sound and avoid depreciation of the local currency unit (inflation): The issuance of local currency into the local currency economy must be matched to the flow of goods and services into the local currency economy. **Money should be issued on the basis of goods and services on their way to market,** not on the basis of long-term investments or loans, nor on the basis of charitable spending. (See appendix B for more background on this point.)

ATTRACTING BUSINESS PARTICIPATION

Many LETS, in which the membership has consisted only of individuals, have been slow to grow. While LETS membership is open to businesses, most LETS have not been very successful in attracting them. I believe it is very important to make a concerted effort to include established businesses as well as individual members in the start-up of a local exchange system. Established businesses, in addition to their name recognition, offer a wider range and volume of goods and services. Since they already are significant players in the local economy, business members provide local exchange systems with the prospect of a faster start and greater impact. The success of Ithaca HOURS is, I believe, largely due to the fact that the organizers have been able to achieve extensive participation of local businesses.

What does it take to attract the participation of the business community in a community currency system? There is no simple answer to that question, but one can start by recognizing that people generally want to have a sense of ownership of whatever they are involved in, particularly where their livelihood is concerned. Most community exchange systems have been started by people at the grass roots—visionaries and idealists and social entrepreneurs who often lack mainstream connections. Thus, they are seen as "outsiders" without established credibility among mainstream businesspeople. Their marginal status makes it an uphill battle to convince the business community to participate. People tend to trust people whom they perceive as being like themselves. They generally want to know who else is "in the game." Thus, the more diverse the organizing group, and the broader the base of initial support, the more likely it is that a community exchange system will be successful. The success of the Toronto Dollar project has been to a large extent derived from social standing of its organizers: people who were part of the local business and academic communities, and who were also well connected to local government. At the very start, dozens of local merchants agreed to accept their local currency, and the mayor of Toronto participated in the launching ceremony.

It seems quite likely that, as the advantages of community currencies become more widely recognized, the business communities themselves will take the initiative to establish local exchange systems. The following chapter focuses on how such a system might be organized.

Overaccumulation — Is It a Problem?

The question has often been raised, What if a member business takes in more vals than it can spend? The answer to this lies in the conditions that determine the val's rate of acceptance by the local community, and in the range of available goods and services being offered by the various members of the system. A community currency, in its sole role of exchange medium, should be spent as fast as it is taken in. If a member business finds insufficient opportunity to spend vals on things that it needs, the surplus would indicate that it overestimated either (1) the value-added component of its business or (2) the willingness and/or ability of others in the community to accept vals. In either case, its logical response should be to reduce the percentage of vals that it is willing to accept in payment and to use its accumulated surplus of vals to reduce its commitment, if any, to the association. This is the proper adjustment mechanism that makes the system self-regulating.

Suppose, for example, that the Record Emporium has been accepting 50 percent vals on all sales of used CDs, tapes, and records. After some months, it finds itself unable to spend them as fast as they are taken in, and it now has a val balance equivalent to $4,000. It has been taking in vals at the rate of about $2,000 a month but has been able to spend only about $1,000 a month. If the Record Emporium would reduce its acceptance percentage to 25 percent, it would then bring its val income into line with its val expenditures.

Of course, in the above example, it would be preferable if the system administration would assist the merchant in finding more ways to spend more vals.

LIMITED OR PERPETUAL LIFE?

I have made the point repeatedly that a community currency should be primarily a medium of exchange, not a savings medium. This means that the currency notes or credits should be spent promptly and not accumulated in large volume.[2] We've already addressed the point at length, as it applies to ledger accounts, in chapter 16. But what about a currency that exists in the form of circulating paper notes held in the hands of members or even, possibly, nonmembers? Among the more promising suggestions is to place an expiration date on every note issued into circulation. Besides preventing the hoarding of notes and the stagnation of circulation, expiration provides another important element of control over the circulation of notes. It is this: Inevitably, some notes will be lost or inadvertently destroyed or permanently taken out of the community as souvenirs. These represent IOUs that will never need to be redeemed by the members of the community. Expiration and recall of the outstanding issue provides an opportunity to determine the amount so lost. That windfall could be appropriated by the system to help cover its administrative costs or to support charitable activity. In addition, a possible redemption fee, such as that applied with Toronto Dollars, could add to the system's fund.

The details of expiration include questions about the currency's life span—should it be a year, two years, or more/less? Should all notes expire on the same date or should the expiration dates be staggered? Should old notes be exchangeable for new notes without cost, and, if so, who should have this privilege? These are all issues that will have to be worked out in practice, but we can anticipate the impact of some possibilities.

A life span of at least two years would seem to be reasonable for a newly founded currency project. That will provide enough time to build the membership base and gain general acceptance in the community before having to deal with the additional administrative burden of redemption and conversion.

Allowing all notes to expire on the same date might be too disruptive, but, on the other hand, too many expiration dates coming too close together might create confusion. It should be possible to find a happy medium. A period of several weeks or even months might be allowed for an orderly process of exchange to take place, new notes being given for old notes.

The general public might dislike having to remain cognizant of the expiration dates of notes they hold and taking the risk of losing out by having a note expire while in their possession. Nonetheless, expiration provides such huge advantages that it ought to be given a fair test. As a way of avoiding the loss of goodwill, expired notes might retain some of their value for a limited time and be exchangeable for new notes at a reduced rate once the expiration date has passed. They might, for example, still be turned in for, say, 80 percent of their value for up to two months after expiration, 60 percent for another two months, 40 percent for a further two months, and so on, with expired notes becoming completely worthless one year after expiration. Also, it should be made easy to distinguish new notes from expiring notes. This might be accomplished by changing the colors and/or designs of the notes.

I am inclined to recommend that only members be allowed to exchange old, expiring notes for new notes. This would force nonmembers to spend their notes prior to expiration, which would help to simplify the exchange process. Members should be allowed to exchange notes without any penalty, one new note for each old note.

Comparing expiration to demurrage, expiration can be looked at as 100 percent demurrage, which can, however, be avoided by spending the notes before they expire or by exchanging old notes for new. If there is an exchange fee that cannot be avoided, such as the 10 percent fee imposed for redemption of Toronto Dollars, that fee can be considered a one-time demurrage charge. It may not work in quite the same way as the stamps on stamp scrip, which must be applied at more frequent intervals, but it does ultimately pull currency out of hiding.

SHOULD "INTEREST" BE CHARGED ON BALANCES?

The question of interest has already been discussed in chapters 13 and 15. While there has been much debate about this point and opinions vary, the weight of evidence, based on both moral arguments and practical arguments, I think, leads to the conclusion that, if charges *are* made on account balances, they should apply to both debit balances and credit balances.

In a sense, a debit balance is actually a loan (of goods and/or services) made by the community to the member whose account is in debit. But, as argued before, since everyone benefits from using the system, the costs of operating the system should be borne by all members in proportion to the benefits they derive from using it. Those who trade more benefit more. With this in mind, it makes sense to levy membership fees in proportion to the volume of trading rather than account balances.

Will such fees inhibit people from using the system to make trades? Only if the fees become excessive. Since the system is a cooperative association, not a profit-making entity, it needs to collect only enough to cover the costs of operating the system, and it is unlikely that excessive fees should ever become a problem. Even systems operated for profit tend to charge bearable fees. Credit card companies charge merchants a percentage fee on the basis of credit card sales volume, and the merchants seem willing to pay it. Fees based on volume of trading should likewise be acceptable to community exchange system users. If the system uses circulating notes as well as account ledgers, members will be able to avoid the transaction fees while the system will also avoid the cost of recording transactions.

ESSENTIAL ELEMENTS VS. MECHANICAL DETAILS

The evolution of money and banking over the years has resulted in the development of many effective and efficient mechanisms for "keeping score" in this game we call the economy. We must be careful to not throw out any babies as we discard the bathwater. In seeking to design and implement exchange systems that are more equitable and democratic, we must distinguish between what is essential and what is a mechanical detail. Devices such as paper currency notes, checks, credit cards, debit cards, smart cards, and electronic wallets have all been developed to make the transfer of credits (money) more convenient and efficient. As argued throughout this book, there is no reason why community exchange systems cannot utilize similar devices to transfer credits from person to person.

Conclusion

To conclude this chapter, let me reemphasize the importance of the fundamental, ongoing commitment of the participants: they must continue their support of the local currency by their willingness to accept it in payment. This commitment need not be enforced legally, but whatever can be done should be done to promote loyalty and solidarity among those who have been empowered to emit credits or currency. I must also emphasize that it is crucial to gain broad-based community support, which includes the participation of local businesses. That support must be deep as well as wide, which is to say it should include not only large numbers of businesses, but also different types of businesses—not only retailers but wholesalers, service providers, and even manufacturers, and above all employees.

If an organizing group can succeed in these areas, and if it follows the organizational and procedural guidelines outlined in this chapter, I believe that it will achieve an amazing result. Community currency would no longer be a novel curiosity associated with the fringes of society but will become "mainstream" and will demonstrate its true potential for building healthy communities and strong local economies.

Chapter 19

︷

A Business-Based Community Currency

*Change occurs when there is a confluence of both changing values and
economic necessity, not before.*

—John Naisbitt

Everyone is familiar with merchant discount coupons. We've all
used them at one time or another, and we know how they work: 10 percent
off any purchase; buy one, get one free; half-price on matinee movies; two
meals for the price of one; a free drink with the purchase of any other menu
item; and so forth. Every merchant knows that coupons can boost sales. But
even though a well-designed coupon campaign can stimulate business, it is not
without its own costs. First there is the cost of designing the coupon, then the
cost of getting it into the hands of the potential customer, and finally the lost
revenue of the discount itself. The hope, of course, is that these costs will be
more than made up for by the increased business that the coupons generate,
but that may or may not result. As competing businesses adopt the coupon
strategy, its effectiveness tends to diminish, and profit margins may be permanently reduced for everyone.

One of the primary factors that makes the use of coupons and other such
gimmicks necessary, even more than the local competitive climate, is the general deficiency of money in circulation. This is especially true during periods
of "recession." But even under normal economic conditions, the customers
of a particular type of business may have their buying potential restricted
because their disposable income is not keeping pace with inflation. This deficiency of money in circulation derives generally, not from any inadequacy in
the resources or productive capacity of the local economy, but rather from
the workings of remote agencies, including the Federal Reserve Board, the

federal government, large commercial banks, and transnational financial institutions such as the World Trade Organization (WTO), the World Bank, and the International Monetary Fund (IMF). These agencies, which are closely interlinked and often act in consort, hold tight control over the supply of money and the allocation of financial resources. By their policies, which they pursue in their own interests, they can stimulate or strangle both national and local economies.

As pointed out, however, local initiatives can be used to preserve the integrity of local economies in the face of adverse external conditions, initiatives that are private, voluntary, democratic, and not dependent on any government-granted privileges. The issuance of community currency is one such strategy that can be employed by local businesses. They can get all the benefits of a coupon campaign without having to incur most of the usual costs. They can do this if they will cooperate, as well as compete. Local chambers of commerce or neighborhood and minority business associations seem to be the ideal agencies for initiating local currency projects.

Community Trading Coupons

Suppose a group of businesses decided to cooperate in jointly issuing coupons that they all agree to accept, not only from the public but from each other as well. Such coupons could easily become a community currency, changing hands again and again and enabling additional trading by supplementing the supply of official money circulating within the local economy.

BASIS AND LIMITS OF ISSUE

How exactly would these coupons be issued? This is the key question. The issuing must be done properly to keep the coupons circulating and in demand. The primary factor is the nature of the agreement among the cooperating merchants. It must be carefully formulated, clearly stated, and strictly adhered to. Ideally, it should be enforced, not by any outside authority or by resort to the legal system, but by the parties to the agreement themselves. Given a well-developed agreement, the opportunity for continued participation should by itself be adequate incentive for adhering to its terms.

Here's how it can work. Each business agrees to accept payment partly in cash and partly in coupons, with each business itself deciding what percentage of the price to accept in coupons. This percentage can be based on the costs and the "value added" of the particular business (subject to some minimum percentage, say 20%). Payment partly in coupons and partly in cash allows the merchant to cover his or her cash costs, while all or part of the value added by the business can be received in coupon form. The percentage of the purchase price that each business is willing to accept in coupons can be advertised and posted on the premises. As an example, Primo Pizzeria might advertise, "We accept community trading coupons for up to 30 percent of the purchase price on any pizza." Of course, those accepting a higher percentage of payment in coupons will probably attract more of the available business than those accepting a lower percentage.

To get started, the cooperative business group distributes to each member standardized, preprinted coupons such as the one pictured in figure 19.1. The recipient business can then place the coupons into circulation in a variety of ways. The primary method of circulating coupons is by spending them, that is, by purchasing needed goods and services from other member businesses. The member business can also donate some coupons to nonprofit or community service organizations or give some of them to customers or prospective customers. It might also use them to pay employee salaries or bonuses, and some might be given to customers as change. In any case, by accepting the blank coupons from the cooperative, the member business obligates itself to redeem them: it must give back to the cooperative an equal amount of coupons over some period of time, or when the business decides to stop participating. If the coupons have an expiration date, this will force their redemption to take place within some finite time period. Of course, any business that is a member in good standing should be issued new coupons in exchange for old, expiring coupons. This maintains the circulation of coupons generally. Members should also agree that if and when they wish to withdraw from the cooperative they will turn over the same amount of coupons they originally received or make up any deficiency by paying in official currency.

Each business should receive any amount of coupons desired, *up to the equivalent of two months' potential average coupon receipts from sales,* just as in the formula for credit limits used in chapter 18. Thus, a business having average

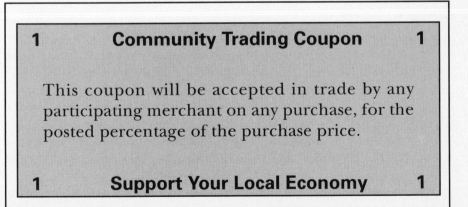

Figure 19.1. Conceptual rendering of a community trading coupon.

monthly sales of $20,000, which agrees to accept 20 percent of payment in coupons, can be issued up to $8,000 worth of coupons:

$20,000 monthly sales x 2 months x 20% payment in coupons = $8,000.

Similarly, a business having average monthly sales of $40,000, which agrees to accept 50 percent of payment in coupons, could be issued up to $40,000 worth of coupons:

$40,000 monthly sales x 2 months x 50% payment in coupons = $40,000

Lost or Expired Coupons

Some coupons will inevitably be lost or remain unredeemed by the expiration date. This amounts to a windfall for the cooperative, which can be credited to an "insurance and public benefit fund" to be used to offset losses due to bankruptcy or default of some member businesses. Any accumulated amount, over and above that needed for the prudent insurance of losses, can be used to support the administrative costs of the cooperative or be donated to local nonprofit community improvement organizations. The cooperative might also impose certain levies on its members for these purposes.

Issuance, Circulation, and Redemption

A coupon first enters circulation when a member business "spends" it on a purchase or donates it. The spender validates the coupon by signing and/or stamping it, and dating it (or dates could be preprinted on the coupons). The recipient of the coupon can then, in turn, spend it on purchases from any other member of the cooperative association. Others who are not members of the cooperative might also be willing to accept the coupons in payment for whatever they sell, knowing that they can spend them at any member business. Thus, the coupons might filter throughout the community, circulating as a supplemental medium of exchange up to their expiration date. This process is depicted in figure 19.2.

The benefits to the member businesses should be apparent. Instead of competing with each other for whatever scarce official money might be circulating within the community, they are cooperating to supplement that supply of money with a local exchange medium, making it possible for them collectively to transact a greater amount of trade. Since the coupons have value only for purchases made locally, they remain in the community instead of being spent outside it, tending to make the community more self-reliant and less dependent on export sales and goods imported from outside. Since anyone is allowed to earn and spend the coupons, their use benefits not only the members of the cooperative but everyone in the community. As the member businesses begin to thrive, others will be inclined to accept the coupons also,

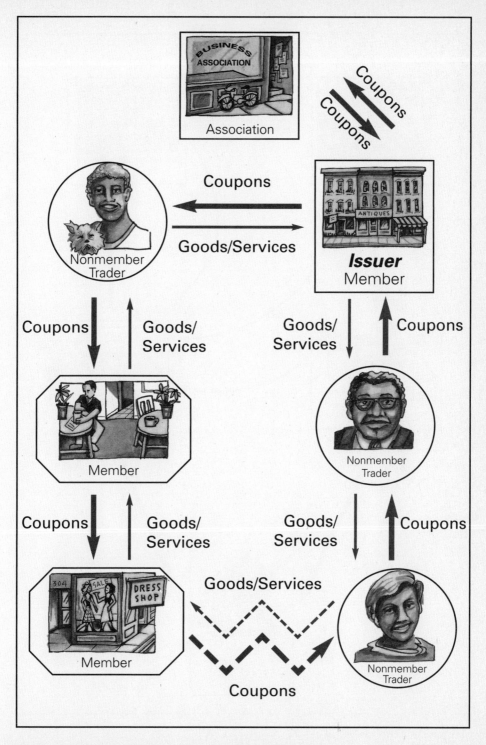

Figure 19.2. The community trading coupon circuit.

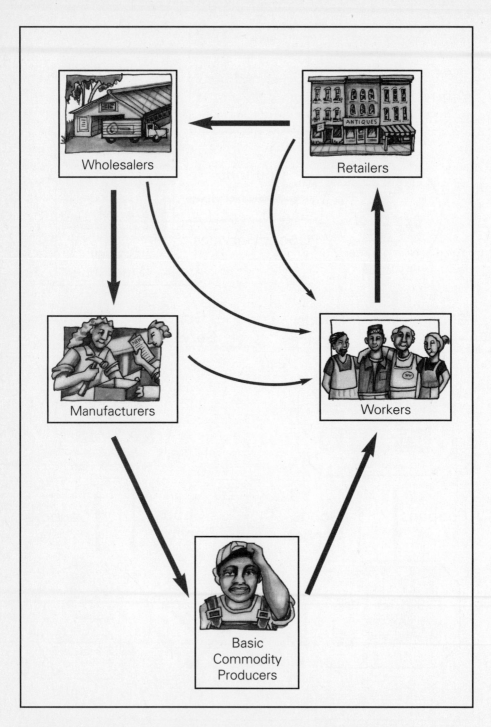

Figure 19.3. Currency circulation through the economic production and distribution circuit.

causing the amount in circulation to increase and giving the community greater and greater control over its own economy and quality of life.

COMPLETING THE PRODUCTION-DISTRIBUTION CIRCUIT

When employees and suppliers of the member businesses agree to accept the coupons, their impact will be greatly magnified. The key issue in establishing any community currency as a major factor in the local economy is to gain acceptance at all levels of the production-distribution circuit. Retail merchants should be able to use it to pay the wholesalers who supply them; the wholesalers should, in turn, be able to use the community currency to pay the manufacturers who supply them; the manufacturers should be able to use it to pay their raw materials suppliers; and the currency should be usable at every one of these levels to pay the workers. This pattern of circulation is shown pictorially in figure 19.3. The organizers of a community exchange system should make every effort to recruit participants from every level of the production-distribution circuit.

Chapter 20

Currency Alternatives for Impersonal Markets

Every person or corporation is entitled to create as much money—by buying, as he or it is able to redeem—by selling.

—E. C. Riegel

The current wave of alternative exchange activity has emphasized the importance of personal commitment within relatively small, limited communities. The social dynamics that exist within such cooperative groups are a very important element in assuring the workability of these approaches. The social and economic interrelationships within a community are mutually reinforcing and evolve simultaneously.

The formation of mutual credit systems such as LETS is one approach to building community while at the same time mobilizing the productive potential of labor that has been undervalued by the market or marginalized by the dominant national and global economic systems. The building of community is not just a byproduct, but an essential requirement, if human needs are to be adequately satisfied overall. To do so, however, we must deal with the current social, political, and economic realities, which include powerful transnational corporate competitors, extremely mobile capital, mobile populations within nations, restricted movement of labor across national boundaries, and transitory and impersonal relationships. Are there exchange alternatives that might be more credible and robust in such circumstances?

As Michael Linton expresses it, "Most regions are communities only in name rather than reality. **An effective community is a process, an ongoing collection of interactions and continuing relationships."**[1] Where these ongoing interactions and continuing relationships are lacking, it might be more effective to approach the problem of exchange by implementing a currency system involving commitments that are more formal and conventional. In an impersonal environment, one may know little or nothing about one's potential trading partners. In that instance it becomes expedient to use a currency that represents a claim to valuable property. Such a currency would tend toward the "hard," impersonal pole of the spectrum, but it could, nevertheless, be designed to be interest-free, and the system for issuing and regulating it could be democratic and cooperative. This could be a type of "funded currency" such as that described in chapter 14. Recall that a funded currency is issued on the basis of, and is redeemable for, real assets held in reserve. Assets used for this purpose might be official money or commodities and goods in inventory, preferably the latter.

Grain Banks and a Commodity-Based Currency

Newly harvested grain, for example, might be deposited in a "grain bank" or warehouse, and new currency would be issued to the farmers in return for their warehouse receipts. The farmers would then be able to spend that currency into circulation. When the grain is finally sold to a miller, say, the miller would pay for it by using community currency acquired in the market. He would first buy the warehouse receipt, then take it to the warehouse, where he would exchange it for the actual grain. That currency then would be extinguished. Having done its job, it is taken out of circulation. The process is shown pictorially in figure 20.1. This is what happens, step-by-step:

1. A farmer takes a load of wheat and deposits it in the bonded warehouse.
2. The warehouse, in return, gives the farmer a receipt showing the physical quantity of wheat deposited.
3. The farmer then takes the warehouse receipt and gives it to a mercantile (or co-op) bank.
4. The mercantile bank, in return, credits the farmer's community currency checking account or gives the farmer paper community currency notes.
5. The farmer now has a spendable exchange medium, which he or she uses to make purchases from any of the various merchants and traders who have agreed to accept the community currency.
6. They, in turn, spend the currency by making purchases from other participating merchants and traders.
7. Such exchanges between traders can occur many times, but eventually the community currency will find its way into the hands of someone who wants to buy the wheat, say, a miller. The miller then takes the currency to the mercantile bank and uses it to buy the warehouse receipt.
8. The miller then takes the receipt to the warehouse and claims the wheat.

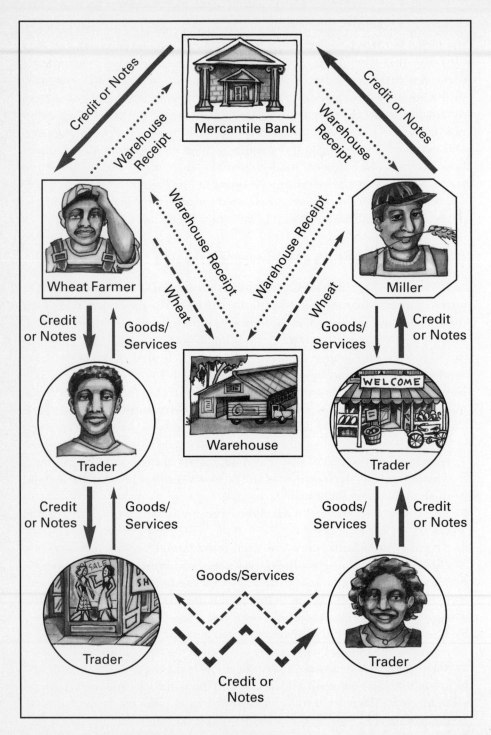

Figure 20.1. A Commodity-based currency circuit.

Note, in figure 20.1, that the warehouse receipt makes a complete circuit. It was issued by the warehouse to the farmer when he or she deposited wheat in the warehouse. The farmer then exchanged the receipt for credits or currency notes at the mercantile bank. The miller bought the warehouse receipt from the mercantile bank using community currency notes or credits acquired from the market in the course of his or her usual business of selling flour and other wheat products. The miller then took the receipt to the warehouse that originally issued it, where he or she exchanged it for the actual wheat. The warehouse receipt, having done its job, and having arrived back at its point of origin, is canceled or destroyed.

Likewise, the community currency notes or credits also make a complete circuit. The mercantile bank created and issued them to the farmer in exchange for the farmer's warehouse receipt. The farmer then spent the notes into circulation, in effect, exchanging them in trade for goods and services. The notes were then used by many other traders to mediate exchanges of goods and/or services. Eventually, they returned to the mercantile bank where they originated, being used to redeem the warehouse receipt that was the basis for issuing the notes in the first place. Once this basis is gone from the bank, the notes or credits must be retired from circulation.

A NUMERICAL EXAMPLE

Now let's put some numbers with the various steps in the issuance, circulation, and retirement of the notes to illustrate the details of how this type of currency works. Suppose the recent history of wheat prices shows them to be fairly stable at around $3.00 a bushel. Mr. Farmer (a likely name) brings in a crop of 20,000 bushels of wheat, which he deposits in a bonded warehouse. On receiving his warehouse receipt, Farmer takes it to the local cooperative mercantile bank, which credits his account or gives him currency at full parity with the recent average price of $3.00.[2] Farmer thus receives $60,000 in community currency or credit ($3.00 x 20,000). Since wheat is perishable, Farmer is not going to wait too long to market it, if he can help it. Wheat has a limited storage life, and proper storage involves significant costs. The longer he waits, the greater his costs and the more the wheat deteriorates. Unless there is an upward fluctuation in the market price sufficient to offset them, these costs will result in Farmer getting a lower eventual total return for his crop.

Suppose Farmer sells his crop two weeks later for a price of $3.20 a bushel or a total of $64,000. His account is then adjusted by adding the extra $4,000 that his crop proved to be worth over the $60,000 originally issued to him. In the unlikely event that the mercantile bank badly misjudged the market and Farmer only got $2.60 for his wheat, his account would be debited for the difference of $8,000. If his account balance was insufficient to cover the debit it could be carried over, and Farmer would receive that much less when his next crop was deposited.

Now suppose Ms. Miller is the buyer of the wheat from Farmer at a price of $3.20 a bushel. Miller must then take $64,000 of community currency to the mercantile bank. Of that amount, $4,000 is credited to Farmer's account, and the remaining $60,000 is used to redeem the warehouse receipt. Miller then takes the warehouse receipt to the warehouse, which allows her to withdraw the wheat. The warehouse receipt is then canceled. Since the bank no longer has the warehouse receipt, the $60,000 that Miller paid to redeem it must go out of circulation.[3] When both the warehouse receipt and the credits or notes that were issued on its basis have made the complete circuit, they are retired. The process begins again when more wheat or other valuable commodities are deposited in the warehouse.

Under this type of system, nobody has to go into debt to bring money into circulation, the amount of money and the amount of value are always in balance, and there is a natural incentive to expedite commerce and keep the money circulating rapidly. There are two reasons for this. First, it is to Farmer's advantage to sell his crop quickly to avoid storage costs and spoilage. Second, it is to his advantage to spend his money into circulation, giving others the means to buy his crop. All that one need do to issue money under such a system is to be productive.

Comparison to Conventional Money

There are, of course, expenses involved in operating warehouses and mercantile banks. These expenses must be covered, but they need not be covered in the usual way of banks, which is to charge interest on loans. In the example discussed above, there are no loans. Both the warehouse and the mercantile bank, like any other business, should be paid fees for the services they perform. They would receive a share of the money created.

Since there is no debt and no interest involved in this method of money creation, it would not suffer from the basic flaw in the conventional money system—the growth of debt beyond the supply of money available to pay it. A major flaw in the present official money system is that the supply of money is *not* automatically expanded to provide the means for purchasing the goods being brought to market. Since the supply of money may be artificially restricted, as well as misallocated, increased production typically drives market prices down. This causes producers to produce less, even though the real need and demand for the product may be far from being satisfied. This is one reason why there is hunger amid plenty; many of those needing food lack the money to buy it. **If the need is there, and the supply is there, the money to match them up should also be there.**

The current system makes producers slaves to money. There are three factors that create this condition. First, because money can come into circulation only through borrowing, a producer, one who owns real wealth, is allowed to convert that wealth to money only by becoming a debtor and using his or her wealth as collateral. Second, because interest is levied on this debt, most of the value, over time, is transferred to nonproducers who control the money and banking process. Third, because the amount of money is artificially regulated and kept in short supply relative to the amount needed for the repayment of debts, some producers will inevitably default on their loans and be forced to forfeit their collateral.

The greater the amount [of goods] produced, the greater the amount of currency in circulation; the more real wealth the community has (in the form of grain, lumber, metals, fuels, and so forth), the more currency there will be. Thus, the real wealth of the community is reflected (symbolically) in the amount of currency in circulation.

Using basic commodities as the basis for issuing currency automatically to producers in proportion to their production makes the producer "king" by placing the money-issuing power in his or her hands. It allows producers to reap their proper reward for their contribution to the community. It creates the amount of currency necessary to allow the purchase of the goods produced. The greater the amount produced, the greater the amount of currency in circulation; the more real wealth the community has (in the form of grain, lumber, metals, fuels, and so forth), the more currency there will be. Thus, the real wealth of the community is reflected (symbolically) in the amount of currency in circulation.

If next year's production falls short of this year's, the amount of money retired in the process of redemption of commodity inventories will be greater than the amount of new money issued. This will cause the money supply to contract along with the supply of commodities, reflecting the relative poverty of the community. If, on the other hand, production should increase from one period to the next, the amount of newly issued money will exceed the amount retired in the process of redemption. The supply of money will thus increase along with the supply of commodities, reflecting the relative prosperity of the community. **This approach to currency issuance would maintain a stable general price level, since there would be no central-bank-created artificial shortage of money, no legalized counterfeit from monetized government debt, no interest, and no misallocated bank credit.**

Producers would not be charged interest on money issued in this manner. The initial amount of money issued on the strength of any particular warehouse receipt would be based on the price history, stability of supply, and perishability of the commodity. The final total received by the producer would be determined by the eventual price received in the market. Producers' accounts would be updated periodically to bring them into line with the actual market results.

I can envision this type of commodity-based currency playing an important role in helping communities to strengthen their local economies and to achieve a measure of self-determination. It can be the foundation that supports a larger structure of local production and exchange. But it should not be the only type of community currency. Some, such as the farmers in our example, have products the value of which can be monetized. Others have only their skills and their labor. Prosperity requires abundant credit that enables everyone to be productive; so everyone should be empowered to some degree. This can be achieved by utilizing the other forms of mutual credit described in preceding chapters as well as those still to come in later chapters.

Chapter 21

⁓

Good Money for Good Work

Our objective should be to create exchange media issued on the basis of human service and Earth service rather than acquisitiveness and domination.

—GRECO

THIS CHAPTER DESCRIBES three innovative currency systems that communities might employ to support local improvements and charitable activities while, at the same time, strengthening the local economy.

Community Service Coupons

Every community depends heavily on its local businesspeople to support community improvement efforts including youth athletics, education, the arts, and other noncommercial activities that benefit the health of the community and the local quality of life. These activities are also heavily dependent on a corps of volunteers who contribute their time and skills. But there is a limit to how much cash the local business community can afford to donate, particularly when forced to compete with large national chain stores and cheap imported goods. Likewise, there is always a limit to the amount of time and energy that volunteers can afford to donate. A Community Service Credit System can transcend these limitations by acknowledging the value of services rendered without the payment of scarce official money. Instead, the organizers issue community service credits backed by the excess capacity of business donors, preferably in the form of circulating notes or "coupons."

A Community Service Credit System provides a way of mobilizing resources to serve local needs. It focuses specifically on volunteer services and community

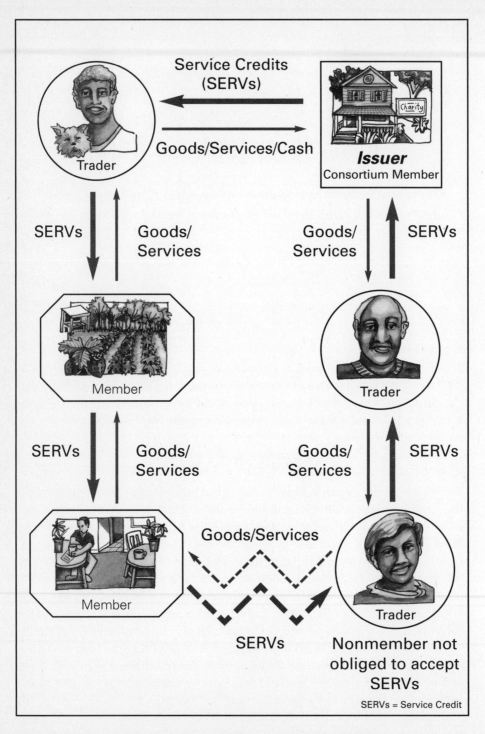

Service Credits
(SERVs)

Goods/Services/Cash

Trader

Issuer
Consortium Member

SERVs

Goods/
Services

Goods/
Services

SERVs

Member

Trader

SERVs

Goods/
Services

Goods/
Services

SERVs

Member

Goods/Services

Trader

SERVs

Nonmember not
obliged to accept
SERVs

SERVs = Service Credit

Figure 21.1, The cooperative community service credit circuit (SERV).

improvement projects, as well as on the support of the local business community. This support takes the form not of donations of cash, which is scarce, but of the donation of part of the participating businesses' excess capacity, which is often abundant. As pointed out in chapter 17, most businesses are able to produce more than they actually sell, and their marginal cost (the cost of additional production) is low in comparison with their average cost per unit of output. Thus, they can afford to donate some of that excess capacity. Further, it is quite likely that their small donations will produce direct and indirect benefits far exceeding their cost. These benefits include not only the goodwill of the community but increases in cash sales resulting from the willingness of business members to accept the community currency as partial payment for goods and services. Under this plan, other local businesses and governmental agencies are also enlisted to accept service credits in full or partial payment for the goods and services they offer for sale. The issuing organization then accepts the credits from them either as donations or in payment for some of the services it provides.

How It Works

Let's consider an example. Let's call the value unit in this system a "SERV." A SERV would be equivalent to one dollar's worth of service. A consortium of social action, community, environmental, self-help, and mutual-aid organizations might agree to jointly publish a periodical for education and outreach. All work would be paid in service credit receipts (SERVs) redeemable by the publication for copy space in the publication, for advertising, and for other related services such as typesetting, layout, or mailing list management. The more space a member organization wants in the magazine, the more service credit receipts it must deliver to the consortium. It can get them as donations or earn them by doing work on the publication or by selling some of its services. Figure 21.1 shows how community service credits are created, circulated, and redeemed.

Businesses can earn SERVs by accepting them in trade, either from individuals who have earned them by working in the consortium or from other businesses that have accepted them in payment. The businesses can then donate the receipts to any member organization or use them to pay for advertising in the consortium's publication. Businesses, by accepting the credit receipts as partial payment for their goods and services, would stimulate their own business just as the use of a discount coupon does. But unlike a discount coupon, service credit receipts can be passed along (spent) for value, or donated to promote activities of benefit to the community. Such a system might be started by making an announcement like the one in figure 21.2. To participate, each business signs an agreement form such as the one in figure 21.3.

Announcing Publication of the Community Weekly

YOUR CHANCE TO SUPPORT
A HEALTHY COMMUNITY
AND A CLEAN ENVIRONMENT

All of our workers are paid for their work in "community service credits," or "*SERVs*." You can support them and our publication by accepting our service credit receipts as you would your own discount coupons, for, say, 20%, 30%, 50%, or more off your regular prices. But unlike discount coupons, community service credit receipts <u>can be used by you to buy things you need</u>. You yourself can spend *SERVs* for goods and services offered by other participating businesses, or you can use them to buy valuable advertising in our magazine, *Community Weekly*. You can also use *SERVs* to pay for our typesetting, design, and layout services. We can do your advertising flyers, menus, business cards, or forms. Or you might prefer to donate *SERVs* to any of our member nonprofit and community improvement organizations that you might wish to support.

Call today and let us add you to our list of participating businesses. We will periodically publish this list in our magazine, indicating for each business the percent of payment that it accepts in *SERVs*. The higher the percentage, the more business you'll attract. And remember, it cost you nothing, because, you, in turn, can spend the *SERVs* you accept. By accepting community service credits, you'll be helping us to improve our community and you'll be boosting your own business at the same time.

Figure 21.2. Typical service credit announcement.

Agreement

(Name of business) agrees to accept (Name of consortium/publication) service credit receipts (*SERVs*) in partial payment for all products and services that it offers for sale, to the extent of ____% of the purchase price. (Name of business) may also limit acceptance of *SERVs* to particular hours or days of the week, as desired.

(Name of business) further agrees to donate ____% of its service credit revenues to (Name of consortium/publication) to be allocated to the member organization(s) of its choice.

(Name of consortium/publication) agrees to accept its own service credit receipts at face value in payment for advertising or other services that it customarily offers, to the extent to ____% of its standard fees.

This agreement may be terminated by either party at any time upon written notice and satisfaction of any outstanding obligations.

Signed _____Date _____
        (for Name of business)

Signed _____Date _____
        (for Name of consortium/publication)

Figure 21.3. Typical service credit agreement.

Earth Rescue Receipts (ERRs)

Earth rescue receipts (ERRs) are paper receipts for contributions made to what we will call "good work" organizations. ERRs would be issued by any organization belonging to a consortium of mutual aid, social action, community improvement, environmental, or other such associations. These receipts, issued in small denominations, would simply acknowledge the donation of money, materials, equipment, or services to a member organization. They would provide evidence that the donor has done "good work." Unlike the usual receipt form used to acknowledge a donation or payment, ERRs would be printed in standardized denominations, say five, ten, twenty, and fifty dollars, and would bear the name and seal of the consortium. When a donor makes a donation, the receipt would be dated and signed and/or validated by the recipient organization and given to the donor. Such a receipt might look like the one shown in figure 21.4. Except for the standard denominations, the steps described above are much the same as current practice in giving a receipt to acknowledge that a donation has been made. So what are the key features of the ERR proposal that make it empowering? Well, what if the donor, who now holds the ERR, were able to get something of value for it? Suppose some local businesses had agreed to accept ERRs in trade? In that case,

10	**Earth Rescue Receipt**	10

This coupon is evidence that a contribution of 10 dollars has been made to a member organization of the Community Improvement Consortium. It may be circulated as currency or it may be exchanged for a permanent tax receipt when donated to any member organization.

Signed _____Date_____

Support your local economy; accept ERRs in trade

10	**For Earth and Community**	10

Figure 21.4. Conceptual rendering of an Earth Rescue Receipt.

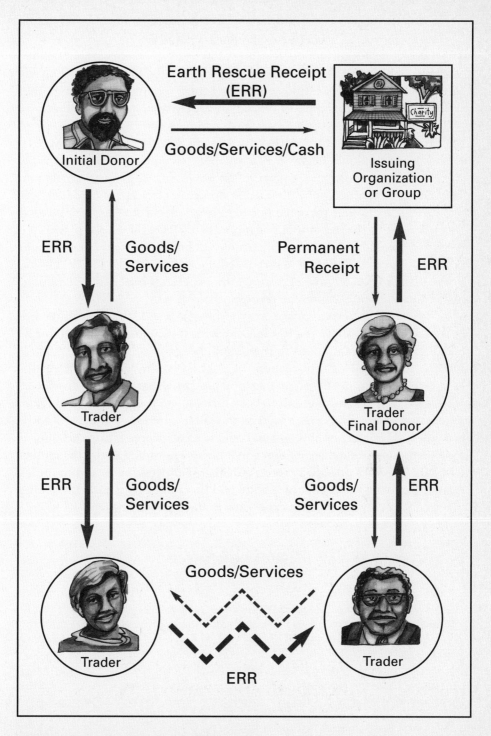

Figure 21.5. The Earth Rescue Receipt circuit.

ERRs could become a circulating currency. The original donor would not be any poorer for having made the donation but would simply have "gotten the ball rolling." An ERR would be considered to be a "temporary receipt" (TR), which could be spent. Thus, ERRs would pass from hand to hand, enabling any number of trades. They would constitute a local medium of exchange that would supplement the supply of official money circulating in the community.

Anyone wishing to make a *permanent* donation would give some amount of the circulating, "temporary" ERRs to any organization in the consortium. In return she or he would be given a "permanent receipt" (PR) to hold for tax purposes.[1] At that point the donated ERRs would be taken out of circulation. They could be reissued only when a new donation of cash, goods, or services was made. If at any time there happened to be an excess of ERRs in circulation (as evidenced by the discounting or refusal of ERRs in the marketplace), the consortium would suspend further issuance until permanent donations caught up with temporary donations and reduced the amount of ERRs in circulation to the proper level. Figure 21.5 shows the process of issuance, circulation, and redemption of Earth rescue receipts.

As the positive effects of this process become more evident, more and more people will want to share the burden of community improvement, either by making additional donations to the member organizations or by accepting ERRs in trade and in the payment of debts. Growing acceptance of this exchange medium, and the increasing local prosperity that it brings, will encourage greater and greater amounts to be contributed to the "good work" organizations and so encourage more work in the public interest. As the use of ERRs expands and proliferates, this process could to some degree replace taxation as a means of supporting the common good. Besides providing a local medium of exchange, it would provide a more participatory process for local community finance, reducing the power of lobbies and special interests and eliminating the need for many government expenditures and transfer payments.

ERR Questions and Answers

Q. Why would anyone accept Earth rescue receipts instead of official currency?
A. ERRs will be acceptable to four groups of people: ERRs will appeal, first, to those who support the community improvement and charitable activities that give rise to their issuance; second, to those who can see the benefits that a local currency provides in strengthening the local economy; third, to those who can see that they represent a sound medium of exchange spendable in the community; and fourth, to businesspeople who can see that accepting them will help increase their cash business as well.
Q. What will make ERRs a sound medium of exchange?

A. ERRs are not issued arbitrarily. They are issued on the basis of actual contributions of value to a participating organization. Each ERR, therefore, represents
a receipt for actual value delivered, either in cash, materials, labor, or services.
The amount of ERRs issued can never exceed the amount of value delivered.
An ERR will circulate only until some holder decides to contribute it back to an
issuing organization. At that point a permanent receipt will be issued to the
donor, to be held for tax purposes, and the ERR will be retired from circulation
until a new donation makes it possible to reissue it.

Q. Suppose not enough ERRs are donated back to member organizations. Won't
the amount in circulation keep building up and cause inflation?

A. That's an excellent question, and it gets to the heart of the monetary problem.
The issuance of ERRs, or any other currency that people are free to discount
or refuse, can never cause inflation. Here's why. As explained in chapter 9,
inflation is an increase in the general level of prices expressed in terms of the
predominant currency unit—in the present case, Federal Reserve "dollars." In
the past, the unit of account that we use, the dollar, was defined as a particular weight of silver or gold. Paper notes were issued to represent silver or gold
dollars and were convertible, on demand of the holder, into precious metal
coins at the bank. When paper notes or bank credits are improperly issued
into circulation, the value of all such notes is diluted; people will then prefer to
hold silver or gold instead of paper. If they accept paper at all, it will be at a
discount: they might accept paper dollar notes in payment for goods or services
but ask a higher price in paper dollars than in silver or gold dollars.

When money is an object of political control, as it has become in every country of the world, the issuing authorities will attempt to prevent the discounting
of their notes and the loss of their precious metal reserves by redemption. They
will refuse to convert the paper currency into silver or gold and declare the
notes to be "legal tender." The effect of these measures is to obliterate the
value standard and force acceptance of the inferior paper currency. When this
happens, sellers have no way of protecting themselves from harm except by
raising prices. Without a forced acceptance of the currency, there can be no
inflation. Thus inflation, which consists of higher prices generally, is really a
symptom that the market is devaluing the official currency. Since traders are
required by law to accept it at face value, the only adjustment they can make
is to raise their prices.

So the answer to your question is that, since ERRs need not be accepted
at face value, an excess of ERRs in circulation will cause them to be discounted
or refused by sellers in the market. If people see this happening, they will
tend to ease off on making initial donations of goods and services, because the
ERRs they would receive could not be spent for full value. At the other end of
the line, permanent donors who can make use of the tax deduction will tend
to accept more ERRs to donate for tax purposes since they can acquire ERRs
more cheaply. For example, if a one-dollar ERR is being accepted in the market at only ninety cents, a permanent donor could obtain a one-dollar tax deduction at a cost of only ninety cents. Whenever the market is free to discount
the value of a note (accept it at less than face value), this fact makes that currency system self-adjusting.

So to sum up, what can happen with an alternative currency is that it might not be accepted at par with the unit of account or official currency. In the past, such discounting of private currencies has in fact occurred. It is the result of improper issuance. In the case of Earth rescue receipts, the amount issued is strictly determined by the amount of value already donated, which itself is a measure of the community's willingness to support the activities of the issuing organizations.

What determines the amount that will remain in circulation is the time period within which the receipts are deemed to be valid in trade. This could be six months, a year, or forever. If an expiration date is specified, an ERR would no longer be accepted in trade after that date, but the holder could still exchange it for a permanent receipt and obtain the associated tax deduction. The experience of the market should make the determination as to whether or not an expiration date should be used.

Q. How will counterfeiting be avoided?

A. Effective anticounterfeiting measures have been well developed over a period of many years. These are commonly employed by governments and issuing banks to protect their currencies. They involve close security over the printing process, special inks and papers, serial numbering, and other measures. There is no reason why these same measures cannot be utilized for local currencies. Indeed, Ithaca HOUR notes are thought by many to be more difficult to counterfeit than Federal Reserve notes. Beyond that, two additional factors will discourage counterfeiting of a local currency. The limited area within which they are accepted and limited time period within which they would be circulated as a payment medium tend to make counterfeiting unprofitable.

Funded Temporary Receipts (FTRs)

While a local currency system such as the Earth rescue receipts might approach more closely the ideals for monetary transformation set forth previously, a funded currency backed by official money might be generally perceived as more conventional and, therefore, more sound and less risky. From that standpoint, it would seem more likely to garner widespread support not only from the local business community, but also local government, nonprofit organizations, and conventional financial institutions—an expectation that has been confirmed by the experience of the Toronto Dollar project. It would also provide better tax advantages to donors under current IRS regulations. Such a funded currency would be similar in many ways to Earth rescue receipts and would work as follows:

1. A consortium of nonprofit, social action, and community improvement groups begins a program under which a trustee accepts, on behalf of its members as a group, deposits of official money from any benefactor.

2. These deposits constitute an endowment fund, to be invested in ways that provide income in official currency to help the organizations meet their cash needs. These funds can be invested in direct obligations of the United States Treasury: bills, notes, and bonds. Alternatively, the funds can be invested in securities of quasi-governmental agencies such as the Government National Mortgage Association (GNMA) and the Federal Farm Credit Bank, which might use them in more socially responsible ways, or in corporate securities screened according to certain social responsibility criteria.[2]

3. These deposits are nonrefundable to the depositor; instead, the consortium issues to the depositor "funded temporary receipts" (FTRs) in standard small denominations, say five, ten, twenty, and fifty dollars. FTRs bear the name and seal of the consortium.

4. These FTRs are spendable with any business or individual willing to accept them.

5. FTRs thus circulate as currency.

6. Any individual wishing to make a permanent contribution to any member organization of the consortium can do so by delivering FTRs to that organization.

7. The organization then issues to the donor a permanent receipt (PR) for tax purposes, allowing the donor to receive a tax deduction for his or her contribution.

8. Such contributions are certainly tax deductible, because they represent the final action in conveying to the recipient organization an entitlement to the deposit of official money.[3]

9. Only recipient organizations that are members of the *good work consortium* are allowed to redeem the temporary receipts for official currency (draw official money out of the endowment pool) and only to a limited extent, preserving most or all of the endowment principal and allowing mainly the income to be withdrawn and spent.[4]

10. Interest earned on the Treasury investments accrues to the consortium and is credited to the members' accounts in proportion to the amount in "funded temporary receipts" donated to each organization in the given period. Thus, the organizations most strongly supported by the community will receive the greater portion of the investment earnings as well.

11. Consortium members need not use the temporary receipts (FTRs) that they receive as donations to draw official money out of the pool but instead may choose to spend them back into circulation, using them to pay employees and suppliers. Likewise, any interest income credited to its account, instead of being withdrawn in dollar currency, can be left on deposit and used as the basis for spending an equivalent amount of FTRs into circulation.

Figure 21.6 illustrates the FTR process.

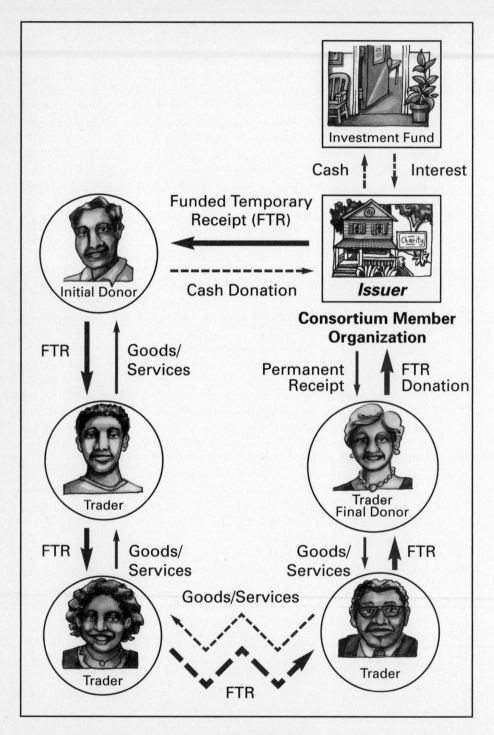

Figure 21.6. The Funded Temporary Receipt (FTR) circuit.

FTR Questions and Answers

—

Q. What's the point of this project?

A. Several beneficial results can be expected from the implementation of an FTR project. The main objective is to shift the bulk of human effort away from conspicuous consumption, waste, and the production of war materiel, toward "good work" that addresses human needs and the needs of the planet.

Q. How does this plan achieve that?

A. First, by encouraging the support of organizations that are taking action toward positive change. Second, by partially substituting a democratic, locally controlled, asset-based exchange medium in place of the official monopolized, centrally controlled, debt-based exchange medium.

Q. Well, how does that work?

A. It encourages the support of good work organizations, because the original depositor need not necessarily be the ultimate donor. Instead, he or she can *spend* the FTRs received in return for making a deposit. The process of donation is begun when the deposit is made and temporary receipts (FTRs) issued but completed only when the FTRs are delivered by the ultimate donor back to some participating organization. Thus, anyone with a dollar can "get the ball rolling" without making any financial sacrifice at all, except to forgo the potential interest income on the money thus deposited. (But if a donor is relatively poor and needs to spend the money instead of investing it anyway, this represents no actual loss to him or her.) Yet the initial donation (exchange of cash for FTRs) does result in a gain for the consortium group. In effect, the official currency becomes a capital pool earning income for the good work organizations; even the poor are empowered to be philanthropic, and the community is provided with a democratic, locally controlled, life-supporting medium of exchange.

   It is conceivable that this approach could ultimately transform the bulk of the official money supply into an endowment fund for good work. Further, it allows the supporters of good work, as a group, to maximize their collective tax advantage. Those who can make the best use of the tax deduction will typically be the ones who make the ultimate donations (of FTRs).

   In the existing system of money and finance, money is first allocated to those enterprises that promise the greatest monetary return, or to those mandated by the existing power structure: the megacorporations, government bureaucracies, military establishments, land and corporate speculators. Under the proposed FTR system, the allocation priorities are reversed. It puts positive change and public service groups first instead of last in the allocation of funds, and it empowers the realization of popular values, not just those of the rich and powerful. It may help to fulfill the prediction that "[the] first shall be last, and the last first."[1]

Q. Can other organizations join the consortium after it is initially formed?

A. Yes. Any organization wishing to participate may be admitted to the consortium by agreeing to the terms of membership.

Q. What if an organization is philosophically opposed to those already in it?

A. In the spirit of conviviality, no nonprofit organization should be excluded. Nor are exclusionary qualifications necessary, because an organization can directly benefit only to the extent that people make donations of FTRs to it. Thus, membership in the consortium in itself does not provide any direct financial benefit to an organization; it benefits only to the extent that it has popular support and receives donations of FTRs.

The foregoing proposals provide variations on the same theme and aim to achieve the same objective: to enhance the strength of the *third sector,* that is, the nonprofit organizations and groups devoted to social improvement and charitable activities, and to reduce its dependence on cash donations and government allocations. Each of the three proposals employs a community currency issued on the basis of donated goods, services, and cash, and thus donations are made to serve also as a medium of exchange, providing a stimulus to the local economy. Each proposal is designed to tap in to particular motivations, take advantage of existing tax laws, and appeal to particular cultural values and attitudes. I would expect that most communities will be able to find something suitable from this catalog of offerings.

Chapter 22

—◤—

Youth Employment Scrip (YES)

. . . one sixth of all 16- to 24-year olds in America—mostly males—are
currently "disaffected and disconnected." They are not associated with
any formal role in society, nor are they in any formal relationship with
another person.

—DAVID PEARCE SNYDER

YES IS AN ACRONYM that stands for both Youth Employment Service and Youth Employment Scrip. I have been promoting the YES project for the past several years. It is an application of the community currency concept that provides a way of mobilizing idle resources, in this case the labor and talents of young people, to serve community needs. Youth can be employed in either the private sector, or the public sector; in for-profit business or nonprofit organizations. YES acknowledges the value of the services they render, without the payment of scarce federal money. Instead, the Youth Employment Service issues Youth Employment Scrip as a way of paying young people for the work that they do.[1]

YES provides a supplemental supply of local currency, which businesses and individuals in the community agree to accept in partial or full payment for the goods and services they sell. The Youth Employment Service, which issues the scrip, then accepts it from others in payment for the services it provides. This approach does not depend on either tax revenues or charity. Rather, it simply provides the missing element required to bring people who need income together with work that needs to be done. That missing element is money. Complementary exchange mechanisms such as scrip have shown themselves to be viable and acceptable substitutes for official money. The YES program empowers youth, supports the local economy, finances important work, and helps to unify the community.

The Youth Problem

Young people are increasingly seen by the general community as a problem. A large percentage of crimes are committed by young people, and about one-quarter of our prison population is under age twenty-five. But crime is just the most extreme aspect of the problem. There are even greater numbers who do not become criminal but who are alienated and hopeless. Lacking self-esteem and basic social and employment skills, they ultimately become non-contributing citizens, immature adults, and ineffective parents. It is both callous and naive to think that police and prisons can contain the effects of the increasing alienation of youth and other marginalized groups. The young are our future. It is in everyone's interest to invest in their preparation and development and to help integrate them into society and the economy—to help them become capable, responsible, and successful, with an adequate degree of self-esteem, and thus able to direct their own lives. The question is how to do that most effectively. The experience of recent years has demonstrated that spending more money on schools and prisons is probably not the answer.

The "system" has rendered young people nonessential to the community, diminishing the well-being of both. Increasingly, adults perceive youths as troublesome, inadequate "others," which reflects back on how the youths perceive themselves. What young people need most is a sense of belonging. The attraction of gang membership is that it provides young people with an identity at a time in their lives when a primary issue is figuring out who they are and how they fit into the wider world. They especially need to have meaningful work and their own sources of income so that they can become independent and self-responsible as they grow into adulthood.

Peter Schwartz, president of the Global Business Network, wrote a book in 1991 titled *The Art of the Long View* (Doubleday). In that book he predicted that, by the year 2000, the earth's population would include more than two billion people between the ages of ten and twenty-one, about one-third of the total population. That prediction has proven to be correct. Schwartz devoted an entire chapter to the phenomenon of "the global teenager," a force that he says will dwarf other demographic factors over the next fifty years. The pressure of their numbers, energy, and idealism, he wrote, "will be so immense that it will reshape the world."

Schwartz pointed out that "in the past, societies with large numbers of adolescent males started wars." According to Gerald Smith, professor of religion and ecology at the University of the South in Sewanee, Tennessee, the youth population of Iran and Iraq rose to 50 percent before the Iran-Iraq war. That war killed millions of young males. Whether or not it was intentional, the war managed to relieve much of the political and economic pressure deriving from the explosion of the youth population in those countries.

Without the experience of being needed and responsible for their communities, and without adequate incomes, the young, as a group, can be expected to express their insecurity and alienation in criminal, antisocial, and self-destructive behavior. Suicide among young people is their leading cause of death.[2] Being largely left out of the mainstream economy, youths find power where they can—in gang membership and commerce in illicit substances. The misguided "war on drugs" is mainly a war against youth and minorities. Older people seem to have little understanding of youth culture and motivations and are all too ready to support "get tough" policies, which lead mainly to further alienation and a mushrooming rate of incarceration for nonviolent "crimes." This situation can only become worse if current economic trends and government policies continue. It will take extensive restructuring of our economic institutions and methods of allocating wealth in order to defuse this time bomb.

Clearly there is no end of work needing to be done. It is equally evident that the vast majority of young people are eager to work. What often is missing is the money to bring work and worker together.

We must find ways to integrate the young more effectively into society. We must provide them with meaningful work that is both edifying for them and valuable to the community. Clearly there is no end of work needing to be done. It is equally evident that the vast majority of young people are eager to work. What often is missing is the money to bring work and worker together. In the private sector, businesses need to keep costs down in order to compete in today's global economy. Their incentives are to minimize the number of people they employ and the amount they pay in wages, salaries, and benefits. As the pace of automation continues to accelerate, there will be an increasing gap between the number of jobs and the number of people seeking employment. In the public sector, there is pressure on all levels of government to keep costs and taxes down. With increasing government indebtedness and interest payments eating up an ever increasing portion of their budgets, and with more money being spent on a direct but futile attack on crime, governmental bodies are cutting back on social programs and releasing employees.

The socialistic approaches, which have been dominant since the Great Depression and Franklin Delano Roosevelt, have proven to be woefully inadequate. Bureaucratic programs, funded and administered by distant government agencies, cannot begin to solve problems that are inherently spiritual, interpersonal, and local. Indeed, such programs often perpetuate or exacerbate the problems they are intended to solve.

One principle seems clear. Those closest to a problem are best equipped to solve it. Effective solutions to community problems can be found only at the community level. The first thing to do is to change our attitudes and shift our focus—away from Washington, away from the state capital, and back to ourselves, our neighborhoods, and our communities.

The Money Problem

Lack of money is the usual reason given for problems not being addressed. Yet, as described earlier, official money is kept purposely scarce in the mistaken belief that scarcity is what gives money its value. As a result, the official monetary system does not provide an adequate supply of money to allow for a fair distribution of the products of the economy, or even to provide everyone with a subsistence level of income. Monetary scarcity also makes it possible for money to be "lent" at high rates of interest and enables those who control its creation to determine the course of the economy and the financial fate of the people. The tragic result is that important work remains undone and human needs often go unmet because of the lack of money. This scarcity is felt most acutely at the margins of society, by those who are less well connected and whose skills are least valued by the market economy. Their numbers include an ever growing proportion of young people.

This situation can, and must, be remedied. As shown throughout this book, money is a human creation. It is just a medium of exchange. Why should money ever be too scarce to match idle workers with work that needs to be done? We can restore the integrity of our local economies, which will, in turn, go a long way toward solving our social and environmental problems. As argued throughout this book, one way to do this is to create our own local medium of exchange to supplement scarce national currency. This has been done many times before, and it is being done now in many places around the world. A local currency can provide the means of connecting buyers and sellers who would otherwise be kept apart by lack of money.

Young people can thus be reconnected to the community and brought into the economy as productive members, learning important skills, building self-esteem, and earning the income that they need to begin to become self-supporting. This can be accomplished by voluntary local action without the need for new legislation or government financing, by using local currency scrip as the bridge.

How Does the YES Program Work?

The project hub is a central coordinating body that we call the Youth Employment Service or yesXchange. It could be a nonprofit organization or government agency or even a private, for-profit business. This coordinating body plays several roles:

- It acts as an employment agency, placing young people in jobs.
- It plays the role of a "bank," issuing and redeeming scrip.
- It acts as a trade exchange, helping to broker trades between participating businesses.
- It collaborates with other agencies in arranging for training, counseling, and other forms of worker support.

The coordinating body can function much like a temporary employment agency, except that, in this case, all the employees are young people within a certain age range and are paid in scrip instead of (or in addition to) official money. The client businesses and agencies needing temporary employees pay their fees to the yesXchange partly in YEScrip and partly in cash. The cash part allows the yesXchange to meet that portion of its overhead expenses that can only be paid in cash and to provide a partial cash wage to the youths it employs. In order to assure the value and continued acceptability of the scrip, the yesXchange must be willing to accept its own scrip in payment of its fees, at par with official currency.

A YEScrip unit is equivalent to one dollar's worth of service. Businesses can earn YEScrip by accepting it in trade, either from individuals who have earned it by working for the Youth Employment Service or from other businesses that have accepted it in trade. The businesses can then use the YEScrip to pay for work done by young workers. Businesses, by accepting YEScrip in partial payment for their goods and services, stimulate their own business just as their use of a discount coupon does. But unlike a discount coupon, YES notes can be passed along (spent) for value or donated to promote activities of benefit to the community.

The following example demonstrates the process by which scrip is issued, circulated, and redeemed. It is shown pictorially in figure 22.1. The YEScrip has to begin somewhere, and in this case it is issued by the Youth Employment Service. Suppose the Berry Farm needs help harvesting its strawberry crop. The owner calls the yesXchange, which agrees to send Carolyn out to pick berries. At the end of the week, Carolyn submits her signed time sheet to the yesXchange, and it gives Carolyn newly issued YEScrip as pay for her work.

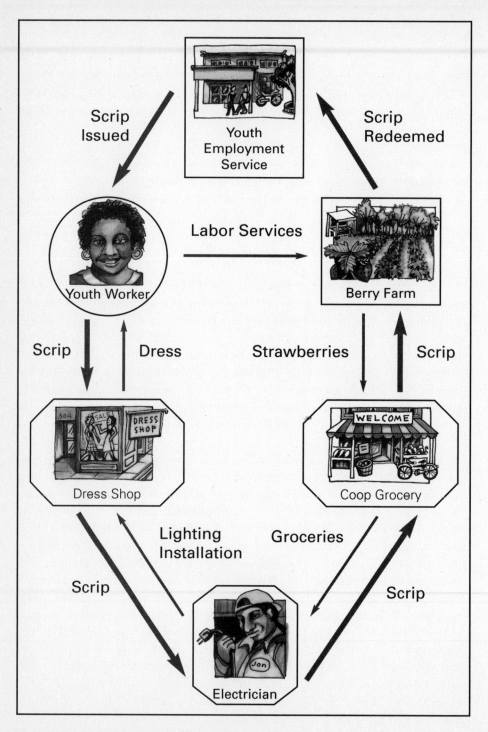

Figure 22.1. Youth Employment Scrip circuit.

What good is the YEScrip to Carolyn? The yesXchange has persuaded several local businesses to accept YEScrip in payment for the goods and services they sell. The Dress Shop is one of them. So Carolyn spends her scrip to buy a new dress. The Dress Shop, in turn, hires an electrician to install new lighting fixtures. The electrician then spends the YEScrip on groceries at the Coop Grocery Store, which uses it to buy strawberries from the Berry Farm. The Berry Farm uses the YEScrip to pay what it owes to the Youth Employment Service for Carolyn's labor. The Youth Employment Service retires the scrip until more work is done. Now the scrip has come full circle. It was issued by the YEService when it paid Carolyn on behalf of the Berry Farm, and it was redeemed by the YEService when it was accepted from the Berry Farm in payment of its debt to the service. Note that the scrip could have changed hands any number of times before making its way back to the Berry Farm and the yesXchange. For the sake of clarity and simplicity, this example has shown just a few transactions.

In practice, each transaction might involve some combination of scrip and official money. The Dress Shop, for example might be willing to accept 50 percent of the price of any merchandise in YEScrip and require the other 50 percent in official money. Thus, Carolyn could buy a $40 dress by paying Y20 (Y is the symbol for YEScrip) and $20. The Dress Shop now has $20, which it can use to cover its cash costs; it also has Y20, which it can use to hire the electrician, who might also require some cash to cover cash costs. But since the electrician's cash expenses are lower, he or she might be willing to accept 80 percent of fees in YEScrip and 20 percent in official money.

Benefits of the YES Project

The implementation of such a project results in several positive effects:

1. It helps to empower a marginalized group of citizens (youths) and make them stakeholders in the community by integrating them into the local economy.
2. It supports the local economy by providing a supplemental local currency to facilitate trade—trade which in many instances could not otherwise take place. Since scrip is recognized only within the local community, this supplemental currency favors local goods and services over imports.
3. It provides a means of financing work that serves the common good, improves the quality of life, and enhances the health of the community.
4. It unifies the community in an effort in which everybody wins.

YEScrip provides an exchange medium issued on the basis of effort put forth by youthful workers, effort that can be applied to commercial enterprises, human service, and/or community improvement. It is completely sound because it is firmly based on the exchange of real value. Although Youth Employment Scrip is described in terms of circulating certificates or notes, it could also take the form of credits in an electronic system using "smart cards" or debit cards or some combination of accounting credits and circulating notes.

Involving Local Businesses

Merchants should be willing to accept YEScrip, not only because of its benefits to the community, but also because it will help them to attract a greater total amount of business and utilize some of their excess capacity. As pointed out earlier, accepting a community currency can stimulate a merchant's business just as discount coupons do, while avoiding most of the costs associated with a coupon campaign.

Sometimes the use of a coupon is restricted to assure that it will be used in a way that takes advantage of a business's excess capacity and will not draw away existing cash business. A movie theater, for example, may accept coupons only for matinee performances when the house is typically only partly filled, or a restaurant may honor coupons only at particular (slack) hours and on slow days, and airlines may honor coupons on a "space available" basis only.

Like a discount coupon, YEScrip gives a participating business a competitive advantage, but, unlike a coupon, accepting YEScrip costs the business little or nothing because the merchant can, in turn, spend it for something that he or she needs. The key difference between YEScrip and a discount coupon is that businesses agree to accept YEScrip not only from the public but also from each other, and while a coupon is accepted only once and then canceled and discarded, scrip can change hands, just like cash, any number of times.

Each business agrees to accept payment partly in cash and partly in YEScrip, with each business itself deciding what percentage of the selling price to accept in YEScrip. This percentage should be based on the cash costs and value added of the particular business. The cash portion allows cash costs to be met, while all or part of the value added by a business can be received in scrip. The percentage of the price that each business is willing to accept in scrip can be advertised and posted on the premises. As an example, the Pizza Parlor might advertise, "We accept YEScrip for up to 50 percent of the purchase price on any pizza."

The issuance of currency at the local level and the willingness of traders in the community to accept this supplemental exchange medium in payment for goods and services, especially the necessities of life, does two things: (1) it gives people more choice over the work they choose to do, encouraging the application of their energies and resources to activities consistent with their values, and (2) it provides the community with a sound medium of exchange that by its very nature is abundant, democratic, and locally controlled.

As the social and economic benefits of such a program become more evident, more and more people will want to participate. Growing acceptance of the local exchange medium will allow for the issuance of additional amounts, which will further encourage work in the public interest. The resultant prosperity should also stimulate an increase in donations to the local nonprofit sector in general. Besides providing a local medium of exchange, YEScrip provides a more participatory process for allocating the resources of the local community, reducing the need for many government expenditures and transfer payments.

Eventually, most of the local merchants will jump onto the bandwagon and accept YEScrip to attract their share of the available business, which will have expanded because of the increased purchasing power that YEScrip brings to the local economy. And, of course, those accepting a higher percentage of payment in YEScrip will probably attract more of the available business than those accepting a lower percentage.

Program Participants and Agreements

Besides the Youth Employment Service, which serves as the hub and central coordinating body, three distinct groups participate in the YES program. First there are the youth workers, whom we refer to as *work partners*. Second there are the businesses that hire the young workers. These are called *employment partners*. The third group is comprised of businesses that have agreed to accept scrip in full or partial payment for the goods and services they sell. These are called *trade partners*. Employment partners will normally also be trade partners, since they are allowed to use scrip to pay their bills to the YEService and thus have a particular reason (in addition to all the community benefits) to earn some scrip income.

Each of these "players" in the program has a particular agreement that defines the terms and conditions of their participation. These agreements must be carefully formulated, clearly stated, and scrupulously adhered to. Participating businesses (employment partners and trade partners) should have maximum freedom to set the terms and limits of scrip acceptance and to be able to opt out of the program at any time. Employment partners, however, must pay whatever they owe to the yesXchange for the value they received (in the form of youth labor). If the program is properly run, businesses will cherish the opportunity for continued participation.

The greatest burden falls upon the yesXchange. The most fundamental feature of any currency issue is the commitment of the issuer to accept it at full face value in payment for whatever the issuer sells. In this case, the yesXchange must be willing at all times to accept the scrip it issues in payment from its employment partners for the youth labor provided. Thus, the basis of issue

Announcement

Say Yes to Youth

PROMOTE A HEALTHY AND PROSPEROUS COMMUNITY
AND A CLEAN ENVIRONMENT

ANNOUNCING THE YOUTH EMPLOYMENT SERVICE (YES) AND
YOUTH EMPLOYMENT SCRIP (YES)

The Youth Employment Service is a nonprofit service agency devoted to the development and empowerment of our young people. All of our workers are paid for their work using a form of "service credits" issued as Youth Employment Scrip (YES). You can support our youth and at the same time promote the local economy by accepting our scrip as you would your own discount coupons, for, say, 20%, 30%, 50%, or more off your regular prices. But unlike discount coupons, YES notes can be used by you to buy things you need. You yourself can spend YES for goods and services offered by other participating businesses, or you can use them to hire youth workers to help you in your own business. Or you might prefer to donate YES to any community improvement organization that you might wish to support.

Call today and let us add you to our list of participating businesses. We will periodically publish this list, indicating for each business the percentage of payment that it accepts in YES. The higher the percentage, the more business you'll attract. And remember, it costs you nothing, because you, in turn, can spend the YES you accept. By accepting Youth Employment Scrip, you'll be helping our youth, our community, our local economy, and yourself.

With YES, Everybody Wins!

Figure 22.2. Youth Employment Scrip announcement.

Agreement

(Name of business) agrees to accept Youth Employment Scrip in partial payment for all products and services that it offers, to the extent of ____% of the purchase price. Th Youth Employment Service agrees to accept YES at full face value in payment for all services that it customarily offers, to the extent of ____% of its standard fees.

This agreement may be canceled by either party at any time upon written notice and payment of any outstanding balance.

Signed_____Date _____
for (name of business)

Signed_____Date _____
for Youth Employment Service

Figure 22.3. Youth Employment Scrip agreement.

for Youth Employment Scrip is labor, and the "backing" for it is the commitment of those who receive that labor to provide an equal amount of value to the community in the form of goods and services, using YEScrip as a vehicle.

As pointed out above, YEScrip first enters circulation when the YEService uses it to pay a worker. The service might validate the scrip by signing and/or stamping it, and dating it (or dates could be preprinted on the notes). The recipient of the scrip can then, in turn, spend it on purchases from any participating merchant or anyone else willing to accept it in payment. Thus, a YEScrip note can circulate as a supplemental medium of exchange up to its expiration date, the holder being assured that it will be accepted by, at the least, any employment partner or trade partner.

The benefits to the participating businesses are significant. Instead of only competing with each other for whatever scarce official money might be circulating within the community, they would also be cooperating to supplement that money with a local exchange medium, making it possible to transact a greater amount of trade while also empowering the youths of the community. Since the YEScrip has value only for purchases made locally, it remains in the community instead of being used to buy from outside the community, tending to make the community more self-reliant and less dependent on export earnings.

A YES system might be started by publishing and distributing an announcement like the one in figure 22.2. Each business would sign an agreement form such as the one in figure 22.3.

YES Questions and Answers

Q. Why would anyone accept Youth Employment Scrip instead of official currency?

A. YEScrip will be acceptable for several reasons. (1) It will be an acceptable form of payment to young people who need work and are unable to find employment that pays official money, because they know that they can spend it at a variety of businesses in the community. (2) YEScrip will be acceptable to businesses that wish to employ youths because they know that they can use YEScrip to pay their wages. (3) YEScrip will appeal also to others who support the activities that give rise to their issuance, namely the employment of young people in meaningful work useful to the community and private sector. (4) YEScrip will appeal to local merchants who can see that accepting it will help to boost their cash business and strengthen the entire local economy. (5) It will be acceptable to anyone in the general public who can see that YEScrip represents a sound medium of exchange that can easily be spent in the community.

Q. What will make YEScrip a sound medium of exchange?

A. YEScrip is not issued arbitrarily. It is issued on the basis of valuable work done by the young workers. Each YES note, therefore, represents a receipt for actual value delivered. The amount of YEScrip issued can never exceed the amount of labor value delivered. A YES note will circulate only until some holder decides to pay it to the Youth Employment Service for services rendered, or donates it to the service. At that point the YES note will be retired from circulation until more work is done to allow it to be reissued.

Q. Won't the issuance of YEScrip cause inflation?

A. As pointed out in the previous chapter, the issuance of YEScrip, or any other currency that people are free to discount or refuse, can never cause inflation. Since YEScrip need not be accepted at face value by anyone except the issuing agency, an excess of YEScrip in circulation will cause it to be discounted or refused by sellers in the market. As people see this happening, they will tend to ease off on their acceptance of it, because the YEScrip they would receive could not be spent for full value. At the other end of the line, businesses that buy labor from the Youth Employment Service will tend to accept more YEScrip since they can thereby get workers more cheaply. For example, if a one-dollar YES note is being accepted in the market at only eighty cents, a business that uses YES services can get five dollars worth of labor for YES that costs it only four dollars. Whenever traders are free to discount the value of a note, that is, accept it at less than face value, the market will automatically force the issuing authority to avoid overissuance; this makes the currency system self-adjusting.

Q. Should YES be issued in the form of accounting credits or paper notes?

A. Conceptually, it doesn't matter whether the YEScrip takes the form of paper notes, tokens, or ledger balances (bookkeeping entries). These are all symbolic representations of the same thing—the values being exchanged—and each is "backed" by the same commitment of the issuer to redeem the scrip by providing value. So checks, notes, cards, and electronic transfers can all be used interchangeably, as they are in the official monetary system. Each form has its particular advantages, but paper notes are the simplest form to implement and handle.

Q. What if a business accumulates too much YEScrip?

A. A local currency, in its sole role of exchange medium, should be spent as fast as it is taken in. If a participating business finds insufficient opportunity to spend YEScrip on things that it needs, the surplus would indicate that it overestimated either (1) the value-added portion of its selling price or (2) the willingness and/or ability of others in the community to accept YEScrip. In either case, a business can remedy the situation by reducing the percentage of YEScrip that it is willing to accept in payment, giving it time to spend down its accumulated surplus of YEScrip.

Q. Should YEScrip have limited or perpetual life?

A. Having a periodic recall feature or expiration date is one way of addressing the problem of keeping the YES notes an exchange medium and limiting their use as a savings or "value storage" medium. As we have discussed previously, it is important to keep these two functions separate. One way to do it is to have the local currency notes expire after a certain length of time, say, one year. Member businesses might be allowed to exchange expiring notes for new notes with a later expiration date.

EPILOGUE

THE FOREGOING CHAPTERS have attempted to communicate, as briefly as possible, my understanding of the essential nature of the money problem and the path toward economic democracy. I have reported some of the more significant developments in the movement toward democratic, community-based systems of exchange and offered some critical direction. My hope is that these efforts will prove helpful to those who carry forward with this important movement.

As the dominant institutions of industrial civilization continue to decay, and as more people find themselves pushed to the margins of the money economy, pressure will build for the implementation of effective alternatives. True democracy can only be forged within the economic realm, and money and exchange are the key elements that must be democratized. Community currency and nonpolitical private exchange systems that are equitable and just will be essential in assuring that the transition to a postmodern society will be smooth and peaceful.

Appendix A

～

Note on Banking as a Profession, and Its Reform

D R. RALPH BORSODI often argued that banking was in great need of reform. I agree, and would suggest that the need is even greater today than it was in his time. Borsodi provided some good direction on how that reform should proceed when he outlined the following principles, which he saw as necessary in reforming the banking profession to serve the common good.

1. Banking is a profession and not a business. The banker, like the lawyer and the doctor, unless he stultifies himself, must put the trust reposed in him before anything else. We entrust our health and even our lives to our doctor. We entrust vital rights and our material interests to our lawyer. We entrust our money and our savings to our banker. The banker is a trustee, and he has not more moral right to exploit the funds entrusted to him than a doctor has the right to exploit the sickness of his patients, or a lawyer the difficulties of his clients. *Professional compensation is one thing, but maximizing profits is something altogether different* [emphasis added].
2. Bankers, like lawyers and doctors, should therefore be licensed and only those qualified to study (usually at an accredited university) and who observe professional standards both in their practice and in their charges for their services, should be permitted by law to engage in banking.
3. The banker, by the essential nature of the service he renders, is a fiduciary trustee. It is malpractice for him to do anything with the funds entrusted to him that he ought to know should not be done with them, just as it is malpractice for a doctor to prescribe treatments that he ought to know endanger the health of his patients. Nobody, no matter how great the profit, has a moral right to betray those who trust him. It is betrayal to exploit the opportunity for profit that trust in his integrity creates.

4. Bankers should not be granted charters to operate banks as business corporations; they should not be legally authorized to earn profits for stockholders, because corporations limit the liabilities of those who own them. In practice the law makes it virtually impossible to hold corporate officers and directors liable for what I am calling malpractice.

   Banks should be owned and operated by sole proprietors, by partnerships, by mutual and cooperative associations; and all those who own them and conduct them should be personally responsible and accountable for the safety of the funds entrusted to them. All laws which exempt bankers, as would be true of all laws which exempted any kind of professional person from full liability for his or her practices, are morally null and void.

There is one point on which I disagree with Borsodi, and that is the reliance on licensing statutes and their enforcement by the state as a means of maintaining professional standards. Licensing often leads to restraint of trade and extortionate fees by placing unreasonable obstacles in the way of those who would enter the profession. It can also be argued that most licenses are a violation of basic human rights guaranteed by the Constitution. I favor the elimination of such statutory privileges and prefer to rely on other, less coercive means. These include (1) open access to information, (2) consumer education, and (3) the certification of practitioners by private accrediting agencies. As Borsodi himself proposes, banks should not be operated as corporate businesses. Without the limited liability protection afforded by the corporate umbrella, banks would tend to be smaller, local in scope, and more responsive to the needs of their clients. The potential for currency abuse would be greatly constrained if the establishment of banks (or the noncorporate exchange systems that might succeed them) was less restricted, and the if depository and credit creation functions were handled by separate agencies.

Borsodi also enumerated a number of measures that he thought would eliminate inflation, reduce unemployment, end the boom-and-bust business cycle, reduce speculation, provide for the capital needs of the local community, and prevent the government "from using the banks of the nation to indulge in its present extravagances by forcing them to finance its deficits."

He argued that, if the following measures were taken, *the whole moral climate of the economy would be transformed:*

1. Bankers, as professionals, should ensure both the safety and proper use of the funds entrusted to them.
2. Professional bankers should see to it that the funds entrusted to them be used only to facilitate commerce.
3. Professional bankers should give priority to financing local needs before investing in projects outside the community.

4. Professional bankers should take over the whole field of investment, taking it "out of the hands of the so-called investment bankers of Wall Street."

It is not appropriate to comment here on each of those points, but they do provide food for thought and debate. There have, however, been some encouraging developments in banking and finance that are worthy of note. The credit union movement, which embraces more democratic principles and emphasizes community finance, is growing ever stronger. There are some notable examples of banks that, while still operating under the umbrella of the corporate charter, have acted to improve their stewardship and give priority to the financing of local needs. Among these is the Shorebank group operating in Chicago, Cleveland, and Detroit, whose "primary business is making loans to local residents in underserved inner city neighborhoods." Others include Community Bank of the Bay in Oakland, California, and the Community Capital Bank of Brooklyn (N.Y.). In addition to these, a wide variety of "socially responsible" investment funds now exist, and dozens of nonbank community loan funds are springing up all over the country.

Appendix B

⌇

Note on the Proper Basis
of Issue for Currency, and the Means
# of Financing Capital Investments and
Consumer Durables

THE FOLLOWING HELPS to clarify a point made earlier: that there are two very different things going on in commercial banking. Commercial banks have the primary responsibility of issuing new money into circulation, which they do by making loans. In this role they are called "banks of issue." They also act as "depository banks," accepting deposits of existing money that people and businesses wish to save.[1] This money is then loaned to consumers who need it to purchase consumer durable goods ("big ticket" items), such as cars and houses, or it is loaned to businesses for tools and equipment. (In actuality, these deposits are held as "reserves" against which new loans are made.) Much of the problem with banking today stems from the confusion caused by the fact that the terminology, forms, and procedures for the two functions are the same. It would, I think, be best to completely divorce the creation of new exchange media from any association with the savings-investment process. I strongly recommend that banks of issue be completely separate from depository banks, as was largely the case in the past, when commercial banks were mainly banks of issue and the depository function was largely handled by savings banks, credit unions, and savings and loan associations.

At any given time, there is a flow of goods and services coming to market. The problem that the instrument called money seeks to solve is to provide each person who has a part in all this production with the means of acquiring his or her share of its total value. Colonel Harwood describes the typical money creation process that prevailed prior to World War I. While banking had serious problems even then, sound principles on the basis of issue were still being followed by most of the larger banks.

As a manufacturer shipped completed things to market, he would prepare a document describing the shipment, take it to his bank, and borrow purchasing media that, in practical effect represented the things en route to market. The bank made the loan by crediting an appropriate amount to the checking account of the manufacturer, but this amount was not deducted from other checking account liabilities of the bank. Thus new purchasing media were created and were placed in circulation when the manufacturer used the addition to his checking account to pay wages, salaries, suppliers, and other costs of processing the things sent to market. (As the things were sold, the receipts from sales were used to repay the bank loan by having that amount deducted from the manufacturer's account. Thus the purchasing media created for temporary use were withdrawn when their purpose had been served.)

Those who received the newly issued purchasing media from the manufacturer then could choose whatever they wanted that the markets offered. . . . The procedure described above has been modified in recent decades as mass production has developed on a broader scale and now occurs almost continuously throughout the year. . . .

The automobile manufacturer arranges with a commercial bank for a "line of credit" and gives a promissory note that may be paid off only once each year during the model changeover period when no cars are en rout to markets. Thus a series of loans continually being repaid as cars are sold is replaced by a single borrowing resulting in the creation of purchasing media that remain in circulation as long as the flow of cars to markets continues. . . .

As commercial banking developed, especially in the United States, two quite different functions have been performed by the same institutions. In addition to the commercial banking function already described, most banks performed an investment function, accepting saved purchasing media and investing it.

The borrower from the bank in the savings-investment transaction is *not* at that time sending to or otherwise offering things of equal value in the markets to be sold. He does not desire purchasing media so that he may distribute it to employees and suppliers who participated in preparing things *for* the markets. His desire is to claim things *from* the markets, either equipment for his factory or a new car for personal use, or any of the multitude of other things available, such as new bricks for construction of a factory, etc. Consequently, **the bank should not create new purchasing media for such a borrower but should lend him purchasing media already in existence that some present owner or owners save and deposit in the bank** [emphasis added].

Probably because the same banks have been performing two functions, each of which involves lender-borrower transactions, similar forms (such as promissory notes), and related procedures, many bankers have confused the two functions. . . . In the first type of procedure, the new purchasing media created represented the exchange value of things en route to or being offered for sale in the local markets; however, in the second, the new purchasing media represented things (such as land, factories, or consumer goods) not being offered by the borrowers for sale but on the contrary being removed by them from the markets.

Perhaps the clearest example of the confusion between commercial and non-commercial banking is provided by the financing of automobiles in or en route to markets in contrast with consumer installment borrowing to purchase a new car. The important distinction that makes all the difference between sound and unsound commercial banking is:

a. When an automobile manufacturer borrows newly created purchasing media and distributes them to employees, suppliers, and others, he is arranging for those potential buyers to obtain their shares (in dollar value) of things in or en route to markets.
b. When an installment buyer arranges to purchase a car [with money he or she borrows], he is not claiming a share corresponding to his participation in producing things for markets, he is claiming someone else's share. [In order for this to be possible, someone else must be willing to forgo claiming his or her share for the term of the loan, that is, be desirous of *saving* his or her share rather than *spending* it.—T.H.G.]

Thus, one can see that a bank's lending transaction may reflect additional things offered in the markets *or it may not.* If it does, creation of new purchasing media [for use until retired by repayment of the loan by the seller] is sound commercial banking. If the lending transaction does *not reflect additional* offerings in the markets, it should be financed by the savings-investment procedures.

My hope is that, as the community exchange movement develops, it will remain cognizant of this distinction between current banking functions, and that as communities begin to develop savings and investment mechanisms, they will be kept separate from the issuance of exchange credits or currency.

ACKNOWLEDGMENTS

IT IS WITH GREAT HUMILITY and gratitude that I present this work, knowing full well that I "stand upon the shoulders of giants." I must acknowledge my debt to scholars and independent thinkers from the past who dared to question the orthodox views. Their dedication and persistence have encouraged my own work, and their keen insights and clear thought have enabled me to find my way through the maze of modern economic confusion and monetary obfuscation. Foremost among these giants is E. C. Riegel, whose penetrating analyses and lucid descriptions have provided the primary foundation for my current understanding of money and exchange. I hope that his work will someday receive the broad recognition that it deserves. Thanks to Spencer Heath MacCallum for preserving Riegel's work from oblivion and introducing me to it. Others who must be mentioned are Ralph Borsodi, Silvio Gesell, Hugo Bilgram, Walter Zander, Irving Fisher, Ulrich von Beckerath, and Frederick Soddy.

Among my contemporaries, I wish to acknowledge the pioneering exchange experiments of Michael Linton, Bob Swann, and Paul Glover. Their efforts have advanced the cause of equity and freedom. I am grateful to each of them for their friendship and for the exchange of views and ideas that we have enjoyed over the years.

There are many who assisted in some way with the preparation of my earlier books, which built the foundation for this one. Thanks to Karen Kennedy, Mary Lin, Laura Till, Greg Meadows, Fred Folvary, Al Andersen, Stephanie Mills, Michael Linton, Bob Swann, Gordon Davidson, Phil Holliday, Neil Shafer, Randy Harris, Mark Fockler, Judy Knox, Matts Myhrman, and the many friends who have provided some form of assistance and encouragement.

With regard to the preparation of this present work, I am greatly indebted to Donna Austin, not only for her continual encouragement and support, but also for her practical assistance in typing, formatting, proofreading, and working out the various diagrams, illustrations, and exhibits.

Finally, I am grateful to Chelsea Green and Alan Berolzheimer for his critical review of the manuscript and specific editorial suggestions, which have undoubtedly resulted in significant improvement of this book.

NOTES

Introduction

1. Taken from an e-mail report by Vicki Robin of the New Road Map Foundation labeled "A Multidimensional View of WTO."
2. A bioregion is a geographic area defined, not by arbitrarily drawn political boundaries, but by its distinctive geophysical features, such as topography, flora, fauna, drainage systems, and climate.

Chapter 1. What's the Matter with Money?

1. J. K. Galbraith, *Money: Whence It Came, Where It Went*, p. 18.
2. *Modern Money Mechanics*, Federal Reserve Bank of Chicago, 1992, p. 3.
3. Ibid.
4. For an excellent and authoritative down-to-earth description of how the Federal Reserve system works, see *Figuring Out the FED*, by Margaret Thoren, 1985 and 1993; available from Truth in Money, Inc., P.O. Box 30, Chagrin Falls, OH 44022.
5. *Two Faces of Debt*, Federal Reserve Bank of Chicago, 1992, pp. 17–19.
6. *The Federal Reserve System: Purposes and Functions*, Washington, D.C.: Board of Governors of the Federal Reserve system, 1961, p. 7.
7. We will return to this point with a more detailed explanation in chapter 4. Also, a fairly thorough but simple and straightforward explanation of the money creation process is contained in *The Truth in Money Book*, by Theodore Thoren and Richard Warner; available from Truth in Money, Inc., P.O. Box 30, Chagrin Falls, OH 44022.
8. *Modern Money Mechanics*, p. 3.
9. Ralph Borsodi, *Green Revolution*, vol. 34, no. 10, December 1977. See appendix A for a more complete statement of Borsodi's views of banking as a profession and his proposals for the reform of banking practice.
10. E.C. Riegel, *Free Enterprise Money*, New York: Harbinger House, 1944, p. xvii.
11. An explanation of the difference between usury and interest will be treated more fully in Chapter 15.

Chapter 1 Sidebar: For Whom the Debt Tolls

1. Margrit Kennedy, *Interest and Inflation Free Money*, 1988. Permakultur Institute. V., Ginsterweg 5, D-3074 Steyerberg, Germany. Fig. 3 facing p. 14.
2. Ibid., fig. 4 facing p. 15.

Chapter 2. Community Currency and the New World Order

The epigraph for chapter 2 is the title of the introduction in Jacques Rueff's *The Age of Inflation*, trans. A. H. Meeus and F. G. Clarke, Chicago: Henry Regnery Co., 1964, p. xii.

1. This is best exemplified in the Gaia hypothesis popularized by scientist James Lovelock and others. See, for example, Lovelock's *The Ages of Gaia, Gaia: A New Look at Life on Earth,* and *Healing Gaia.* Another excellent source is *GAIA: The Human Journey from Chaos to Cosmos,* by Elisabet Sahtouris.
2. Hebrews 11:1.
3. Ethereal in the sense of "less substantial or material." Exchange media, representing individual choices and decisions, take the form, not of gold or silver or even paper, but of ledger entries and electronic pulses moving with the speed of light from place to place. Such "electronic funds transfers" routinely take place in today's banking system, but the people's own credit is sold back to them for interest as if it were gold or silver.

Chapter 3. The Power and Place of Money

1. 1 Timothy 6:10.
2. Jane Jacobs's book, *Cities and the Wealth of Nations*, provides excellent insights into the principles of economic life.

Chapter 4. What Is Money?

1. See also part 3 of my book *Money and Debt: A Solution to the Global Crisis*, and see my article "New Money: A Creative Opportunity for Business," in *Perspectives on Business and Global Change*, vol. 11, no. 3, 1997.
2. Hugo Bilgram and L. E. Levy, *The Cause of Business Depressions*, Philadelphia: J. B. Lippincott Company, 1914, p. 95.
3. Ibid.
4. E. C. Riegel, *Flight from Inflation: The Monetary Alternative*, 1978, pp. 15–16. Available from the Heather Foundation, Box 180, Tonopah, NV 89049. Any serious student of money and exchange should read this entire volume but especially chapter 2, which explains the essential nature of money. Other books by Riegel are also available from this source.
5. E. C. Riegel, *Private Enterprise Money: A Non-Political Money System*, New York: Harbinger House, 1944.
6. The subjects of interest, usury, equity, and social justice are interrelated, and there is much more to be considered. I will attempt to clarify these issues and give a more complete answer to this question in chapters 15 and 16.

Chapter 5. The Disintegration of Local Economies

The epigraph at the beginning of chapter 5 comes from Wendell Berry, "Does Community Have a Value?" in *Home Economics: Fourteen Essays*, New York: Farrar, Straus and Giroux, 1987.

1. Karl Polanyi, *The Great Transformation*, p. 35.
2. It was at this point that the separation should have been made between the unit of account and the form of payment. The dollar, for example, as a unit of account, could have continued to be defined as the value of so much fine gold, while government notes and/or bank notes or credits might have been stipulated as the means of settling accounts. But the value of these notes and credits in terms of gold would have to be determined by the market, not by statute.
3. Frederick Soddy, *The Role of Money*, 1935. It is significant to note the context of this quotation as well: "The 'money power' which has been able to overshadow ostensibly responsible government, is not the power of the merely ultra-rich, but is nothing more nor less than a new technique designed to create and destroy money by adding and withdrawing figures in bank ledgers, *without the slightest concern for the interests of the community* [emphasis added] or the real role that money ought to perform therein. . . ." For more of Soddy's analysis of money and finance, see also his *Wealth, Virtual Wealth and Debt*.
4. Perhaps the United States should consider basing congressional representation only partly on geography and more on voluntary association. A person could choose the organization through which to cast his or her vote. Each such association, which would have to be some minimum size, would be entitled to elect a representative.
5. Manfred Max-Neef, "Reflections on a Paradigm Shift in Economics," in *The New Economic Agenda*, Mary Inglis and Sandra Kramer (eds.), Findhorn Press, The Park, Forres IV36 OTZ, Scotland, 1985, pp. 147, 148. Other works that deal more thoroughly with the theme of human scale are *The Breakdown of Nations*, by Leopold Kohr, New York: E. P. Dutton, 1957 and 1978; and *Human Scale* by Kirkpatrick Sale, New York: Coward, McCann & Geoghegan, 1980.
6. The work of Manuel Castells is particularly insightful. See his three-volume work, *The Information Age: Economy, Society and Culture*. See also David Korten, *When Corporations Rule the World* and *The Post-corporate World*.
7. *Rethink, reorganize and restructure* is the motto that I sound when I speak of transformation. Many individuals and groups are doing good work in each of these topical areas. The CIRC Web site contains links to some of them. Log on at http://azstarnet.com/~circ.
8. This aspect is well developed in Sharif Abdullah's book, *Creating a World That Works for All*.

Chapter 6. Money, Power, and the U.S. Constitution

1. More about this fascinating history can be found in Edwin Vieira's booklet *What Is a Dollar?* See references.
2. William Dunkman, *Money, Credit and Banking*, pp. 284, 285.
3. Ibid., pp. 360–63.

Chapter 7. Restoring Local Economies

The epigraph opening chapter 7 comes from G.D.H. Cole and W. Mellor, *The Meaning of Industrial Freedom,* London: Geo. Allen and Unwin, Ltd., 1918, p.4. Quoted by Erich Fromm in *The Sane Society,* p. 249.
1. Max-Neef, "Paradigm Shift," pp. 147–48.

Chapter 8. A Brief History of Community Currencies and Private Exchange Systems

The epigraph opening chapter 8 comes from Ralph A. Mitchell and Neil Shafer, *Standard Catalog of Depression Scrip of the United States: The 1930s Including Canada and Mexico,* first edition, Iola, Wisc.: Kraus Publications, 1984.
1. Ibid.
2. Ibid., p. 13.
3. Ibid., p. 70.
4. This account was taken from *New Zealand GREEN$QUARTERLY,* no. 6, November 1991, which cites the original source as *The Fig Tree,* "a Douglas Social Credit Quarterly Review," June 1937.
5. Silvio Gesell, *The Natural Economic Order,* San Antonio, Tex: The Free Economy Publishing Co., 1934 (translated from the sixth German edition). Originally published in 1913.
6. Ibid., p. 9.
7. *The American Heritage Dictionary of the English Language,* New York: American Heritage Publishing Co., 1973.
8. Irving Fisher, *Stamp Scrip,* New York: Adelphi Company, 1933.
9. Ibid., p. 18.
10. This historical information was derived primarily from two sources: Richard Gregg, *The Big Idol,* Navajivan Press, Ahmedabad-14, India, 1963; and Irving Fisher's *Stamp Scrip,* cited above.
11. This is another way of bringing scrip or currency into circulation, but the use of official currency is not really necessary and, in fact, limits the power and impact of a community currency, as I shall explain later.
12. This account appears to be inaccurate in stating that the stamp was 2 percent. Fisher's figure of 1 percent per month appears to be the correct one.
13. Gregg, *The Big Idol.*
14. Fisher, *Stamp Scrip.*
15. Ibid.
16. From *Michael Ende and the Money-Go-Round,* a video production of NHK, Japan (2000).
17. Lewis D. Solomon, *Rethinking Our Centralized Monetary System,* New York: Praeger, 1996.
18. Fisher, *Stamp Scrip,* p. 18.
19. Ibid., p. 24.
20. *Annals of Collective Economy* 9, no. 3 (December 1933): 355–68. This paper proposed a new issue of railway money to help alleviate the effects of the Depression. This information was obtained from an English version published in *Peace Plans #9* compiled by Libertarian Microfiche Publishing Company, Berrima, NSW, Australia. See Sources and Resources, at the end of this book, for the complete address.
21. Bilgram and Levy, *Cause of Business Depressions,* p. 416.

Chapter 8 Sidebar: The "Constant" Currency of Ralph Borsodi

1. Dr. Borsodi was the author of several books. One of his first, *This Ugly Civilization*, published in 1928, was widely read and anticipated the work of many of our contemporary social critics. Seeing the many social dysfunctions and unhealthy habits of the modern American lifestyle, Borsodi took his family to the country, where they established a modern rural homestead. Much of this experience is documented in another of his books, *Flight from the City*. Borsodi founded the School of Living in 1934 to promote the further exploration of healthy living and healthy communities. Over the years, the School of Living has evolved into a nationwide educational network of people who are oriented toward personal responsibility, cooperative self-reliance, and ecological and societal improvement. This author was involved with the school for many years, during which he served as president, trustee, and coeditor of its journal, *Green Revolution*.

2. For a more detailed summary of the features of the Constant see appendix C of *Money and Debt*. For a complete description of the Constant experiment see Ralph Borsodi's *Inflation and the Coming Keynesian Catastrophe: The Story of the Exeter Experiment with Constants*, published jointly by the E. F. Schumacher Society, 140 Jug End Rd., Great Barrington, MA 01230, and the School of Living, 432 Leaman Road, Cochranville, PA 19330, 1989. The manuscript for this book was written in the early 1970s.

Chapter 9. Global Finance, Inflation, and Local Currencies

The epigraph opening chapter 9 comes from Jacques Rueff, *The Age of Inflation*, p. xii.

1. *The Charlotte Observer*, Thursday, November 28, 1985, sec. A, p. 50.
2. *American Heritage Dictionary*.
3. Borsodi, *Inflation and the Coming Keynesian Catastrophe*, pp. 6–7.
4. In the words of former auto industry executive Lee Iacocca, "Historians will look back someday on how we tried to cure inflation, and they will think it as silly as bloodletting." Quoted by William Greider in *The Trouble with Money: A Prescription for America's Financial Fever*, p. 77.
5. See Murray Rothbard's *The Fed as a Cartelization Device*.
6. This subject of the proper basis of issue is addressed more completely in appendix B, which contains excerpts from "The Lost Art of Commercial Banking," by E. C. Harwood, taken from *How Safe Is Your Bank*, published by the American Institute for Economic Research, Great Barrington, MA 01230, 1989.
7. *American Heritage Dictionary*.
8. "Bonds That Brought a Boom," by José Reissig, in *New Economics*, no. 20, winter 1991, London, England.
9. Ibid.
10. I have information from Mr. Reissig that on January 1, 1992, "four zeros were dropped from the national currency, which was renamed the peso instead of austral." From personal correspondence dated March 10, 1992.
11. Personal correspondence dated April 20, 1992.
12. Ibid.
13. As mentioned earlier, the government of Argentina, in 1992, reformed its currency and renamed the monetary unit "peso."

Chapter 10. New Wave Pioneers

The epigraph opening chapter 10 comes from *Ithaca MONEY*, no. 14, December 1993–January 1994.

1. IRTA fact sheet, "The Commercial Barter Industry."
2. IRTA fact sheet, "The International Reciprocal Trade Association."
3. IRTA, "The Commercial Barter Industry,"
4. Paul E. Suplizio, "Commercial Barter Exchanges in Society," an address presented to the Chicago Association of Commerce and Industry, Chicago, September 18, 1985.
5. See also the description of LETS that appeared in an illustrated article titled "The Local Employment and Trading System," by Michael Linton and Thomas Greco, in *Whole Earth Review*, no. 55, summer 1987.
6. This may be a shortcoming of LETS groups. The help of a "broker" to stimulate trading might enhance the usefulness of LETS for many members. Brokers might be compensated for their efforts in LETS credits.
7. A few community exchange systems that began as LETS have supplemented their ledger accounts with paper "receipts" or notes, which circulate hand to hand like paper currency. Circulating notes have a number of advantages including a reduction in the labor and expense of operating the system. More will be said about this later.
8. Detailed information about how to start and operate a LETS can be obtained from sources given in the Sources and Resources section at the back of this book. This section also contains a list of selected operating LETSystems and software sources.
9. Ruth Hobson, "The Amazing Growth of LETS in the UK," in *LETSlink Newsletter*, May 1993.
10. Ibid., and conversations with Michael Linton in September 1993.
11. See *The Washington Post*, Monday, May 20, 1991, sect. A, p. 1. This article describes Deli Dollars and Berkshire Farm Preserve Notes. See also *The Berkshire Record*, April 26, 1991, sect. B, p. 1, which describes all four scrip issues.
12. Based on e-mail messages and a personal visit with Paul Glover, October 2000.
13. Based on e-mail message from Paul Glover, hours@lightlink.com, dated March 15, 1999.
14. "A Public Service Economy: An Interview with Edgar S. Cahn," *Multinational Monitor*, April 1989, pp. 17–21.
15. Colin Greer, "What's an Hour of Your Time Worth?" *Parade Magazine*, August 20, 1995, p. 20.
16. *Directory of Volunteer Service Credit Programs*, University of Maryland, Center on Aging, College Park, Md., April 1993.
17. Ibid.
18. Cahn interview, *Multinational Monitor.*
19. From "The Barter Industry." ITEX Corporation literature found at www.itexbayarea.com/ixidust.htm.

Chapter 11. Recent Models and Developments

1. This section of chapter 11, on Toronto dollars, is based, in part, on an e-mail message, "Evolution of Toronto Dollars," from John Flanders to the HOURS list: hourslist-l@lightlink.com, Tuesday, December 29, 1998.

2. E-mail correspondence from David Walsh, dated October 22, 1999, and November 8, 2000.
3. News release via Canada NewsWire, "Two Toronto Branches Sell Toronto Dollars," June 21, 1999.
4. Based on information supplied by Sergio Lub, e-mail messages dated December 20, 2000, and January 15, 2001.
5. Resources for Human Development, corporate brochure, Philadelphia, Pa., 2000.
6. This section is based largely upon material and information supplied by Heloisa Primavera, one of the active organizers of RGT. Quotes are taken from her working paper "Social Money: Well Timed Permanence or a Break from Normality?" Information was also acquired from personal observation during a visit to Argentina in April 2001, and from conversations with many involved people.
7. Indeed, there is hardly any need for visitors from the United States to exchange currency, as dollars are readily accepted and circulate widely throughout the Argentine economy. In Buenos Aires, one may draw cash from an ATM in either pesos or United States dollars.
8. The term *multireciprocal barter* is used in South America to distinguish traditional barter trading from what we call *mutual credit* or *community credit.*
9. SEL is a loose federation of more than three hundred LETS-style mutual credit circles in France. The evolution of SEL was inspired by the British LETS experience. SEL clubs typically use credit checks as a way of transferring credits from one person to another.
10. Literally, "small papers."
11. The text of the agreement can be found at http://ccdev.lets.net/latin.html, Argentina section.

Chapter 12. Currency Fundamentals

1. Bilgram and Levy, *The Cause of Business Depressions,* p. 383.
2. For a thorough and relatively rigorous exposition of the fallacy of the volume theory of the value of money, see ibid., pp. 136–55.
3. Greco, *Money and Debt,* sect. 3.
4. Friedrich von Hayek, *Choice in Currency: A Way to Stop Inflation,* London: Institute of Economic Affairs, 1976.
5. Riegel, *Private Enterprise Money,* p. 109.

Chapter 13. Mutual Credit: The Foundation for Community Currencies

The epigraph opening chapter 13 comes from Riegel, *Flight from Inflation,* p. 143.

Chapter 14. Basic Currency Types: A Classification Scheme

1. An individual may, of course, issue his or her own currency (a personal IOU) by his or her own authority; however, its acceptability will be limited in comparison to a currency that many people are committed, by agreement, to accept.

Chapter 14 Sidebar: Harvey Bucks

1. Steven Wangen, vice president, First State Bank of Harvey (N. Dakota). Personal correspondence dated July 18, 1996.

Chapter 15. A Note on Interest

The epigraph opening chapter 15 comes from R. K. Narayan, *The Financial Expert*, Chicago: University of Chicago Press, 1981.
1. See, for example, part 1 of my book *Money and Debt*.
2. I have treated this subject somewhat more completely in my book *Money and Debt*.
3. Sidney Homer, *A History of Interest Rates*, New Brunswick, N.J.: Rutgers University Press, 1963.
4. There are two basic forms of financial investment, debt and equity. They are both contractual agreements. An equity contract gives the holder an ownership share of an enterprise or asset. The compensation is a share of the profits, which, of course, are not guaranteed. In an equity contract risk is shared, while in a debt contract, the risk is placed almost entirely upon the borrower. In the securities markets, debt takes the form of bonds, which offer a fixed rate of interest return, while equity takes the form of shares of "stock." Stockholders, being part owners of a company, expect that they will receive a portion of the profits in the form of "dividends." Narrowing the gulf between the "haves" and the "have-nots" might be accomplished through a more generalized distribution of ownership within our economy. How that might be achieved is expounded by Jeffrey Gates in his book *The Ownership Solution*.
5. The cost of the stamp used in some forms of stamp scrip is a form of demurrage.
6. For a more complete elaboration on this point, see Greco, *Money and Debt*, pp. 54–59.

Chapter 15 Sidebar: A Story of Robinson Crusoe

1. The text in this sidebar is edited and adapted from Gesell, *The Natural Economic Order*.

Chapter 16. Medium of Exchange or Savings Medium?

1. This description of JAK is based on information provided by Cal Schindel, who cites the original source as Simon Goldin, editor of *Pengar* magazine. See the JAK Web site for more details (given in the Sources and Resources at the back of this book).
2. For a more complete explanation of this banking error, see appendix B.

Chapter 18. How to Design and Implement a Community Exchange

The epigraph opening chapter 18 comes from Riegel, *Flight from Inflation*, p. 49.
1. This limit might eventually be relaxed or eliminated as the system becomes established and stable operation is demonstrated. Accepting 100 percent payment in vals on some sales is sound so long as there are enough cash sales to cover cash costs overall.
2. For a comprehensive discussion of the importance of segregating the traditional functions of money, see part 3 of my book *Money and Debt*.

Chapter 19. A Business-Based Community Currency

The epigraph opening chapter 19 comes from John Naisbitt, *Megatrends*, New York: Warner Books, 1982, p. 183.

Chapter 20. Currency Alternatives for Impersonal Markets

The epigraph opening chapter 20 comes from E. C. Riegel, *Private Enterprise Money*, p. 119.

1. "Local Currencies," brief, Landsman Community Services, May 8, 1991 (see Sources and Resources at the back of this book).
2. Some might argue that some amount less than full parity should be credited, say 80 percent. This, however, would place into circulation an amount of money insufficient to purchase the deposited commodity at par, thus tending to force prices down and preventing the producer from obtaining an adequate return or recovering costs.
3. In actual practice, the details of the procedure might be somewhat different, but the effect would be as described. The bank, which maintains a continuous inventory record and issues release certificates for withdrawal of wheat from the warehouse, would begin to retire currency from circulation as it came in to pay for the wheat. This is somewhat similar to existing bank practice with regard to financing automobile dealers' inventories of vehicles, except that banks charge interest at substantial rates.

Chapter 21. Good Money for Good Work

1. As I understand it, the Internal Revenue Service (IRS) currently does not recognize the donation of services as a tax-deductible contribution. Only cash and in-kind donations qualify. Some change in the tax regulations might be necessary to gain tax advantages for donation of ERRs, or the donation of services might have to be excluded as a basis of issue for ERRs.
2. The socially responsible investing movement is well established and growing. There are numerous sources of information and guidance on this subject, including *The GREENMONEY Journal*. See the Sources and Resources section for contact information.
3. Donations of services, on the other hand, are not deductible under current IRS regulations.
4. Ideally, there should be no liquidation of the security fund at all. As the pool of government securities increases, more official money would be replaced with FTRs, transforming the medium of exchange from a debt-based medium to a service-based medium. As a practical matter, though, the interest income from the endowment fund would probably be distributed to member organizations to help meet their cash needs.

Chapter 21 Sidebar: FTR Questions and Answers

1. Mark 10:31.

Chapter 22. Youth Employment Scrip (YES)

The epigraph opening chapter 22 comes from David Pearce Snyder, "The Revolution in the Workplace," in *The Futurist*, March–April 1996, pp. 8–13.

1. It is not clear what the legal obstacles might be. While legal constraints may require that the minimum wage be paid in official money, a community currency could certainly be used to provide wage supplements in excess of the minimum.
2. Carl Hammerschlag and Howard Silverman state that "suicide and homicide account for one-third of all deaths in [the 14–21] age group." They also point out that "cultures with intact initiation rituals that promote the work of adolescence do not have high death rates from crime, suicide, or homicide." Carl A. Hammerschlag and Howard D. Silverman, *Healing Ceremonies*, New York: The Berkeley Publishing Group, 1997, p. 43.

Appendix A. Note on Banking as a Profession, and Its Reform

This appendix is based on material contained in "The Nature of Banking," an article, by Dr. Ralph Borsodi, which appeared in *Green Revolution*, vol. 34, no. 10, December 1977, published by the School of Living, 432 Leaman Road, Cochranville, PA 19330.

Appendix B. Note on the Proper Basis of Issue for Currency, and the Means of Financing Capital Investments and Consumer Durables

This appendix is based on material contained in "The Lost Art of Commercial Banking," an article by E. C. Harwood, in *How Safe Is Your Bank*, published by the American Institute for Economic Research, Great Barrington, MA 01230, 1989. All quoted passages in the following text are taken from that article, which was originally published in 1974. I thank the AIER for granting permission to reprint it here.

1. Or that they wish to make readily available for transfer via checks, debit cards, automatic payment schedules, and the like.

REFERENCES

"A Public Service Economy: An Interview with Edgar S. Cahn." *Multinational Monitor,* April 1989, pp. 17–21.

Abdullah, Sharif, *Creating a World That Works for All.* San Francisco: Berrett-Koehler Publishers, 1999.

Berry, Wendell, "Does Community Have a Value?" in *Home Economics: Fourteen Essays.* New York: Farrar, Straus, and Giroux, 1987.

Bilgram, Hugo, and L. E. Levy, *The Cause of Business Depressions.* Philadelphia: J. B. Lippincott Company, 1914. Reprinted by Libertarian Book House, Bombay, India, 1950.

Borsodi, Ralph, *Inflation and the Coming Keynesian Catastrophe: The Story of the Exeter Experiment with Constants.* Published jointly by The E. F. Schumacher Society, 140 Jug End Rd., Great Barrington, MA 01230 and the School of Living, 432 Leaman Rd., Cochranville, PA 19330, 1989.

———, *Flight from the City.* New York: Harper, 1933.

———, *This Ugly Civilization.* New York: Simon and Schuster, 1929.

Cahn, Edgar S., "Time Dollars." *Co-op America Quarterly,* spring 1993.

Cahn, Edgar, and Jonathan Rowe, *Time Dollars.* Emmaus, Pa.: Rodale Press, 1992.

Castells, Manuel, *The Information Age: Economy, Society and Culture* (3 volumes). Cambridge, Mass. and Oxford, U.K.: Blackwell Publishers, 1996–98.

Cole, G. D. H., and W. Mellor, *The Meaning of Industrial Freedom.* London: George Allen and Unwin, 1918.

Del Mar, Alexander, *The History of Money in America: From the Earliest Times to the Establishment of the Constitution.* 1899; Hawthorne, Calif.: Omni Publications, 1966.

Directory of Volunteer Service Credit Programs. College Park, Md.: University of Maryland, Center on Aging, April 1993.

Douglas, C. H., *The Monopoly of Credit.* 1931.

Douthwaite, Richard, *Short Circuit: Strengthening Local Economies for Security in an Unstable World.* Totnes, U.K.: Green Books, 1996.

Douthwaite, Richard, and Dan Wagman, *Barataria: A Community Exchange Network for the Third System.* Strohalm, Oudegracht 42, 3511 AR Utrecht, Holland, 1999.

Dunkman, William, *Money, Credit and Banking.* New York: Random House, 1970.

Fisher, Irving, *Mastering the Crisis.* London: George Allen & Unwin, 1934.

———, *Stamp Scrip.* New York: Adelphi Company, 1933.

Fromm, Erich, *The Sane Society.* Greenwich, Ct.: Fawcett Publications, 1955.

Galbraith, John Kenneth, *Economics in Perspective.* Boston: Houghton Mifflin, 1987.

———, *Money: Whence It Came, Where It Went.* Boston: Houghton Mifflin, 1975.

Gates, Jeffrey R., *The Ownership Solution: Toward a Shared Capitalism for the 21st Century.* Perseus, 1 Jacob Way, Reading, MA 01867, 1999.

George, Henry, *Progress and Poverty*. 1879; New York: Robert Schalkenbach Foundation, 1975.

Gesell, Silvio, *The Natural Economic Order*. 1913; San Antonio, Tx.: The Free Economy Publishing Co., 1934 (translated from the sixth German edition).

Greco, Thomas H., *New Money for Healthy Communities*. Thomas H. Greco, Publisher, P.O. Box 42663, Tucson, AZ 85733, 1994.

———, *Money and Debt: A Solution to the Global Crisis*. Second edition, Thomas H. Greco, Publisher, P.O. Box 42663, Tucson, AZ 85733, 1990.

Gregg, Richard, *The Big Idol*. Navajivan Press, Ahmedabad-14, India, 1963.

Greider, William, *One World, Ready or Not*. New York: Touchstone Books, 1998.

———, *The Trouble with Money*. Whittle Direct Books, 505 Market Street, Knoxville, TN 37902, 1989.

———, *Secrets of the Temple: How the Federal Reserve Runs the Country*. New York: Simon and Schuster, 1987.

Hammerschlag, Carl A., and Howard D. Silverman, *Healing Ceremonies*. New York: The Berkeley Publishing Group, 1997.

Harwood, E. C., "The Lost Art of Commercial Banking," in *How Safe Is Your Bank*. Great Barrington, Mass.: American Institute for Economic Research, 1989.

Hayek, Friedrich von, *Denationalization of Money: The Argument Refined*. London: The Institute of Economic Affairs, 1990.

———, *Choice in Currency: A Way to Stop Inflation*. London: The Institute of Economic Affairs, 1976.

Hobson, Ruth, "The Amazing Growth of LETS in the UK." *LETSlink Newsletter* (U.K.), May 1993.

Homer, Sidney, *A History of Interest Rates*. New Brunswick, N.J.: Rutgers University Press, 1963.

Jacobs, Jane, *Cities and the Wealth of Nations*. New York: Vintage, 1984.

Kennedy, Margrit, *Interest and Inflation Free Money*. Permakultur Institut e.V., Ginsterweg 5, D-3074 Steyerberg, Germany, 1988.

Korten, David C., *When Corporations Rule the World*. 2nd edition, San Francisco: Berrett-Koehler Publishers, 1995.

———, *The Post-Corporate World: Life After Capitalism*. San Francisco: Berrett-Koehler Publishers, 1999.

Kohr, Leopold, *The Breakdown of Nations*. New York: E. P. Dutton, 1957, 1978.

Linton, Michael, and Thomas Greco, "The Local Employment and Trading System." *Whole Earth Review*, no. 55, summer 1987.

Lovelock, James, *Healing Gaia: A New Prescription for the Living Planet*. New York: Crown Publishing Group, 1991.

———, *The Ages of Gaia*. New York: Norton, 1988.

Max-Neef, Manfred, "Reflections on a Paradigm Shift in Economics," in *The New Economic Agenda*. Mary Inglis and Sandra Kramer, eds., Findhorn Press, The Park, Forres IV36 OTZ, Scotland, 1985.

Mitchell, Ralph A., and Neil Shafer, *Standard Catalog of Depression Scrip of the United States: The 1930s Including Canada and Mexico*. Iola, Wisc.: Kraus Publications, 1984.

Modern Money Mechanics. Federal Reserve Bank of Chicago, 1992.

Naisbitt, John, *Megatrends*. New York: Warner Books, 1982.

Narayan, R. K., *The Financial Expert*. Chicago: University of Chicago Press, 1981.

Reinfeld, Fred, *The Story of Paper Money*. New York: Sterling Publishing, 1957.

Reissig, José, "Bonds That Brought a Boom." *New Economics*, #20, winter 1991 (London, England).

Riegel, E. C., *Flight from Inflation: The Monetary Alternative.* The Heather Foundation, Box 180, Tonopah, NV 89049, 1978.

———, *Private Enterprise Money: A Non-Political Money System.* New York: Harbinger House, 1944.

Rothbard, Murray, *The Federal Reserve as a Cartelization Device: The Early Years, 1913–1930.* In Barry Siegel, ed., *Money in Crisis.* San Francisco: Pacific Institute for Public Policy Research, and Cambridge: Ballinger Publishing Company, 1984, pp. 89–136.

Rueff, Jacques, *The Monetary Sin of the West.* New York: Macmillan, 1972.

———, *The Age of Inflation.* Trans. by A. H. Meeus and F. G. Clarke, Chicago: Henry Regnery Co., 1964.

Sale, Kirkpatrick, *Human Scale.* New York: Coward, McCann, and Geoghegan, 1980.

Sahtouris, Elisabet, *GAIA: The Human Journey From Chaos to Cosmos.* New York: Pocket Books, 1989.

Soddy, Frederick, *Wealth, Virtual Wealth, and Debt.* Third edition, Hawthorne, Calif.: Omni Publications, 1961. Reprinted from the second edition, 1933.

———, *The Role of Money.* New York: Harcourt, 1935.

Solomon, Lewis, *Rethinking Our Centralized Monetary System: The Case for Local Currency.* Westport, Ct.: Praeger, 1996.

Suplizio, Paul E., *Commercial Barter Exchanges in Society,* an address presented to the Chicago Association of Commerce and Industry, Chicago, September 18, 1985. International Reciprocal Trade Association, 9513 Beach Mill Road, Great Falls, VA 22066, 1985.

The Commercial Barter Industry. IRTA fact sheet, International Reciprocal Trade Association, 9513 Beach Mill Road, Great Falls, VA 22066.

The Federal Reserve System: Purposes and Functions. Board of Governors of the Federal Reserve System, Washington, D.C., 1961.

The International Reciprocal Trade Association. IRTA fact sheet, International Reciprocal Trade Association, 9513 Beach Mill Road, Great Falls, VA 22066.

Thoren, Margaret, *Figuring Out the FED.* Truth in Money, P.O. Box 30, Chagrin Falls, OH 44022, 1985, 1993.

Thoren, Theodore, and Richard Warner, *The Truth in Money Book.* Revised second edition, Truth in Money, P.O. Box 30, Chagrin Falls, OH 44022, 1984.

Timberlake, Richard H., *Gold, Greenbacks, and the Constitution.* The George Edward Durell Foundation, P.O. Box 847, Berryville, VA 22611, 1991.

———, and Kevin Dowd, eds., *Money and the Nation State.* New Brunswick, N.J.: Transaction Publishers, 1998.

Two Faces of Debt. Federal Reserve Bank of Chicago, 1992.

Understanding the M's in Monetary Policy. Federal Reserve Bank of New York, 1994.

Vieira, Edwin, *What Is A "Dollar"?: An Historical Analysis of the Fundamental Question in Monetary Policy.* Monograph No. 6. National Alliance for Constitutional Money, P.O. Box 3634, Manassas, VA 22110.1996.

Weatherford, Jack, *The History of Money: From Sandstone to Cyberspace.* New York: Crown, 1997.

Yeager, Leland B., "From Gold to the Ecu: The International Monetary System in Retrospect," in *Money and the Nation State.* Kevin Dowd and Richard H. Timberlake, eds., Oakland, Calif: The Independent Institute, 1998, pp. 77–104.

Yunus, Muhammad, *Banker to the Poor: Micro-lending and the Battle Against World Poverty.* New York: Public Affairs, 1999.

Zander, Walter, "Railway Money and Unemployment." Annals of Collective Economy 9, no. 3 (December 1933): 355–68.

SOURCES AND RESOURCES

The purpose of this section is to help the reader to find additional information about community currencies and exchange systems, community economic development, and sustainability. Contact and resource information is ever changing and can quickly become outdated. This section, therefore, provides only a limited number of the more established "gateway" sources from which a multitude of other sources can be derived.

INSTITUTIONS

Community Information Resource Center (CIRC)
Thomas H. Greco, Jr., Director
P.O. Box 42663
Tucson, AZ 85733
Ph: 520–795–8930
E-mail: circ2@mindspring.com
Web site: www.azstarnet.com/~circ
CIRC is a nonprofit consulting organization and networking hub dedicated to promoting economic equity, social justice, and community improvement. It specializes in community currency and mutual credit design, development, and implementation. It provides advice, facilitation, staff training, research, and technical and administrative support for community improvement and restructuring. Particular areas of expertise include community economic development, financial equity, money and banking, information and educational technology, sustainable practices, survey research, and statistical analysis. The CIRC Web site contains numerous links to progressive organizations and groups that are active in these areas.

E. F. Schumacher Society
140 Jug End Road, Great Barrington, MA 01230
Ph: 413–528–1737
E-mail: efssociety@aol.com
Web site: www.schumachersociety.org
Named in honor of the late author of *Small Is Beautiful,* the Schumacher Society works to foster appropriate technology, human scale, and right-livelihood. It has sponsored several local exchange experiments, plus micro-finance, and community land trusts. It maintains the Decentralist Library and publishes the quarterly *Local Currency News.*

Geonomy Society
Jeffery J. Smith, President
1611 SE Nehalem St, #2, Portland, OR 97202-6700
Ph: 503–236–1968; Fax 503–760–4932
E-mail: geonomist@juno.com
Web site: www.progress.org/geonomy
The Geonomy Society promotes solutions that advance the cause of economic equity
and social justice. It blends green values with the philosophy of Henry George.

Libertarian Microfiche Publishing Company
John Zube
P.O. Box 52 or 35 Oxley St., Berrima, NSW 2577 Australia
Ph.: 02–48–771–436
E-mail: jzube@acenet.com.au
Web site: www.acenet.com.au/~jzube
Libertarian Microfiche is a unique and phenomenal source of material on free money,
free banking, alternative exchange, and decentralism. Zube has converted to micro-
fiche form more than 300,000 pages of material, much of which is primary resource
material (letters, unpublished papers) that is hard to find or not available elsewhere.

School of Living
432 Leaman Road, Cochranville, PA 19330
Ph: 610–593–2346
E-mail: SOL@s-o-l.org
Web site: www.s-o-l.org
Since 1934, the School of Living has been promoting right-livelihood, decentralism,
social justice, sustainable economics, communities, and cooperative self-reliance. It
publishes a quarterly journal, the *Green Revolution*. SOL is a primary developer of the
community land trust model. SOL founder Ralph Borsodi created and circulated a
private currency called the Constant during the 1970s.

ELECTRONIC SOURCES

WEB SITES

Barataria
www.barataria.org
"A Community Exchange Network for the Third System." Barataria is a federation of
four community exchange systems operating in Ireland, The Netherlands, Scotland,
and Spain.

Community Currencies
www.communitycurrency.org
Carol Brouillet, cbrouillet@igc.org

Community Currencies in Asia, Africa, and Latin America
http://ccdev.lets.net
Stephen DeMeulenaere, stephen@lets.net

A well-maintained site that provides a gateway to complementary exchange activities around the world, especially the south, and contains much useful information, including the full text of Silvio Gesell's book, *The Natural Economic Order.*

Community Way
www.communityway.org
The Web site for information on the Community Way initiatives being promoted by LETS originator Michael Linton, Ernie Yacub, and others.

Future of Money
www.transaction.net/money
Brian Zisk
Covers the developing field of community exchange systems and contains links to a number of related sites.

International LETS List
www.cyberclass.net/turmel/urlsnat.htm
Compiled and maintained by John Turmel, this international list has Web sites and e-mail contacts for more than seven hundred local currency systems in more than forty-five nations.

LETSystems—the Home Page
www.gmlets.u-net.com/
The official Web site for LETS information and developments. Includes the LETS Design Manual and downloadable software.

Money Page
www.ex.ac.uk/~RDavies/arian/money.html
Roy Davies, Rdavies@exeter.ac.uk
Provides a wide range of materials on monetary history and theory, including information on recent developments such as electronic money or "e-money."

Project LETS List—LETS Directory
Chris Hohner, Peterborough, Ontario
http://lentils.imagineis.com/letslist
This site, started in 1998, provides an online database that allows social currency systems to enter and update their own information. It also provides a search engine by keyword and country. As of spring 2001, there were 218 managed listings. A statistics section shows total Web links, e-mail contacts, systems by country, and recent changes to the database. The database also currently contains 186 e-mail contacts and links to 175 Web sites. Hohner estimates that there are more than 1,600 systems around the world.

E-MAIL LISTS

Econ-lets
econ_lets@jiscmail.ac.uk
This is the main list for dialogue among LETS organizers and participants worldwide. To subscribe, send a message to jiscmail.ac.uk, with the text: subscribe econ_lets. For further information see www.jiscmail.ac.uk/docs/transition.htm.

Hourslist-L

hourslist_l@lightlink.com

This is a list for community currency practitioners and developers. While the focus is mainly on currencies that follow the Ithaca HOURS model, the discussions often involve ongoing issues relating to community exchange generally and community economics. The list is officially described as follows:

> "The HOURSlist is the online forum for opinions, ideas and questions about the operation of local currency systems, serving managers of and participants in local currency systems." To subscribe, send e-mail to majordomo@lightlink.com with the following command in the body of your e-mail message: subscribe hourslist <your e-mail address>

Ozlets

This e-mail list is intended for LETS activists in "Australian, New Zealand, and Regional LETSystems." The issues discussed range from "local system difficulties, to setting up new LETS, to definitions of a LETS, and beyond." To subscribe, send e-mail to: Majordomo@mena.org.au with the text: subscribe ozlets

turmel@egroups.com

This is another group for correspondence among monetary reform and community exchange advocates. A main focus is the promotion of a "world-wide L.E.T.S. interest-free time-currency system on the Internet." To subscribe, contact John Turmel, the group's moderator at turmel@freenet.carleton.ca or see www.cyberclass.net/turmel.

PUBLICATIONS

Monetary Reform Magazine

Ian Woods, Editor

RR2, Shanty Bay, Ontario, Canada L0L 2L0

Ph: 705–726–7300

E-mail: editor@monetary-reform.on.ca

Web site: www.monetary-reform.on.ca/main.shtml

An excellent publication that contains articles on various aspects of the "money problem," monetary reform proposals, and the problems of corporate dominance in a globalized economy.

COMMUNITY CURRENCY AND EXCHANGE CONTACTS AROUND THE WORLD

The following is only a partial list, but it includes key contacts and a few of the well-established systems in each region. Other contacts and up-to-date changes can be found on the various Web sites indicated above.

AFRICA

Senegal's "Bons" System

Hassan Aslafy Graf

E-mail: graf@enda.sn

Web site: http://ccdev.lets.net/

The South African New Economics (SANE) Foundation
Wayne A. M. Visser
P.O. Box 53057, Kenilworth 7745, Cape Town, South Africa
Ph: +27–21–615418, fax: +27–21–642718
E-mail: wayne@stones.co.za or sane@iafrica.com
Web site: http://sane.org.za/
"An autonomous network for the creation of a humane, just, sustainable and cultur-
ally appropriate economic system in South Africa."

ASIA

Indonesia
Indonesia Community Currency Systems (ICCS)
Stephen DeMeulenaere
Jl. Pedati Raya No. 20, Rt 007/09, Jakarta 13350 Indonesia
Ph: 62–21–819–1623, fax +62–21–850–0670
E-mail: iccs@indosat.net.id or stephen@lets.net

Japan
Dept. of Advanced Social and International Studies
Prof. Makoto Murayama
University of Tokyo
3-8-1 Komaba Meguro-ku, Tokyo, 153-8902, Japan
Ph: +81–3–5454–6466, fax: +81–33–5454—4339
E-mail: murayama@waka.c.u-tokyo.ac.jp

Gesell Kenkyuukai (Gesell Research Society Japan)
Eiichi Morino, President
3-321 Koyasudohri, Kanagawa-ku, Yokohama 221-0021, Japan
Ph: +81–45–441–0407, fax: +81–45–441–0428
E-mail: e-mail:morino@alles.or.jp
Publishes a magazine (in Japanese) and is generally recommended as a starting point
for researching local money movements in Japan.

Local Money Movements in Japan
Miguel Yasuyuki Hirota
Web sites: www3.plala.or.jp/mig/japan-uk.html;
www3.plala.or.jp/mig/interactive/english/index-uk.html (English translation of lots
of information on Japanese local money movements)
This Web site is maintained by Miguel Hirota, a postgraduate student at Tokyo University. It contains a great deal of useful information about developments in Japan. Most of
the information is available in English and Spanish as well as Japanese.

Seikatsu Club Consumer's Cooperative
Shigeki Maruyama
3-2-28 Mikasaka, Setagaya-Ku, Tokyo, Japan
Ph: +81–3–3706–0036, fax: +81–3–3472–9401
E-mail: shuei@sannet.ne.jp

AUSTRALIA/NEW ZEALAND

Australia
LETS in Australia
Web site: www.lets.org.au
A page of links to Australian LETSystems and Web sites.

SALETS and *Ozlets News*
Annie Lowe
P.O. Box 480, Nairne 5252, South Australia
Phone/fax: +61–08–8391–3909
E-mail: salets@olis.net.au
Web site: http://members.ozemail.com.au/~tpnet/lets
This is "South Australia's LETSystem and Multi LETS Register." *Ozlets News* is a national quarterly publication for LETS organizers in Australia and overseas.

VicLETS
c/o Borderlands Cooperative P.O. Box 8018, Camberwell North 3124
Ph: +61–03–9882–6887, fax: +61–03–9882–6601
E-mail: viclets@borderlands.org.au
Web site: www.borderlands.org.au/viclets/welcome.htm

New Zealand
New Zealand LETS Review (formerly *Green$Quarterly*)
P.O. Box 11,708 Manners St., Wellington, New Zealand
E-Mail: review@ihug.co.nz
Web site: http://homepages.ihug.co.nz/~cave/
This is a bi-monthly publication which provides "New Zealand Trading Exchanges with a forum in which to share their ideas, experiences, opinions and information."

New Zealand LETS Support and Information Group (SIGS)
Bryan Duxfield
E-mail: duxb@xtra.co.nz
Web site: http://sigs.freeservers.com
This group was set up in 1998 to provide support and information for NZ LETS generally. It is working to build up a network of people and information that can assist individuals and exchanges.

NZ G$ (New Zealand Green Dollar) Information
Maureen Mallinson
E-mail: plumbing@ihug.co.nz
Ph: +64–07–868–2642, fax: +64–07–868–2645
Provides information about LETS/green dollars activity in New Zealand, "including a list of all the exchanges, how to set up a system, how we intertrade and more."

EUROPE

France
Système Échange Local, S.E.L.
Web site: http://asso.francenet.fr/sel

A resource for community currency and mutual credit systems in France. As of February 1999, the SEL page listed 320 systems. Offers a French-language handbook, Guide des Sel.

Ireland
Enterprise Connacht-Ulster
Gerry Mc Garry
Clare St., Ballyhaunis, Co. Mayo, Ireland
Ph: +353–907–30170, fax: +353–907–30679
E-mail: gererdmcgarry@tinet.ie

The Netherlands
Aktie Strohalm
Oudegracht 42, 3511 AR Utrecht, Netherlands
Ph: 030–231–4314, fax: 030-234 3986
E-mail: info@strohalm.nl
Web site: www.strohalm.nl
An activist organization which promotes social and economic development and community exchange. "One of the first Dutch NGOs actively committed to the cause of a socially, environmentally and culturally sustainable society." Includes links to Dutch LETSystems. Contains some English language content.

Amstelnet
Naima Challioui; Werner Barendrecht
Sint Pieterspoortsteeg 23a, 1012 HM Amsterdam, Netherlands
Ph: +31–204–208–280, fax: +31–204–288–081
E-mail: naima@mail.intouch.nl

Spain
3-er Sector
Txamina Arrieta, Janvier de Miguel 92, Bloque 2, 28018 Madrid, Spain
Ph: +34–91–77–79–435
E-mail: 3sector@nodo50.org

Sweden
JAK Medlemsbank
Vasagatan 14, 541 50 Sköövde, Sweden
Ph: +46–0500–46–45–00, fax: +46–0500–46–45–61
E-mail: jak@jak.se
Web site: www.jak.se
JAK is a well-established bank that provides for interest-free lending based on a member's saving record. "The bank is owned and managed by its 21,000 members. There are two main aspects to the activities of the JAK Members Bank: To provide its members with interest-free loans and, through subsidiary ventures, local risk-sharing investment opportunities based on their interest-free savings." JAK is an important model to study and emulate.

Switzerland
Talent Experiment
Postfach, CH-5001, Aarau, Switzerland
Ph: +41–0–62–822–84–86, fax: +41–0–62–836–40–44
E-mail: incontact@inwo.org
Web site: www.talent.ch
"The Talent Experiment was founded in Switzerland in 1993 and has grown rapidly, spreading around the country and into Austria, Germany, and the German-speaking part of Italy. By mid-1995, there were several autonomous Talent groups, structured along similar lines. The Swiss group alone had grown to over 700 members, including 100 businesses, and the cumulative turnover for this group was reported to have been about 400,000 Tt. (Talents), equivalent to about US$320,000.

"Talents are described as interest-free money, created by local users, with a twofold goal . . . to stimulate the local economy, and . . . to promote global monetary reform in order to overcome the global crisis.

"The founders of the project report that the experiment has attracted strong public interest and extensive media coverage."

WIR Bank
Auberg 1, 4002 Basel, Switzerland
Ph: +41–61–277–911
Web site: www.wir.ch
WIR is a very large and successful credit clearing and cooperative trading circle. Its sixty-five-year history has established it as one of the most important models for non-monetary exchange. The Web site provides information in German, French, and Italian.

United Kingdom
LETSLink UK
Liz Shephard
54 Campbell Road Southeast, Hants P.O.5 1RW, United Kingdom
Ph: +44–0–1705–730–639
E-mail: lets@letslinkuk.org
Web site: www.letslinkuk.org/
Founded in 1991, LETSLink UK is a private agency that promotes "testing, researching and developing sustainable models for local and community-based LETS and complementary currencies." It offers a variety of resources and services and maintains a database of such systems located throughout the United Kingdom.

North America

Canada
Bow Chinook Hours
Sarah Kerr
c/o The Arusha Centre
233 10th St. NW, Calgary, Alberta, Canada T2N 1V5
Ph: 403–270–8002
E-mail: bcbc@calcna.ab.ca
Web site: www.bcbc.ab.ca
Landsman Community Services, Ltd.
Michael Linton

1600 Embleton Cres., Courtenay, BC V9N 6N8, Canada
Ph: 250–338–0213/0214
E-mail: lcs@mars.ark.com
Web sites: www.gmlets.u-net.com; www.communityway.org; www.cctrading.net;
www.openmoney.org.
Landsman is operated by Michael Linton, originator of LETS, a type of mutual credit system. This is the definitive source for information about LETS theory and operation.
Michael is available to work with groups who wish to set-up LETSystems. He has been
promoting a community economic development model called Community Way as well
as the use of "smart cards," which can handle transactions involving multiple currencies.

LETS Toronto
44 St George St., Toronto M5S 2S2 Canada
Ph: 416–595–5477, fax: 416–595–0383
E-mail: lets@web.net
Web site: www.web.net/~lets
A large, well-established system that has hundreds of active members.

Toronto Dollars
Toronto Dollar Community Projects Inc.
49 Wellington St. E., Fifth Floor, Toronto ON M5E IC9
Ph: 416–361–0466, fax: 416–361–1123
E-mail: tordoll@torontodollar.net
Web site: www.web.net/~tordoll

Mexico
Tianguis Tlaloc
Contact: Luis Lopezllera M.
Promocion del Desarrollo Popular (PDP)
Tlaloc 40-3, Col. Tlaxpana, 11370 Mexico D. F., Mexico
Ph: +52–5566–4265, fax: +52–5592–1989
E-mail: espacios@laneta.apc.org
A community exchange system that uses both currency notes and account ledgers.
Sponsored by (PDP), a nonprofit social action organization, which also publishes a
quarterly magazine, LA OTRA Bolsa de Valores (THE OTHER Stock Exchange), which
is distributed to 850 organizations and groups in seventy countries.

United States
Commonweal, Inc./Commonweal HeroCard
Kevin Ryan
CHC Data, Inc.
219 Main Street SE, Suite 500, Minneapolis, MN 55414
Ph: 612–378–7887, fax: 612–617–1001
E-mail: kryan@chcdata.com
Web site: www.commonweal.com
Has been conducting a dual currency pilot project, using community service dollars as
a reward for community volunteer contributions. Issues a Community HeroCard.™
This "system uniquely combines loyalty programs with community volunteer service
on a single 'intelligent' card."

dualcurrencyTransactional Business Systems (dcTBS)
Joel Hodroff
P.O. Box 16299, Minneapolis, MN 55416-0299
Ph: 612–872–8765, fax: 612–874–1595
E-mail: joelhodroff@dualcurrency.com
Offers a patented dual currency transaction system designed to make multiple currency transactions more convenient, and to promote community economic development.

Equal Dollars
Vanessa Williams
Resources for Human Development, Inc.
4700 Wissahickon Ave., Suite 126, Philadelphia, PA 19144
Ph: 215–951–0300, ext. 3377; fax: 215–849–7360
E-mail: EqualDollars@rhd.org
Web site: www.rhd.org/equal.html
A unique inner-city community currency project sponsored by Resources for Human Development, Inc., a large nonprofit social service organization.

Friendly Favors
Contact: Sergio Lub
3800 Vista Oaks Dr., Martinez, CA 94553
Ph: 925–229–3600, ext. 101
E-mail: Mail@Favors.org
Web site: www.favors.org
Friendly favors is a Web-based voluntary association of people who acknowledge one another by awarding THANKYOUS. It resembles a mutual credit system in its essential features. This is an interesting and impressive development effort in making use of the internet to facilitate exchange. Anyone wishing to join should: (1) go to www.Favors.org, click apply, fill out the form, and submit, or (2) send a request for sponsorship to Mail@Favors.org with a short biography, references, and a jpg color picture of yourself (or you can mail your nonreturnable color picture to the address above).

Ithaca HOURS/*Hour Town*
Paul Glover, founder
Box 6578, Ithaca, NY 14851
Ph: 607–272–4330
E-mail: hours@lightlink.com
Web site: www.ithacahours.org
Hour Town, previously called *Ithaca MONEY,* is a tabloid newspaper that issues Ithaca HOUR community currency notes to its advertisers. In addition to classified listings and display ads of goods and services offered and requested, it provides information about community economics, local exchange and self-help options. Communities wishing to institute similar programs can obtain a Home Town Money Starter Kit for forty dollars. The kit "explains step-by-step start-up and maintenance of an HOURS system, and includes forms, laws, articles, procedures, insights, samples of Ithaca's HOURS, and issues of *Hour Town.*" The proprietors state that the kit has so far been sent to more than one thousand communities in forty-seven states. They offer several informative videos that describe HOURS in various languages, including Spanish, French, Italian, and Japanese.

Solomon, Prof. Lewis
Ph: 202–994–6753
E-mail: lsolomon@main.nlc.gwu.edu
Lewis Solomon is a law professor at George Washington University and author of
Rethinking Our Centralized Monetary System: The Case for a System of Local Currencies
(Praeger, 1996), a book that addresses the legal aspects of unofficial currencies and private exchange systems.

Sound Hours
Web site: www.olywa.net/roundtable/sound_hours/exchange.html
A large-scale community currency organized by Sustainable Community Roundtable.

Time Dollar Institute
5500 39th St. NW, Washington, DC 20015
Ph: 202–686–5200
E-mail: yeswecan@aol.com
Web site: www.timedollar.org/
National clearinghouse for information about service credit/time dollar programs, including a directory, and organizing assistance. "The Time Dollar Institute, established by Edgar Cahn in 1995, is a non-profit organization based in Washington, DC that assists in the design and operation of cutting-edge programs that are the cornerstone of community rebuilding and revitalization efforts across the country. The Institute utilizes Time Dollars, a local, tax-exempt currency, as a way of rewarding people for helping others and building community. The Institute's commitment to community rebuilding extends beyond the District of Columbia to cities throughout the U.S. as well as programs in Japan and the United Kingdom."

Tucson Traders
Contact: Debbie Daly
P.O. Box 1842, Tucson, AZ 85702
Ph: 520–388–8844
E-mail: debbiedaly1@juno.com
Web site: www.tucsontraders.org
A well-run mutual credit system that utilizes circulating currency notes. Members draw Tucson token notes against their line of credit and agree to repay them if and when they terminate membership.

Valley Trade Connection
324 Wells Street, Greenfield, MA 01301
Ph: 413–774–7204, ext. 127
E-mail: vtc@shaysnet.com
Web site: www.valleydollars.org A well-established and active community exchange organization operating under the umbrella of a nonprofit corporation. Issues a circulating currency called valley dollars. Directory is published both in print and on-line.

WomanShare
Diana McCourt and Jane Wilson
680 West End Ave., New York, NY 10025
Ph: 212–662–9746

E-mail: wshare@aol.com
A remarkably successful skills exchange and mutual support network for women in the New York City area. Activities include outreach ("Inter-actions"), a biannual directory, monthly potlucks, group trading, and educational workshops. Runs a computer-based service exchange system.

SOUTH AMERICA

Red Global de Trueque in Argentina (RGT) (Global Barter Network)
Contact: Heloisa Primavera
E-mail: trueque@clacso.edu.ar; primavera@clacso.edu.arg
Contact: Horacio Covas, Carlos De Sanso Zeballos 398, CP 1876 Bernal, Gran Buenos Aires, Argentina
E-mail: Horacio_Covas@hotmail.com; Desanzo@abaconet.com.ar
Web sites: www.geocities.com/RainForest/Canopy/5413/index.html;
www.truequeclub.com
RGT is a collectively run trading network of more than 500 "barter" groups nationwide with combined membership approaching 300,000 households. These Web sites contain all the essential information about the organization and operation of trading clubs, including a list of clubs and a schedule of their trading fairs. The Geocities site contains and English translation of a fascinating article entitled "Re-shuffling For A New Social Order: The Experience Of The Global Barter Network In Argentina." It also contains the network charter, of which the first principle is "Our fulfillment as human beings need not be conditioned by money." E-mail lists may be subscribed from these sites.

INDEX

A

accountant, mutual credit system, 184
accounting credit. *See* credit balance
accounting system
  community currencies used for (*See* community currencies)
  ledger (*See* ledger accounts)
advertising, community currency as form of, 203
advertising fees, mutual credit systems, 143
agent (currency distributor), 185–86, 189
Argentina
  Global Trading Network (*See* Global Trading Network (Red Global de Trueque, RGT))
  local money printed by individual provinces of, 76–77, 82–85
Art of the Long View, The, 242
Australia, LETS in, 92–94, 282
Austria, stamp scrip in, 66–67

B

bank credit, 5–8, 11, 26, 29–33, 159, 165. *See also* debt; interest
  creditworthiness, determination of, 129
  depositors' money loaned by bank, 6, 174
  monetization process, 29–32
  secured loans, 8–9, 159 (*See also* collateral)
  unsecured loans, 159
banking, politicization of, 10
banking profession, reform of, 257–59
banks. *See also* central banks
  capital fund, 191

depositories, role as, 6–8, 174, 260
  licensing of bankers, 257–58
  loaning of deposits by, 174
  political influence of, 44
banks of issue, 6, 260. *See also* bank credit
barter trade, 18
  commercial, 87–88
  indirect barter, 25–26
  legality of, 68
  limitations of, 172
  tax implications, 88
  two-person transaction, 86–87
Bilgram, Hugo, 24–25, 74–75, 127
bills of credit, 42
Borsodi, Ralph, 9, 73, 78, 257–59
Britain, LETS in, 92–94, 284
budget deficits, government. *See* government, monetization of debt by
business-based community currencies, 213–19. *See also* commodity-based community currencies; community trading coupons
businesses, attracting participation in community currencies of, 208–209

C

Cahn, Edgar, 98–99
campaign contributions, role of, 38, 44
Canada, 284–85
  LETS in, 92, 285
  Toronto Dollars (*See* Toronto Dollars)
Canadian Imperial Bank of Commerce, 110
capital, control of, 35
capital formation
  defined, 174

mutual credit systems, 175–78
capital fund, mutual credit system, 191–96
cash-based community currencies, 107, 147–59. *See also* Toronto Dollars
  advantages/disadvantages, 156, 161–62
  gift certificate type, 148–51
  Harvey Bucks, 156, 158
  for impersonal markets, 221
  special purpose cash-substitute scrip, 153–56
  traveler's check type, 151–53
  uses for cash paid into system, 156–59
cash redemption
  circulation prior to, 151–52
  funds for, investment of, 159
  gift certificates, 151
  regulation of, 199
  stamp scrip, 152
  Toronto Dollars, 155–57
  waiting period for, 155
cash-substitute scrip, 153–56. *See also* Toronto Dollars
Caslow Recovery Certificates, 57–61
central banks. *See also* Federal Reserve
  local currencies, objections by central government to, 76–82
  role of, 133
centralized political institutions, disintegration of, 40
chain stores, 49
charitable giving, 182, 208, 227. *See also* nonprofit organizations, contributions to
Christmas Cash, 156, 158
citizen participation, constraints on, 38

coinage provisions, U.S.
Constitution, 42
collateral, 11, 134, 159, 225
for scrip, 70
WIR cooperative, 68, 134
commercial banks. *See* banks
commodity-based community
currencies, 221–26
comparison to conven-
tional money, 224–26
example, 223–24
commodity money, 25–26,
35–36
community banking. *See* community exchange systems
community currencies, 18,
137. *See also* cash-based
community currencies;
Ithaca HOURS program;
ledger accounts; Toronto
Dollars; Youth Employ-
ment Service/Scrip
(YES)
advantages of, 202–204
backing of, 130, 134, 146
(*See also* membership
agreement)
basis of issue, 146, 162,
208, 216
business-based, 213–19
central government/bank
objections to, 76–82
classification of, 145–48
commodity-based, 221–24
(*See also* wealth-based
community currencies)
conversion of official currency to, 206–208
as credit instruments,
127–28, 146, 182–83
credit limits, 200–203 (*See
also* credit balance)
debit balance (*See* debit
balance)
empowerment of commu-
nity members by, xvii,
147, 161
Equal Dollars, 114–15
examples of, 162–63
expiration dates, 112,
210–11, 236, 253
gift certificate-type, 148–51
gift exchange and, 182
Global Trading Network,
117–18, 120
for impersonal markets, 51,
220–26

improvements in, 181–96
inflation and, 81–82, 186,
206, 235
interest and, 52
originators
(principal/agent),
185–86, 189–90
reciprocal exchange,
importance of (*See*
reciprocal exchange)
role of, 13–14, 51–54
self-regulation of supply of,
209–10, 236
traveler's checks, 151–53
Tucson Traders, 101–106,
287
unit of account, 131–32
wealth-based, 147–48,
159–63
community economic devel-
opment, 21, 220–21, 226.
See also nonprofit organizations, contributions to
Equal Dollars program,
114–15
strategies for, 48–49
community exchange sys-
tems, 50–51, 197–212
business participation,
attracting, 208–209
credit creation
power/credit limits,
198, 200–202
currency convertibility, 199
(*See also* cash redemp-
tion)
employee participation,
202
fees (*See* fees, community
exchange systems)
governance, 198, 200
guidelines for, 198–99
membership (*See* member-
ship)
networking of, 51
organizational form,
198–99
overaccumulation of cred-
its in, 209–10
system trading account,
199, 204–206
types of (exchange mecha-
nisms), 198–99,
202–204 (*See also* com-
munity currencies;
mutual credit (MC)
systems)

Community Hero Card,
192–93
Community Reinvestment
Act, 9
Community Service Credit
System, 192–93, 227–31
community trading coupons
basis and limits of issue,
214–16
benefits to member busi-
nesses of, 216–19
completing production-distribution circuit, 219
issuance, circulation, and
redemption, 216–19
lost or expired coupons,
216
Community Way, 192–93
computerization of accounts,
103
Constant currency, 73
coresponsibility groups, 143
corporations
large, community domi-
nated by, 49
scrip issued by, 69–70
counterfeit, legal, 78
counterfeit scrip
anticounterfeiting tech-
niques, use of, 108,
236
Global Trading Network
paper currency, 111,
123
coupons, discount, 192,
213–19
credit
bank (*See* bank credit)
definitions of, 128
lines of, 68, 134, 198 (*See
also* debit balance)
credit balance, 128, 138, 178,
183–84
demurrage on, 62–64, 143,
167–68
overaccumulation of cred-
its, 209–10, 253
system stagnation and,
174–76, 210
credit clearing system, 74–75
credit instruments. *See also*
bank credit
money alternatives as,
127–28, 146, 182–83
money as, 127–28
credit limit. *See* debit balance,
limits on

credit money, 25–26. *See also* bank credit
credit unions, 259
credit-worthiness, determination of, 129
currency fundamentals, 127–35. *See also* community currencies; money
  agreement, authority based on, 130–31
  backing for currency, 132–34
  basis of issue of, 128
  forms and devices, 134–35
  power to issue, 129–30
  redeemability, 132–34
  supply of exchange media, regulation of, 128–29
  surety, 134
  unit of account, 131–32

D
daily reflux, 201
Davies, Roy, 85
debit balance, 129, 138–39, 183–84, 198, 200–202, 211
  community currencies and, 203
  interest on, 91, 143, 167–68, 199, 211–12
  in LETS, 90–91
  limits on, 104, 106, 140, 142, 203
  as loan, 105–106
  system stagnation and, 174–76, 210
debt, 7–8, 78, 165. *See also* bank credit; interest; loans
  imperative, 5
  money as acknowledgment of, 127
  trap, 11–12, 34
decentralization, 39
deflation, 70, 80–81
Deli Dollars, 148, 159
demand deposits
  banks, 174
  mutual credit systems, 175–78
democracy
  forms of, 38–39
  local control of money and markets, 50
demurrage, 62–64, 143, 167–68

depression, 32
discount coupons, 192, 213–19
dollar, defining, 43
döMAK barter circle, 106–107
donations. *See* nonprofit organizations, contributions to

E
Earth Rescue Receipts, 232–36
economic credit, 128
economic development. *See* community economic development
economic interaction, modes of, 18
economic system, 20–21
economies, local. *See* local economies
e-mail lists, 279–80
empires, end of, 39–40
employee participation, community exchange, 202, 219
employer-employee relationship, 37
enclosure acts, 34–35
Equal Dollars (=$s), 114–15
excess business capacity, mutual credit system supported by, 191–96
exchange, 18–20, 37. *See also* community exchange systems; reciprocal exchange; trade exchanges
  effective mechanisms for, 47
  role of money in, 19, 25, 87, 172

F
Farm Preserve Notes, 148
Federal Reserve, 5–7, 36, 79, 213
  constitutionality of money issued through, 43–44
  notes, 6–7, 26
  policies of, 7, 9, 33
fees, community exchange systems, 143, 176–77, 191, 199
  for advertising, 143, 199
  interest, as alternative to, 224–26

volume of trading, based on, 211–12
finance
  control of, 37
  politicization of, 10
Fisher, Irving, 63–66, 69
Flanders, John, 107, 109
fractional reserve banking, 36
fraud, 107
freedom, constraints on, 38
free trade agreements, xvii–xviii, 80,
Friedman, Milton, 10
Friendly Favors, 112–14, 286
Friend to Friend Program, Miami, 99
funded currencies. *See* cash-based community currencies
funded temporary receipts, 236–40

G
gaia consciousness, 16
Galbraith, John Kenneth, 5
General Agreement on Tariffs and Trade, 80
Germany
  döMAK barter circle, 106–107
  stamp scrip in, 64–66
Gesell, Silvio, 62–64, 167–71
gift certificate currency type, 148–51
gifts, 18, 189–90
globalization, xvii–xviii
Global Trading Network (Red Global de Trueque, RGT), 115–24, 288
  Argentinean government, support of, 121–22
  current state of, 117–20
  development of, 116–17
  membership, 117–18, 120
  organization and operation of, 120–21
  political factionalism in, 123–24
  principles of, 122–23
  problems and prospects of, 123–24
  success, factors in, 122
  volume of trading in, 121
Glover, Paul, 94–95
governance, community exchange systems, 198, 200

government. *See also* United
States government, role
of
Argentinean government
support of Global
Trading Network,
121–22
legislated wealth redistribution, 173
local currencies, objections
by central government
to, 76–82
monetization of debt by,
10, 44, 70, 79
grain banks, 221–24
Great Depression, 57–62
greenbacks, 43, 131
Grey, Victor, 113
growth, costs of, 49
growth imperative, 5, 165

H
Harwood, E. C., 260
History of Interest Rates, A, 166
Hodroff, Jeff, 192
Homer, Sidney, 166
*Home Town Money: How to
Enrich Your Community,*
98
"Home Town Money Starter
Kit," 98
HOURS program. *See* Ithaca
HOURS program
HOUR Town, 96–98, 184–86,
190, 286
human needs, fundamental,
46–47
human unity, 15–16

I
impersonal markets, currency
alternatives for, 51,
220–26
import replacement, 21
indirect barter, 25–26. *See also*
community exchange
systems
inflation, 10, 258
causes of, 78–80
community currencies and,
81–82, 186, 206, 235
defined, 77–78
exporting inflation
through free trade
agreements, 80
provincial bonds, effect of
issuance of, 81–82

Youth Employment Ser-
vice/Scrip (YES) and,
252–53
interest, 11–12, 29, 32–33,
164–71
commodity-based commu-
nity currency fees as
alternative to, 224–26
debit balance (loans),
mutual credit systems,
91, 143, 167–68, 199,
211–12
Gesell's Robinson Crusoe
vignette, 167–71
interest-free mutual credit
systems, 52, 91, 106
savings deposits, mutual
credit systems, 176–77
usury compared, 165–67
International Monetary Fund
(IMF), 214
International Reciprocal
Trade Association
(IRTA), 87–88
investment, 143, 173, 260
involuntary transfer, 18
IOUs, 26–29, 87, 146, 160,
182–83. *See also* bank
credit; debit balance
issue, basis of,
128–129177–178, 146,
183, 195–96, 208, 260–62
community trading
coupons, 216
wealth-based community
currencies, 162
Youth Employment Ser-
vice/Scrip (YES),
249–51
Ithaca HOURS program,
95–98, 100, 109, 131–32,
280, 286
business participation,
attracting, 208
debasement of currency,
186, 190
LETS compared, 183–85
method of operation,
189–91

J
Jacobs, Jane, 21
JAK system, 177, 283

K
Kennedy, Margrit, 12
Keynes, John Maynard, 70

Kinney, Mark, 19
Kogawa, Joy, 107

L
Larkin merchandise bonds,
61–62
ledger accounts, 101–104,
137, 183, 202–3. *See also*
credit balance; debit
balance
centralized system, prob-
lems of, 106
personal logbooks, 106–107
legal tender, 6, 42
lesser developed countries
(LDCs), 39, 47. *See also*
Global Trading Network
(Red Global de Trueque,
RGT)
LETS (Local Employment
and Trading System),
23–24, 50–51, 75, 86,
89–94, 131, 137–38
business participation,
attracting, 208
costs of, 91
debits in, 90–91
example, 91–92
information sources,
279–80, 282, 284–85
interest, charging of, 91
Ithaca HOURS compared,
183–85
operation of, 90–91
Toronto, 109
worldwide interest in,
92–94, 100
Levy, L. E., 24–25, 74–75, 127
lines of credit. *See* credit, lines
of
Linton, Michael, 23–24, 50,
89, 192, 220, 284–85
liquidity, 21–23
loans. *See also* bank credit;
IOUs; mortgages
debit balance as, 105–106
depositors' money loaned
by banks, 6, 174
example, 176–77
fees for, 178–77 (*See also*
interest)
inner city micro-lending
program, 115
of Ithaca HOURS, 98
secured, 8–9, 159 (*See also*
collateral)
unsecured, 159

local control, 39, 48–50, 214
local currencies. *See* community currencies
local economies
    disintegration of, 34–40
    health of, 47
Lub, Sergio, 112

M
marginal cost, 191
market economy, 18, 37, 182.
        See also exchange
    local control, 39, 48–50,
        214
    reducing reliance on, 48
Marshall, John, 41
Martinez, Enrique, 121
Max-Neef, Manfred, 39, 46
mechanistic models, 47
membership, 198–200
    coresponsibility groups,
        143
    as governing body, 198
    group/organizational/family, 143
    inclusiveness of, 198–99
    LETS system, 183–84
    periodic renewal of membership, 130–31
membership agreement,
        105–106
    account settlement provisions, 143
    commitment, failure to
        honor, 131, 175
    credit and debit balance,
        controlling, 175–76
    issuing authority based on,
        130
Miami Friend to Friend program, 99
misinformation system, monetary system as, 4
Missouri service credit programs, 99
monetary instruments, 26
monetary system
    as misinformation system, 4
    problems with, 4
    wealth moved from poor to
        rich by, 11–12
monetization of debt, 29, 44,
        159, 258
monetization of value of
        goods/labor, 160, 195
money
    circuit, 26–29

commodity-based community currency compared, 224–26
conflicting roles of, 172
creation of, 4–8
as credit instrument,
        127–28, 182–83
defined, 21–24
evolution of, 35–36
as exchange medium, xvii,
        19, 25, 87, 172,
historical forms of, 25–26
human interaction, place
        in, 19–20, 182
improper bases of issue
        and inflation, 78–79
informational content of,
        24–25
liberation of, 13
local control of, 48
measuring value of, 43
misallocation of, 9–11
new money, creation of, 7–8
politicization of, 10, 19–20
power of, 18–19
purpose of, 24–25
reducing reliance on, 48
scarcity of (*See* money
        supply)
social control through
        control of, 37
soundness of, factors in,
        127–28
U. S. Constitution and,
        41–45
money alternatives. *See also*
        barter trade; community
        currencies; community
        exchange systems; currency fundamentals;
        mutual credit (MC)
        systems; scrip
backing of, 130, 134, 146
as credit instruments,
        127–28, 146, 182–83
for impersonal markets, 51,
        220–26
legal considerations, 68
soundness of, factors in,
        127–28
*Money and Debt: A Solution to
        the Global Crisis,* xvi, 132
money supply
    balanced, 128, 184
    insufficiency of, 8–9,
        52–53, 78, 213–14,
        224–25

regulation of, 128–29
self-adjusting, 128, 209–10,
        236
value of goods/labor, monetization of, 160, 195
mortgages, 11, 29, 32. *See also*
        loans
mutual credit (MC) systems,
        18, 50–51, 75, 87,
        136–44, 197–98. *See also*
        community currencies;
        ledger accounts
acceptance and enhancement of, strategies for,
        144
account settlement agreements, 143
advantages of, 51–52
basic steps in organizing,
        140–42
basis of issue, 128–29,
        177–78, 195–96
capital fund, 191–95
continuing issues, overview
        of, 142–43
coresponsibility groups,
        143
credit balance (*See* credit
        balance)
debit limits (*See* debit balance)
defaults, 184
defined, 136–38
demand *vs.* capital
        accounts, 175–78
disadvantages, 106
dōMAK barter circle, 106–7
excess business capacity
        used for support of,
        191–96
fees (*See* fees, community
        exchange systems)
forms and devices, 134–35
fraud in, 107
interest and (*See* interest)
issuing authority, 130
loans, 176–1777
membership (*See* membership)
method of operation,
        138–40
money supply in, 184
operating revenues, 191
operation costs, 191
registrar/accountant, 184
savings and investment provisions, 143

stagnation, preventing,
174–75
taxability/reportability,
143
Tucson Traders, 101–106
unit of account, 131–32

N
National Bank Act of 1863, 44
Natural Economic Order, The,
62
New Economics Foundation,
100
*New Money for Healthy Commu-
nities,* xvi, 192
new world order, 14–15
humane aspects of, 47
sustainability of, 47
New Zealand, 92–94, 282
nodos, Global Trading Network, 116–17, 120
nonprofit organizations, contributions to, 108,
227–36
Community Service Credit
System, 227–31
Earth Rescue Receipts,
232–36
excess business capacity,
use of, 192
funded temporary receipts,
236–40
Toronto Dollars, 110–11
North American Free Trade
Agreement (NAFTA), 80

O
overdrawn accounts. *See* debit
balance

P
paper money, 26, 36. *See also*
scrip
Philadelphia, Resources for
Human Development
(RHD) Equal Dollars,
114–15
Pilling, David, 85
Polany, Karl, 35
precious metals, 25–26, 35–36
primary economic unit,
20–21
Primavera, Heloisa, 116
principal (currency originator), 185–86, 190
promissory notes, 42, 159. *See
also* loans

proportional representation,
38–39

R
railway notes, 70–74
recession, 81, 213
reciprocal exchange, 18,
86–87, 182–84, 190
redemption. *See* cash
redemption
Red Global de Trueque
(RGT). *See* Global Trad-
ing Network (Red Global
de Trueque, RGT)
reflux rate, 61, 201
registrar, mutual credit system, 184
Reissig, José, 82–84
resources, informational,
277–88
Resources for Human
Development (RHD),
114–15
*Rethinking Our Centralized
Monetary System,* 68
Riegel, E. C., 10, 26–29, 134,
200

S
saving, 173, 260
methods of, 173–74
mutual credit systems, 143,
175–78
as purpose of money, 172
Schwanenkirchen, stamp
scrip in, 64–66, 69
Schwartz, Peter, 242
scrip, 137. *See also* community
currencies
Caslow Recovery Certifi-
cates, 57–61
common types of, 57
corporations, issued by,
69–70
counterfeit (*See* counterfeit
scrip)
demurrage, 62–63
forms and devices, 134–35
Gesell, Silvio, system of,
62–63
gift certificates, 148–51
Global Trading Network,
117, 120
Great Depression, use in,
57–62
Harvey Bucks/Christmas
Cash, 156, 158

Larkin merchandise bonds,
61–62
municipal/state govern-
ment, issued by, 69
railway notes, 70–74
reflux rate, 61
retailers, issued by (goods
foundation), 70
SHARE program, 94–95
special purpose cash-substitute, 153–56 (*See also*
Toronto Dollars)
stamp scrip, 62–70
targeted to assist specific
groups, 155 (*See also*
Youth Employment
Service/Scrip (YES))
terminology, choice of,
134–35
traveler's checks, 151–53,
159
Tucson Traders, 104–106
secured loan, 8–9, 159
service credit plans, 98–99
service credit receipts
(SERVs), 229–31
SHARE (Self-Help Associa-
tion for a Regional
Economy), 94–95
slavery and wage slavery,
34–35, 225
Smith, Gerald, 242
social contracts, errors in,
16–17
social control through control of money and
finance, 37
social disintegration, 37–39
social money movement. *See*
Global Trading Network
(Red Global de Trueque,
RGT)
Soddy, Frederick, 36
Solomon, Lewis, 68
South America, social money
in. *See* Global Trading
Network (Red Global de
Trueque, RGT)
specialization of function, 37
special purpose cash-
substitute, 153–56. *See
also* Toronto Dollars
stamp scrip, 62–70
demurrage, 68–69
in Germany and Austria,
64–68
redemption of, 152

self-liquidating, 68–69
transfer tax style, 69
weekly tax style, 69
surety. *See* collateral
Swedish JAK system, 177, 283
Switzerland, 67–68, 75, 134, 283–84
symbolic money, 25–26
system administrators, role of, 103–5
system trading account, 199, 204–206

T
taxation, 18
commercial barter trade, 88
Earth Rescue Receipt program, 234–35
funded temporary receipts, tax advantages of, 236
Global Trading Network trade fairs, 118
mutual credit systems, taxability of, 143
value added tax, 118, 201
Tax Equity Act of 1982, 88
THANKYOUS, 113–14
Time Dollars, 98–100
Timm, Hans, 63
Toronto Dollar Reserve Fund, 107–11
Toronto Dollars, 107–12, 153, 156–57, 285
business benefits and considerations, 111–12
business participation, attracting, 209
Community Trust Fund, 108, 110–11
current status, 109–10
essential features, 107–108
evolution of, 108–109
example, 111
method of operation, 110–11
notes, expiration of, 112
redemption, 151, 155–57
start-up costs, 112
Toronto Dollars Community Projects Inc., 107

trade credit, 138, 172
trade dollar, 88
trade exchanges, 86
commercial, 87–88
legality of, 68
method of operation, 87–88
trade fairs, 103, 118–20
transaction fees. *See* fees, community exchange systems
transfer payments, 38, 81, 173
traveler's checks, 151–53, 159
Tucson Traders, 101–106, 287

U
United States Constitution, money in, 41–45
coinage provisions, 42
issuance of money based on promise to pay, 43–44
measuring value of money, 43
United States government, role of, 6, 214. *See also* Federal Reserve
budget, 11
budget deficits, 10, 44
unsecured loan, 159
usury, 164–67. *See also* interest

V
vals, 200–202
value added tax (VAT), 118
von Hayek, Friedrich, 133

W
wage slavery, 35, 225
Walsh, David, 107, 109
Wära, 63–64, 69
warehouse receipts, 221–24
wealth
creation, 5
movement from poor to rich of, 11–12
wealth-based community currencies, 147–48, 159–63
advantages/disadvantages, 161–62
basis of issue, 162

characteristics of, 160
commodity-based community currencies, 221–26
examples of, 162–63
inventories used as reserves for, 161–62
nonfunded and funded currencies compared, 160–61
WIR business cooperative, 67–68, 75, 134, 284
Wörgl, stamp scrip in, 66–67, 69
work styles, changes in, 39–40
World Bank, 214
World Trade Organization (WTO), 214, xviii
World Wide Web
Friendly Favor system, 112–14
informational web sites, 278–79

Y
Yacub, Ernie, 192
Youth Employment Service/Scrip (YES)
basis of issue, 249–51
benefits of, 247–48
inflation and, 252–53
local businesses, role of, 248–49, 251–52
method of operation, 245–47
money problem, effect of, 244
overaccumulation of credits, 253
program participants and agreements, 249–53
trade partners, 249
work partners, 249
yesXchange as issuer, role of, 249–51
youth problem and, 242–44

Z
Zander, Walter, 71–72

CHELSEA GREEN

Sustainable living has many facets. Chelsea Green's celebration of the sustainable arts has led us to publish trend-setting books about organic gardening, solar electricity and renewable energy, innovative building techniques, regenerative forestry, local and bioregional democracy, and whole foods. The company's published works, while intensely practical, are also entertaining and inspirational, demonstrating that an ecological approach to life is consistent with producing beautiful, eloquent, and useful books, videos, and audio cassettes.

For more information about Chelsea Green, or to request a free catalog, call toll-free (800) 639-4099, or write to us at P.O. Box 428, White River Junction, Vermont 05001. Visit our Web site at www.chelseagreen.com.

Chelsea Green's titles include:

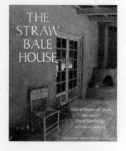  

The Straw Bale House	The Neighborhood Forager	Believing Cassandra
The Independent Home	The Apple Grower	Gaviotas: A Village to
The Natural House	The Flower Farmer	Reinvent the World
Serious Straw Bale	Breed Your Own	Who Owns the Sun?
The Beauty of	Vegetable Varieties	Global Spin:
Straw Bale Homes	Passport to Gardening	The Corporate Assault
The Resourceful Renovator	Keeping Food Fresh	on Environmentalism
Independent Builder	The Soul of Soil	Hemp Horizons
The Rammed Earth House	The New Organic Grower	A Patch of Eden
The Passive Solar House	Four-Season Harvest	A Place in the Sun
Wind Energy Basics	Solar Gardening	Beyond the Limits
Wind Power for Home &	Straight-Ahead Organic	The Man Who Planted Trees
Business	The Contrary Farmer	The Northern Forest
The Solar Living Sourcebook	The Co-op Cookbook	The New Settler Interviews
A Shelter Sketchbook	Whole Foods Companion	Loving and Leaving the
Mortgage-Free!	The Bread Builder	Good Life
Hammer. Nail. Wood.	Simple Food for the	Scott Nearing: The Making
Stone Circles	Good Life	of a Homesteader
Toil: Building Yourself	The Maple Sugar Book	Wise Words for the Good Life